PRAISE FOR
OCCUPATION: ORGANIZER

"In left-wing circles and right-wing fever dreams, the professional organizer has recently been a key protagonist. *Occupation: Organizer* casts a sympathetic yet rigorously critical light on that position. Petitjean's contribution is vital to figuring out what the barriers are to remaking our world into the more democratic, just, and peaceful place we know it can be." —**Micah Uetricht**, coauthor of *Bigger than Bernie: How We Go from the Sanders Campaign to Democratic Socialism*

"An essential read for everybody interested in the history and contradictions of community organizing in the US." —**Eric Blanc**, author of *Red State Revolt: The Teachers' Strike Wave and Working-Class Politics*

"*Occupation: Organizer* is a deeply thought-provoking book that approaches community organizing—and critically, the role of the organizer—from the standpoint of the development of a profession, with all the ironies and difficulties that entails. With a sharp and unsparing sociological eye, Clément Petitjean asks how the job of "community organizer" emerged over decades and how identifiable but unstable boundaries formed around it. It is a story that highlights both key figures and strategies in the professionalization process and the movements and institutions that made them effective. Petitjean leaves the reader with both an appreciation of the work organizers do and a deep unease about the profession itself. *Occupation: Organizer* brings new perspectives to current thinking about nonprofits, foundations, and the weakening of grassroots movements and challenges us to think more clearly about present contradictions and the real futures that may emerge from them." —**John Krinsky**, City College of New York

OCCUPATION: ORGANIZER

A CRITICAL HISTORY OF COMMUNITY ORGANIZING IN AMERICA

CLÉMENT PETITJEAN

Haymarket Books
Chicago, Illinois

Published in 2023 by
Haymarket Books
P.O. Box 180165
Chicago, IL 60618
773-583-7884
www.haymarketbooks.org
info@haymarketbooks.org

ISBN: 978-1-64259-914-5

Distributed to the trade in the US through Consortium Book Sales and
Distribution (www.cbsd.com) and internationally through Ingram Publisher
Services International (www.ingramcontent.com).

This book was published with the generous support of Lannan Foundation and
Wallace Action Fund.

Special discounts are available for bulk purchases by organizations and institutions. Please call 773-583-7884 or email info@haymarketbooks.org for more
information.

Cover design by Benjamin Koditschek.

Printed in Canada by union labor.

Library of Congress Cataloging-in-Publication data is available.

10 9 8 7 6 5 4 3 2 1

To Marie—for the laughter and the windmills

CONTENTS

LIST OF ABBREVIATIONS

ACORN	Association of Community Organizations for Reform Now
BYNC	Back of the Yards Neighborhood Council
BPP	Black Panther Party
CAA	Community Action Agencies
CAP	Campaign Against Pollution
CAP	Chicago Area Project
CAP	Community Action Program
CCCO	Coordinating Council of Community Organizations
CCHD	Catholic Campaign for Human Development
CIO	Committee of Industrial Organizations, later renamed Congress of Industrial Organizations
CORE	Congress of Racial Equality
CSO	Community Service Organization
CTWO	Center for Third World Organizing
EOA	Economic Opportunity Act
FBI	Federal Bureau of Investigation
FIGHT	Freedom, Integration, God, Honor, Today
FSA	Farm Security Administration
IAF	Industrial Areas Foundation
IFCO	Interfaith Foundation for Community Organization
IJR	Institute for Juvenile Research
JCUA	Jewish Council on Urban Affairs
JOIN	Jobs or Income Now
KOCO	Kenwood-Oakland Community Organization
NAACP	National Association for the Advancement of Colored People
NCCC	National Conference of Catholic Charities

NNG	National Network of Grantmakers
NOA	National Organizers Alliance
NPA	National People's Action
NTIC	National Training and Information Center
NWRO	National Welfare Rights Organization
PICO	Pacific Institute for Community Organization
PWOC	Packinghouse Workers Organizing Committee
SCLC	Southern Christian Leadership Conference
SEIU	Service Employees International Union
SON-SOC	Save Our Neighborhoods, Save Our City
TWO	Temporary Woodlawn Organization, later renamed the Woodlawn Organization
UFW	United Farm Workers
ULU	United Labor Union
VISTA	Volunteers in Service to America
WCMC	Welfare Council of Metropolitan Chicago
WTO	World Trade Organization

THE COMMUNITY ORGANIZING MYSTIQUE

Kelly Viselman, a Chicago-based community organizer specializing in housing issues, always has a hard time explaining to people what she does for a living. "I'm thinking of a lot of weddings I've gone to, people don't really understand what organizing is." But it's not just that people cannot wrap their heads around her occupation. When Kelly tells them that she is an organizer, the words conjure up in them blurred memories of Barack Obama's 2008 election, and they very often react in the same way: "Oh! You run for president?"[1]

Kelly's mishaps are far from isolated or mundane events. Rather, they point to the unique position that community organizing occupies in US politics and political imagination. It's hard to think of another occupation that people assume leads directly to the highest political office in the country. But the fantasies surrounding this mysterious label go beyond electoral politics. Over the years it has gained an almost mythic flavor connoting an authentic bond with the marginalized and the oppressed as well as the ability to generate and sustain effective social change in ways that are superior to other forms of collective action.[2] Former community organizer Mike Miller and social scientist Aaron Schutz, for instance, see it as "among the most promising approaches to social change in the country and world."[3] But at the same time, community organizing is often described as hard, at times tedious work. "Community organizing is often romanticized," Black Lives Matter activist and former community organizer Alicia Garza writes, "but the actual work is about tenacity, perseverance, and commitment. . . . Community organizing is the messy work of bringing people together, from different backgrounds and experiences, to change the conditions they are living in. It is the work of building relationships among people who may believe that they have nothing in common so that they can achieve a common goal."[4]

Thinking about community organizing almost immediately conjures up a variety of larger-than-life icons—Barack Obama, of course, and Saul Alinsky, who's often hailed as the "founding father" of community organizing and whose writings are considered classic organizing primers. More recently, against the backdrop of a long-overdue revision of commonly held narratives about US history, civil rights activist Ella Baker has also been presented as another inspirational figure, one whose defense of "spadework"—the backbreaking labor that patiently prepares the ground for collective action—set an alternative tradition, grounded in feminist and antiracist struggles.[5]

Beyond these celebratory narratives, community organizing is also the object of a whole range of misconceptions, misguided assumptions, and sheer ignorance, which come not only from its conservative or liberal detractors but also from people who share similar commitments to fighting for justice, equality, and emancipation, either because they uncritically aggrandize community organizing's merits or because they dogmatically dismiss it as a puppet show driven by nonprofits and running on ill-gotten philanthropic money.

My goal in this book is to challenge these misconceptions and take community organizing as a serious object of critical analysis. In order to do so, we need to look at community organizers not so much as individuals, with their stories and backgrounds, but as the members of a particular social group, with its own values, norms, and material and symbolic interests, which exists as a relatively autonomous entity. A group with more or less clearly defined notions of what is or isn't an organizer, what organizers do or do not do. A group that performs particular work tasks and interacts with a particular set of other actors and institutions.

Despite the fact that the "community organizing" and "community organizer" labels have gained so much currency since 2008, their actual meanings are still extremely vague and confusing. A good example of this is Alicia Garza's assertion, for instance, that "as an organizer, you help different parts of the community learn about one another's histories and embrace one another's humanity as an incentive to fight together. . . . Organizers are engaged in solving the ongoing puzzle of how to build enough power to change the conditions that keep people in misery."[6]

And yet, little is known about the actual people who self-identify as community organizers. What are their employment conditions? What are their social backgrounds, race, gender, and class identities or the political education they received before entering their jobs? Apart from a few niche surveys conducted more than twenty years ago, there are no solid answers to these questions.[7] Such information matters because community organizers are not just transparent "helpers" or "problem solvers" who recede in the background to let the oppressed find their voices and stand up for their rights. Like any of us, community organizers are not free-floating rational individuals; they are shaped by the multilayered social conditions in which they live; like any of us, their social attributes and positions within relations of power (in terms of race, class, gender, sexuality, age, and citizenship, for instance) affect the work they do and how they conceive of that work.

Comradely but rigorous critique is all the more necessary given the politicizing role that the (mostly paid) positions that the label "community organizing" encompasses have played over the past couple of decades. Indeed, community organizer positions have become one of the main recruitment channels for new generations driving an unprecedented politicization to the left. Alicia Garza, US representatives Alexandria Ocasio-Cortez and Rashida Tlaib, and countless others across the United States who have dedicated themselves to the Movement for Black Lives, to feminist, LGBTQ, environmental, immigrants' rights, and labor struggles, who have been instrumental in building a rejuvenated socialist movement, have received their political training as community organizers or have proudly claimed the title as their own.[8]

These are remarkable developments. They point to the central position that community organizing occupies as a site for politicization on the left. They point to its ability to recruit among marginalized groups along age, race, class, gender, and sexuality lines. Few other social sites that directly or remotely contribute to building counterinstitutions and power among the oppressed can boast a similar track record.

But such developments are also the product of a particular history, one that has, since the early twentieth century, been shaped and driven by the professionalization of the organizer's role. To put it briefly, community organizing's history of professionalization is about how a particular portion of political work, which the "community organizer" label now encapsulates, came to be defined as a full-time activity connoting effectiveness and self-effacement to let the oppressed and marginalized speak, an activity that required not only that the people performing it be paid for their work but also that their skills and competence be recognized too. That history raises difficult questions about how the advent of professional organizers as a group has affected prospects for democratic emancipatory politics. It also raises questions about the conditions and constraints that make concrete political work possible, particularly the vexed issue of funding, and whether the drive to professionalization necessarily means the door is open for establishment sources to swoop in and neutralize radical demands. Finally, it raises questions about potential ways to avoid the pitfalls of professionalization.

To provide some answers to these questions, I argue that the professionalization dynamics that shaped what is now called community organizing gave birth to a contradictory hybrid. As a semiautonomous entity transcending individual organizations, the professional group of community organizers is best seen as an infrastructure straddling the worlds of social movements, institutionalized politics, nonprofits, and philanthropy and having conflicted ties with these worlds. Because of the group's historical trajectory, there is an inbuilt tension between what I call the volunteer management consultant and the radical spadeworker. This unbridgeable tension makes it fundamentally ambiguous and contradictory.

Any serious history of community organizing must at one point or another reckon with Saul Alinsky. A sociologist by training and a juvenile-delinquency prevention social worker by trade who worked in Chicago's immigrant working-class neighborhoods in the 1930s, he embarked on a singular career as a political entrepreneur who sold his expertise in producing rationalized civic participation. Over the course of three decades, from 1940 until his death in 1972, he institutionalized and disseminated his work, building local groups across the country, training hundreds of people in his "organizational procedures," and writing books that synthesized his experience and expertise (*Reveille for Radicals* in 1946 and *Rules for Radicals* in 1971). Of crucial (and lasting) importance was the claim that there were certain universal principles of organization and "change," distinct and independent from ideological battles, that can build powerful citizen organizations, rejuvenate US democracy, and improve people's lives. Alinsky posited that only organization could produce meaningful change, but organization did not happen spontaneously. It requires the skilled, outside intervention of people he called "organizers," who identified and trained local volunteer community "leaders," who then unified the community's multiple interests in a single entity and around common interests. Without organizers, the participation of marginalized groups in public affairs would not exist.

The (few) biographical works memorializing Alinsky emphasize his position as a maverick and a radical.[9] Not only is he often presented as the "Sigmund Freud"[10] of community organizing, but in these texts he appears as someone who was deeply committed to democracy and ordinary folks reclaiming their full citizenship.[11] This book, however, is not a biography of Alinsky. While it does bring to the fore key biographical elements that have received little analytical attention but that affected professionalization dynamics in long-lasting ways, it is not primarily concerned with Alinsky's life, per se. Rather, it seeks to illuminate the importance of Alinsky's contribution in setting in motion professionalization dynamics that have driven community organizing's history. Furthermore, it shows how alternative roles and practices developed outside of, or even against, Alinsky's expanding turf and how much the current definitions and understanding of the community organizer's role owe to the conflicts and tensions between these competing options.

After laying out in chapter 1 the value of understanding the community organizer's role in terms of professionalization, professionalism, and professional work, I chart that ambiguous history through three main moments. The first moment, covered in chapters 2 and 3, looks at how Saul Alinsky's career as a political entrepreneur institutionalized a form of "militant liberalism" that was fundamentally professional in nature.[12] Such militant liberalism can be described as a political crème brûlée, with a crisp layer of conflict tactics and antiestablishment rhetoric on top of a mellow cream of commitment to class harmony, compromise, and liberal pluralism. Significantly, the professional dimension of the work was baked into the crème from the beginning.

The second moment, which I take up in chapters 4 and 5, spans the civil rights revolution of the Long Sixties, from the late 1950s to the early 1970s. The decade-long wave of protest fundamentally altered the institutional course that Alinsky had charted. On the one hand, it pushed Alinsky and his Industrial Areas Foundation (IAF) to emphasize his work as a "professional slum organizer." On the other hand, it led to the emergence of innovative radical practices that evolved in complex opposition to Alinsky's approach. In the wake of Ella Baker and the Student Nonviolent Coordinating Committee (SNCC),

Students for a Democratic Society (SDS) and its short-lived Economic Research and Action Project (ERAP), and Black power groups like the Black Panthers, a different definition of the organizer's role took shape: the organizer was not a human resources management consultant of sorts, as was the case at the IAF, but a radical spadeworker, whose work was not premised on a professional project but grounded in and oriented toward social movements and collective struggles.

Chapters 6 and 7 show how the third moment, which started in the late 1970s, welded together these two distinct, even sometimes antagonistic, threads. During Alinsky's career and after his death in 1972, a whole range of actors involved in the burgeoning community organizing movement criticized his own definition of the organizer's role as an outside, detached, manipulating expert. The contours of the roles were challenged by white New Leftists, organizers of color, and women who (rightfully) felt that Alinsky and the IAF completely overlooked central issues of race, gender, and ideology.[13] But such criticisms never called into question the existence of the organizer's role itself and its centrality. That coming together happened as former sixties radicals who were trying to find ways to sustain protest activity and engagement outside of movement waves found a home in the various groups that came out of the IAF tradition. Despite enduring divergences over the meaning of the organizer's role and position, a common agreement consolidated over the need to pursue a professionalization strategy as the best solution to bring about effective social change. The process culminated in 2008 with Barack Obama's election to the White House. But in order to legitimize its place within the political ecosystem, community organizers as a group turned to philanthropic foundations not just for increased financial stability but also for social recognition, which led to its structural subordination to philanthropy.

To tell this story, the book focuses primarily on Chicago. From Saul Alinsky to Barack Obama, the city has occupied a unique position in the history of community organizing and continues to do so. An unsuccessful attempt at comparing community organizing scenes in

Chicago and Detroit during my PhD work drove that point home: there is no equivalent in the rest of the US to the tightly knit, highly self-conscious, dense institutional fabric that is the community organizing milieu in Chicago. Not even New York or Los Angeles, whose larger sizes might make you think otherwise. But precisely because of that singular position, Chicago offers a fruitful vantage point from which to look at how that history unfolded—and why professionalization was such a major piece in the puzzle.

The book weaves together anecdotes, individual biographies, and broader social processes, but it should not be read as a collection of biographies of Chicago's known, lesser-known, and forgotten community organizer figures. The main subject is the professional group of community organizers, an entity that transcends individual organizers and individual organizations. Although I spend quite some time looking at people's backgrounds and stories, my goal is not to paint a collective picture of noble commitment and self-dedication but to uncover the social conditions that make such commitments possible and how, in return, they affect concrete political work. Neither does the book contain the usual David versus Goliath stories of how small community groups won significant victories despite the odds against powerful institutions.[14]

Hagiography has its merits, undoubtedly, but it is too often written to the detriment of critical analysis. Organizing work is hard and essential work, and it is important that the organizers I met in Chicago and the groups they work for exist and keep fighting for social justice. But as a social scientist, I am also deeply convinced that understanding the tensions and power dynamics at play in community organizing is a crucial and necessary step in identifying alternative courses of action. My hope is that the book will provide tools, insights, and perspectives that can contribute to urgent debates on the struggles for justice and emancipation.

CHAPTER 1

UNPACKING PROFESSIONALIZATION

To set the record straight about community organizing and to show why professionalization dynamics have been so central to its history, a good place to start is the 2008 presidential election. Kelly Viselman's experience, which will resonate with anyone who has ever described themselves as a community organizer, is a significant reminder that 2008 did not just represent the election of the first Black president in US history. It was also the first time a former paid, full-time community organizer was elected to the highest political office in the country. Suddenly, the words "community organizing" and "community organizer," which the vast majority of Americans had never heard of until then, became associated with Barack Obama.

2008, OBAMA, AND ALINSKY

When he first ran for elected office—an open seat in the Illinois Senate—in the mid-1990s, Obama had already been out of his community organizer job for eight years but had kept ties with the milieu of progressive Chicago politics that partly overlapped with the community organizing world. Obama graduated from Columbia University in 1983. Like many other recent college graduates, he had vague ideas about what he wanted to do for a living, but he was intent on advancing the cause of social justice. In 1985, he ended up working for the Developing Communities Project organization on the Far South Side of Chicago, without being fully aware of what the job entailed. He stayed there until 1988, setting up a job-training program and building a tenants' rights organization, among other things, with residents from the Roseland neighborhood. He then went to Harvard Law School, becoming in the process the first African American president of the prestigious *Harvard Law Review*. In 1991, after getting his law degree, he returned to Chicago, where he soon made a name for himself within local progressive politics as the director of Project VOTE. The project was a nationwide voter registration organization put together by the Chicago chapter of the Association of Community Organizations for Reform Now (ACORN), one of the largest national community organizing federations at the time, and Service Employees International Union Local 880, which organized homecare and child-care workers. Registering tens of thousands of new voters, especially in predominantly Black neighborhoods, Project VOTE gave a meaningful push to the election of Carol Moseley Braun as the first African American woman senator in US history.[1]

After his stint at Project VOTE, Obama joined a law firm specializing in civil rights and urban development. He kept a foot in the world of professional community organizing, however, by joining the board of the Woods Fund of Chicago, one of the main philanthropic foundations funding community organizing efforts in the city. He remained on Woods's board until 2001. In 1996, Obama was elected to the Illinois Senate. Eight years later, after failing along the way to unseat US Representative Bobby Rush—a four-term incumbent and former Black Panther Party member—Obama was elected to the US Senate. In the summer of 2004, his opening speech at the Democratic National Convention turned him into a national political figure.

During the 2008 Democratic primaries and general election, the Obama campaign insisted on his prior experience as a community organizer to highlight his proximity to ordinary citizens, his relational and listening skills, his firsthand knowledge of the issues people dealt with on a daily basis, and also his intimate ability to reach compromises and to think pragmatically. The election crystallized the positive connotations associated with a label, "community organizer," that remained obscure to most people. In response to direct attacks made by Republicans at their party's convention in September 2008, Obama and his campaign manager reasserted the positive value they attached to the term. While Obama underlined the pettiness of Republicans who "mocked, dismissed, and actually laughed out loud at Americans who engage in community service and organizing," his campaign manager went even farther: "Community organizing is how ordinary people respond to out-of-touch politicians and their failed policies."[2] The implications were clear: in the stark opposition between out-of-touch politicians and ordinary people, Obama clearly belonged with the latter. As a result, he would bring forward policies that enjoyed genuine popular support—and he would turn things around in the process.

Such an intentional self-presentation was not crafted overnight during the 2008 campaign. It was years in the making. As early as December 1995, when Obama announced his candidacy for a seat in the Illinois Senate, he already pitched his community organizer experience in the following terms:

> What if a politician were to see his job as that of an organizer as part teacher and part advocate, one who does not sell voters short but who educates them about the real choices before them? As an elected public official, for instance, I could bring church and community leaders together easier than I could as a community organizer or lawyer. We would come together to form concrete economic development strategies, take advantage of existing laws and structures, and create bridges and bonds within all sectors of the community. We must form grass-root structures that would hold me and other elected officials more accountable for their actions.[3]

At the time, Obama had just published his autobiography *Dreams from My Father*, where he presented his experience in Chicago, to which about a third of the book was devoted, as the best political and moral education he had ever received. The book was reissued in 2004, right at the time when he gained prominence on the national stage. At every step in his political career, as he made his way up the political echelons, Obama presented elected office not only as a continuation of earlier roles in his career (as a community organizer, as a lawyer) during which he strove to "create bridges and bonds" between people and groups but also as an upgraded, more effective one because the job wielded more power.

The Obama campaign did not just use this aspect of his past as a communications resource to highlight his proximity to ordinary people and his deep-seated faith in democratic accountability processes. With the help of Marshall Ganz, a former United Farm Workers (UFW) organizer who by then had become a renowned Harvard professor, the Obama campaign set up a mass volunteer training program powered by two thousand full-time organizers to launch a national canvassing operation.[4] The move was meant to reach out to potential voters who did not appear in the various voter databases used by political consulting firms. In total, around four million volunteers reached out to between fifty and sixty-five million voters. After the election, all the data was collected in a new, "enormous database of email addresses collected during the campaign to mobilize support on behalf of the administration's agenda."[5]

That community organizing was suddenly exposed to unprecedented media coverage and social recognition does not mean that its meaning was clarified, however. Quite the opposite. The year 2008 put the spotlight on a hitherto unknown line of work and the individuals who performed that work, but the dazzling light prevented the general public from seeing clearly what the actual work entailed. In a way, the 2008 election produced a huge amount of symbolic capital, but Obama privatized all the profits that could have trickled down onto the occupation. Community organizing remained largely invisible, in the margins of the political field. Hence Mike Miller and Aaron Schutz's bittersweet remark that "Barack Obama put 'community organizing' on the lips of millions who had never heard of it. That was both a service and disservice to the work. It is good that it be known. It is not good that so few people understand what the 'organizing' is and are told (mostly incorrectly) that Obama's electoral apparatus embodies it."[6] In 2014, community organizing specialist Peter Dreier still lamented that "not a single daily newspaper has a reporter assigned full-time to cover community organizing."[7]

Furthermore, that the community organizer and community organizing labels were inextricably woven into the narrative around Obama's election does not mean that all voters, media outlets, and elected officials acknowledged the positive connotations they were endowed with. The establishment of a chain of equivalences between "community organizer," "community," "grassroots," "proximity," and other similar positively charged—but rather empty—signifiers meant nothing for Republican officials and voters. The Republican Party convention in Saint Paul, Minnesota, in September 2008 made this abundantly clear. Several prominent Republican figures took turns to single out Obama's organizing experience as a ridiculous joke. Former New York City mayor Rudy Giuliani sneered that Obama "worked as a community organizer. What? Maybe this is the first problem on the résumé." In the speech where she accepted running on the Republican ticket with Senator John McCain, Alaska governor Sarah Palin quipped that "a small-town mayor is sort of like a community organizer, except that you have actual responsibilities."[8]

Republicans' fixation on Obama's past as a community organizer went far beyond his individual biography. Every individual and organization that had crossed paths with Obama became an object of intense, obsessive attention. This was the case for ACORN, the national community organizing federation that was instrumental in putting Project VOTE together in the early 1990s. By the late 2000s, ACORN, which started out as a small organization in Arkansas in 1970, had reached national prominence. With its one hundred chapters scattered in forty-two states, more than six hundred staff, and tens of thousands of low- and moderate-income members, it was an important political force to be reckoned with. During the Democratic primaries, Obama had sought ACORN's endorsement. But during a televised debate between him and John McCain in October 2008, the Republican candidate accused ACORN of "[being] now on the verge of maybe perpetrating one of the greatest frauds in voter history in this country" by submitting invalid voter registration forms. ACORN "may be destroying the fabric of democracy," McCain prophesized.[9] And because the group had endorsed Obama, it followed that he represented a threat to US democracy too. Media coverage went into overdrive: in October, there were almost two thousand news stories about ACORN, which turned the organization into an object of public scorn and derision. The group was a threat to US democracy, a dangerous radical left organization promoting a socialist revolution. As one writer sympathetic to the group noted, "For months preceding the 2008 presidential debates, Republican Party and right-wing echo politicians, bloggers, columnists, editorial writers, and TV and radio talk show hosts led an orchestrated campaign blaming ACORN for widespread voter fraud."[10] The day after the debate, "several ACORN community organizers received death threats, and the antipoverty group's Boston and Seattle offices were vandalized."[11]

After Obama was elected and sworn in as president, ACORN remained a prized target for conservative attacks. In the summer of 2009, two conservative activists posing as a sex worker and a pimp goaded ACORN workers in Baltimore into giving advice on how to set up a prostitution business. The encounter was secretly taped. The videos were released on far-right commentator Andrew Breitbart's BigGovernment. com website and soon relayed by Fox News. Republican lawmakers at the state and federal levels took the baton and turned the media scandal, which mainstream outlets like the *New York Times* and the *Washington Post* contributed to feeding, into a series of government investigations and attempts at criminalizing the organization. In mid-September, Republican House leader John Boehner introduced a bill called "Defund ACORN" to cut all federal funding to the group. A vast majority of representatives voted in favor of the bill (345 to 75), although it was later struck down by a federal judge.[12]

The combination of various salvos of conservative-led media controversies, the lack of support from the Obama administration, and a deep internal leadership crisis at ACORN proved too overwhelming for the forty-year-old community organizing group.[13] In the early days of 2010, seventeen chapters seceded from the organization to create separate statewide groups. ACORN as a national entity disappeared altogether.

ACORN's demise points to a broader, paradoxical phenomenon that unfolded in the early years of the Obama presidency: although community organizing groups became the object of vicious attacks from the right, they also enjoyed more legitimacy than ever before. While ACORN's grave was being dug in 2008–2009 by a motley group of individuals and institutions with different, if not opposed, interests and motivations, another significant development was underway: the unearthing of someone who, by the late 2000s, had been mostly forgotten—Saul Alinsky.

Republicans played a leading role in resurrecting Alinsky while turning him into a left-wing bogeyman. Former Republican speaker of the House of Representatives Newt Gingrich saw him as a diabolical, "radical" un-American socialist guru who had Obama under his spell. Conservative talk show host Glenn Beck, who deemed Alinsky a Marxist radical, ran a four-part series on "the most important man in America today," whose "vicious tactics" were still very much alive and who represented a "Jesus" figure to "progressive ideologists."[14] The fact that Hillary Clinton had written an undergraduate paper on Alinsky's community organization practices,[15] and had exchanged several letters with him back in the early 1970s, further confirmed Republicans in their belief that the entire Democratic Party was devoted to fulfilling what they described as Alinsky's radical vision.

Although Alinsky's name had been all but erased from mainstream collective memory, in certain activist circles he was known for his practical advice on how to build effective organizations and for coming up with creative, unexpected protest tactics. By then, *Rules for Radicals* in particular had become something of a go-to book for a lot of people who wanted to get involved in radical politics but did not really know where to start. It's no small irony that Tea Party activists, infuriated with the Obama presidency but also dissatisfied with what they perceived as the Republican Party establishment's weak response to it, actually went to Alinsky's books for training tool kits and manuals.[16]

Contra lofty ideas about how civic and political engagements grow out of disinterestedness or moral indignation, Alinsky had provocatively claimed throughout his thirty-year career that power dynamics and self-interest were the fundamental forces driving people's behavior and that anyone willing to change people's living conditions should not only take them into account but also embrace them. He excelled in the art of polarization through his verbal attacks against "the status quo" and "the liberal establishment," his defense of a Machiavellian "the end justifies the means" approach to action, and his calls for "[rubbing] raw the sores of [people's] discontent" or "mass political jujitsu."[17]

During the 2008 sequence, a series of actors and institutions (Obama's campaign, the mainstream media, the Republican Party establishment, conservative media outlets, and Tea Party activists, mostly) struggled with one another over the meaning of Obama's candidacy and election, and in the process they forged solid symbolic links between Obama and the "community organizing" and "community organizer" labels (and Alinsky to a lesser extent) that made it into collective representations. Years later, the equivalence still holds, as Kelly's wedding anecdote indicates. But because these words are so ubiquitous and positively charged, it is all the more necessary to pause to clarify their meanings.

WHY WORDS AND HISTORY MATTER

In the US the word "organizer" and its variations—community organizer, labor organizer, political organizer, faith organizer—are so taken for granted that they hardly ever appear in book indexes as items that readers might want to look up. Moreover, pretty much everyone, from journalists, academics, and politicians to left-wing writers and the general public, uses "organizer" and "activist" interchangeably, as synonyms, or consider the "activist" label to be a generic, neutral term covering all forms of collective action.[18] A recent example of this lexical confusion is Eric Blanc's otherwise compelling *Red State Revolt*. The book offers a detailed, firsthand account of the teachers' strike wave that swept the US in 2018, emphasizing the role played by a small group of dedicated teachers who, contra the mainstream narrative in the media of an entirely spontaneous upsurge, intervened consciously to organize and lead these revolts. But the way Blanc refers to these individuals also provides a telling example of lexical muddiness: over just three pages, they are synonymously called "experienced," "grassroots," or "workplace activists," "rank-and-file organizers," "militant teachers," "workplace militants," and "militant teacher organizers."[19]

If you zoom in on the "community organizer" label and you start looking at the ways it has been used over the past couple of years, you soon realize that its meaning is quite hazy. On the broadest of levels, it suggests that someone is or was involved in some sort of collective action at the local level, but it's never quite clear if they acted in a paid or volunteer capacity. Sometimes it could be replaced with "volunteer neighborhood activist," but it casts a more sympathetic light on the subject at hand because of the positive connotations of rigor and skill.[20] Sometimes it is used as a generic term to describe someone who worked as paid staff in a nonprofit organization, but regardless of the work they actually did.

For people who work or have worked as paid community organizers, who claim the title as a source of pride, there are actually strong qualitative differences between "activists" and "organizers." If you speak with community organizers and you call them "activists," they will most certainly correct you right away. Indeed, for community organizers, "activist" connotes forms of direct action and disruptive protest disconnected from mass support; it implies social and cultural distance between the individuals engaging in action and the people on whose behalf they are acting. "Organizer," on the other hand, connotes connection to a base of support, an objective and subjective proximity to the mobilized group, and a rational mind that lays out strategic plans of action to harness existing resources toward success. Both figures are related to two modes of action: organizing and activism (the latter is also often called "mobilizing").

According to Mike Miller, the distinction was first drawn in the 1960s, during the civil rights movement. It originated in the willingness on the part of members from the Student Nonviolent Coordinating Committee (SNCC), who in the early 1960s were engaged in painstaking, under-the-radar voter registration campaigns in the Deep South, to dissociate themselves from Martin Luther King Jr.'s charismatic, attention-grabbing, media-oriented national leadership (even if King's aura trickled down on them and bolstered their legitimacy among local residents). They drew a distinction between King's "mobilizing" and their own mode of action, "organizing," which, for practical and symbolic purposes, they defined as "slow, respectful work."[21] Several academic studies on SNCC took up this practical distinction and consolidated it into a conceptual one: "organizing" and "mobilizing" referred to distinct traditions and "models" that developed in the crucible of the civil rights movement and extended to other sectors of society.[22] In the 2000s, other social scientists used the distinction to talk about the civil rights movement, the New Left, and other sixties movements.[23] What emerges from these scholarly texts (and ordinary uses) is that "organizer" is a label undergirded by highly positive connotations, a mystique that has no real equivalent. "Activist" can be appropriated positively, but often it carries a stigma people try to get rid of. And "mobilizer" is hardly ever claimed with pride and gusto. When labor organizer and author Jane McAlevey calls Alinsky a "mobilizer" rather than an organizer, for instance, she does not mean it as a compliment.[24]

Bundling diverse forms of collective action under the generic category "activism" is a fairly recent phenomenon. Until 1949, *Merriam-Webster's* dictionary did not reference "activist" under that sense. Activism, instead, was defined as "any doctrine or tendency that emphasizes activity; the advocacy of action or of a policy of action."[25] It is in the 1950s and 1960s that the category was increasingly used in the media and by political leaders to talk about the ongoing social upheavals—more precisely to disqualify protesters who joined the civil rights and antiwar movements. The "activist" label came to evoke the futility of disruptive action conducted by a radical minority or the threatening "outside agitator," who caused trouble and disturbed the peace, and whose specter was so often used to defend white supremacy whether it be in Birmingham or in Chicago. Chapter 7 shows how community organizers' discrediting the "activist" label is the symbolic product of their collective, intentional drive toward professional status.

What about the "community organizer" label? Archival records suggest that when the label emerged it had little to do with protest politics, contrary to a close cousin, "union organizer," which had been around US organized labor since at least the 1880s. In all likelihood the "community organizer" category first emerged in the 1910s in the burgeoning world of professional social work. It was used within institutions that defended a form of neighborhood-level intervention called "community organization" that challenged social work's growing insistence on individual rather than more structural solutions to poverty and other issues brought about by rapid urbanization and industrialization. The category spread after the US entered World War I in April 1917 and took on a slightly different meaning: the soldiers who were stationed in military camps, waiting to be sent over to Europe or demobilized, were taken care of by "community organizers" who worked for social institutions promoting group cohesion and patriotism through leisure activities.[26] In the 1920s, the category spread even further, following the institutional development of community organization as a subfield of professional social work.[27]

These social-work roots resonate with and shed new light on another important element. Although Alinsky is lionized today as the "father of community organizing," he actually never described what he did as "community organizing." He talked about "community organization," "mass organization," or just "organization," but never about "community organizing." This is not hairsplitting. The difference between "organizing" and "organization" is thin but real. While "organizing" has clear political, collective action connotations, "organization" can also be used in nonpolitical environments. Second, even if it's hard to pinpoint the exact origins of the label, archival evidence suggests that the "community organizing" label started being used sometime in the mid-1960s in movement circles—either among SNCC members or by New Leftists who took their cues from SNCC.[28] Finally, it is only in the late 1970s and early 1980s, when professional community organizing became national in scope, that mainstream institutions started using the label as well, thereby legitimizing it. Philanthropic foundations, who played such a crucial role in the institutionalization and professionalization of community organizing, started to use the term to label their own grant-making activities in the mid-1980s.

It is very likely that these linguistic concerns have to do with how I approached the topic. As a Frenchman embedding myself within Chicago's community organizing milieu for my PhD in sociology, I had a hard time understanding why the organizers I met felt so strongly about not being mistaken for activists. The distinction did not make sense to me because in French there is only one default, generic word, *militant*, which can be used both as a noun and an adjective. And it took me years to realize that the organizer/activist distinction was actually grounded in a professional versus amateur divide. This is probably due to the fact that the professionalization dynamics affecting political commitments writ large have unfolded differently in the French context. More generally the ties that have developed for a couple of centuries between labor, the left, the state, social movements, and nonprofits are not the same as in the US. These sometimes radically different histories bear on the thought categories that people use to talk about these ties.

PATRICK'S TWO PILES OF BOOKS

In February 2017, as I was conducting ethnographic research in Chicago for my PhD, I visited the home of an organizer named Patrick, on the city's South Side.[29] A Chicago native who was raised Catholic and became active in Catholic youth organizations, Patrick worked as a senior staff member for the IAF throughout the 1970s. He went on to become a consultant in organizational development, a diversity project manager in a large philanthropic foundation, and an educator for school principals at a public university. When I interviewed him, he was long retired. On the table in the living room, where we talked for several hours, Patrick had carefully arranged two piles of books. The first consisted of books on community organizing—Alinsky's *Reveille for Radicals* (1946), *The Professional Radical* (1965), and *Rules for Radicals* (1971); two biographies of the man, *The Radical Vision of Saul Alinsky* by P. David Finks (1984) and Sanford Horwitt's *Let Them Call Me Rebel*; and two books written by Alinsky's successors at the helm of the IAF, Edward Chambers and Michael Gecan.

The other pile was far more bewildering. It comprised three management books that Patrick had often used in his career: *Leading Change* (1996), by John Kotter, the self-proclaimed "world's foremost expert on business leadership" and a professor at the Harvard Business School; *Leadership on the Line* (2002), a best-seller written by Ronald Heifetz and Marty Linsky, two Harvard Kennedy School of Government faculty members; and management consultant Jim Collins's *Good to Great* (2001). Patrick picked up *Leading Change* and explained, "[This is] one of the clearest descriptions of organizing for change . . . that I've ever seen, and it aligns almost perfectly with what I have done as an organizer." He opened it to a page he had earmarked with a Post-it note and, with his index finger skimming down the page, he laid out Kotter's "eight-step process for leading change." He then grabbed *Leadership on the Line*, and he said, "To me, as an organizer, I read this and I think, 'Alinsky could have written this book.'"[30]

The whole situation floored me. Why did Patrick think that Saul Alinsky should sit next to a pile of books written by business leadership experts and management consultants? Why should he insist that Alinsky could have written them? And why did he do and say all that while positively identifying as an organizer? Without even taking into account the ridiculous right-wing narrative that Alinsky was a radical evil genius, nothing in the dominant story about him being one of the greatest champions of grassroots democracy could help me make sense of this puzzling interaction. In the literature written by Alinsky enthusiasts, Patrick's pile of management books simply does not exist.

Of course, there are a number of books that have voiced serious criticisms of Alinsky's work and legacy and debunked the myths and fantasies surrounding him. In his masterful account of the rise and fall of the United Farm Workers, educator Frank Bardacke argues that there is a coherent body of thought that he calls "Alinskyism." He defines this approach as "a codified discipline, with core theoretical propositions, recognized heresies, disciples, fallen neophytes, and splits. It is a political theory, with the emphasis on the political, and Alinsky is the grand theorist."[31] Under the guise of what Alinsky presented as a pragmatic, nonideological worldview, "so many of his ideas are taken straight from the almost invisible ideology that we live and breathe: the ideology of American democracy."[32]

More recently, in a book that has become a must-read for many on the left, Jane McAlevey also turns the romanticized view about Alinsky on its head. After warning that "talking about Alinsky can be just as tricky as talking about Marx" because "there is what they wrote, and what they did, and what has been done by their followers," McAlevey contends that Alinsky did not engage in "organizing," which develops long-lasting working-class power by engaging with workers comprehensively, both in the workplace and in the community, but in shallow "mobilizing," which fails to grasp workers' "organic ties" to their communities. Alinsky has usurped the "organizer" title; instead, "he was a mobilizer, outside the factories."[33]

Bardacke and McAlevey zero in on Alinsky's contradictions: the ideological impetus behind his professed aversion for ideology, the flawed portrait of the organizer as a lonesome cowboy that he painted throughout his career. Despite its undeniable merits, the more accurate picture they paint leaves little room for the pile of management books, however. To put it differently, if you follow Bardacke's and McAlevey's lines of criticism, you can vaguely guess that Alinsky-style practices were not fully aligned with fostering self-activity and self-organization of the oppressed, that their underlying politics are not necessarily radical in themselves, but you cannot satisfactorily account for the link with management consulting and organizational development that made so much sense to Patrick. You cannot explain why he decided to juxtapose the two piles of books next to one another or why he claimed that, "as an organizer," he thought that Alinsky could have written the management ones.

Patrick is not the only one who praised Alinsky as a pioneer in management consulting. John Sheridan, a major professional union buster who trained hundreds of his colleagues from the 1970s on and who was considered "the contemporary dean of antilabor consulting" in the 1990s, cited Alinsky as someone who deeply influenced his work.[34] Similarly, Art Kleiner, a management thinker and longtime editor-in-chief of the management journal *strategy+business*, dedicated an entire chapter to Alinsky in his book on the "heretics" who "reinvented corporate management."[35] Although these takes on Alinsky have not made it into the dominant narrative around Alinsky's career, they offer essential insights on Patrick's decision to stack a second pile of management books: the professional dimension of the organizer's work.

PROFESSIONALIZATION UNPACKED

"Professionalization" is a loaded word that must be dealt with carefully, particularly when applied to politics and commitment writ large.

First, when the notion of professionalization is used, it's almost always in conjunction with other related words, so much so that they often feel like synonyms. In academic studies, the concept is intimately tied with processes of institutionalization. One of the most convincing perspectives argues that professionalization is a process that creates a particular group of specialists who are cut off from the rank and file. Sociologist Charles Tilly, for instance, sees professionalization as a threat to the social movement as a form of innovative collective action because it creates a body of specialists whose narrow focus, material interests, and increased distance from volunteer mass movement participants can stifle the potentially new demands, groups, identities, and tactics that these movements can give birth to.[36] Along the same lines, sociologist Theda Skocpol shows how the large, nationwide, cross-class voluntary associations that were organized from the first half of the nineteenth century to the middle of the twentieth in the US were replaced, from the 1970s on, by increasingly specialized, professionally run organizations with no real membership. Instead, they rely for funding on foundations, corporations, or large individual donors. Skocpol calls this a shift "from membership to management."[37]

Another critical take on professionalization considers that professionalization is the result of the bureaucratization of organizations. This perspective has a long and rich history on the left, particularly when applied to party and union bureaucracies and the role they have played in taming, diverting, or betraying radical demands coming from the rank and file. With the advent of formal, self-reproducing organizations, organizational functions become specialized, and full-time positions are created for people to perform them. But in the process, these full-time cadre develop a vested interest in the organization's survival. According to these accounts, what's often called an "iron law of oligarchy" is woven into the organization's fabric, creating a structural gap between the leadership and their base, which strips rank-and-file members of their ability to debate and decide over the organization's course.

A third take on the professionalization issue focuses more specifically on organizational forms. Scholars and activists alike have emphasized the threats posed by "NGOization" or "nonprofitization"—the increasingly central place that nongovernmental organizations (NGOs) and nonprofit organizations occupy in contemporary social justice movements and their stifling effect on radical movements. The process seems particularly ubiquitous, transcending national borders: it's been observed in Palestine, in the Dalit movement in India, amid the post-Katrina situation in New Orleans, and in queer politics in Chicago and Minneapolis.[38] This line of criticism was popularized in 2007 by the INCITE! Women of Color against Violence collective in a seminal book called *The Revolution Will Not Be Funded: Beyond the Non-Profit Industrial Complex*. Since then, the concept of the nonprofit-industrial complex has been integrated into activists' common sense and everyday language. Riffing on Dwight Eisenhower's denunciation of the "military-industrial complex," the concept sheds light on the objective alliance with the carceral state, the commodification of social justice activity, the interdependence between nonprofits, capitalist interests, philanthropic actors, and public administrations, and the power relations that underlie them. Nonprofitization, this argument goes, channels, neutralizes, co-opts, and betrays the radical and authentic demands of the grassroots through one indirect mechanism in particular: the subordination to philanthropic funding. When nonprofits file for a tax-exempt status called 501(c)(3), they spend more and more time looking for grants or reaching out to large donors rather than developing their own sources of income, such as membership dues. As INCITE! puts it, the advent of the nonprofit-industrial complex has translated into a shift from "mass-based organizing capable of actually transforming society" to "career-based modes of organizing."[39]

Several voices have applied this critical framework to make sense of community organizing. Some of them are community organizers themselves reflecting on their work and the structural constraints that weigh down on them. In 2010, community organizer Rosemary Ndubuizu urged other organizers to acknowledge their predicament: "Because of this nonprofit industrial complex, we have created a cult of organizational preservation. . . . We assume that this work cannot be done without a paid staff, hierarchical organization, and paternal leadership. . . . We must answer for ourselves whether our unilateral adoption of traditional processes and structures can lead us to the radical change many of us believe is possible."[40]

From these standpoints, professionalization is the process that creates a group of specialists who sell their labor to social justice movement organizations in exchange for financial compensation, which in turn blunts these organizations' radical edges. The underlying assumption, therefore, is the following equation: professionalization = depoliticization. In other words, the pursuit of professional status has a depoliticizing effect that hampers radicalism and militancy.

This simple equivalence raises a series of problems, however. First, these analyses are predicated on a truncated view of what professional groups are and what they do. It's undeniable that modern professions are organized "to exchange their services for *a price*," that they obey the broader capitalist logic of commodification—that is, "the extension of capitalist exchange relations to all areas of human activity."[41] But there are other processes at play in what is usually meant by "professionalization," such as credentialization through academic degrees, rationalization of the division of labor imposed by management, or the establishment of specialized groups and associations defending the profession's standing, which can take place independently from commodification.[42] The fact that a lot of paid community organizers (or organizers in other fields, for that matter) are college graduates who majored in social science cannot be fully accounted for through the lenses of the commodification narrative. Similarly, the fact that community organizing positions can actually introduce the people who hold them to radical politics or radicalize them, as Alicia Garza makes clear in her autobiography, for instance, is something that the professionalization = depoliticization equation ignores completely.

Second, one central aspect of professionalization processes that the narratives on bureaucratization or nonprofitization mostly overlook is the mechanisms binding a professional group together. A key component in that regard is a common basis of training, access to relatively abstract knowledge, and a common language. As professionals mobilize this body of knowledge and know-how to perform their work, they draw a crucial distinction between themselves and "amateurs" (in both senses of "unpaid" and "unskilled"), which creates a sense of cognitive superiority separating them from "the laity."[43] Professionals know what they are doing and why they are doing it—they can take their own actions as an object of critique and reflect on them; amateurs can, at best, make educated guesses based on instinct, but they cannot elicit the principles that guided their actions. This sense of cognitive superiority does not mean that organizers feel that they are superior to the community leaders they develop but that they have a sense of the bigger picture and the next steps that should be taken to reach their goals.

Lastly, it is necessary to distinguish between two types of professionalization. The push toward professionalization can be imposed from without by forces external to the professional group (government agencies or philanthropic foundations, for instance), as a series of injunctions to change the performance of work over which professionals and workers in general have little to no control. But this is quite different from professionalization from within, where claiming some sort of professional status can be a way to promote one's image to clients and competitors or to secure social recognition for work tasks deemed essential but that are performed in the shadows.[44]

In the case of activism and commitments in general, the drive to create more stable paid positions (higher wages or access to health care, for instance) can be seen as a positive way to retain people's commitments and avoid movement burnout, as well as help them find ways to balance their personal and work lives. Because of the cultural and historical associations between voluntarism, disinterestedness, and the nobility of a given cause, the introduction of money inevitably conjures up the specter of interest and moral and political corruption.[45] As former UFW lead organizer Marshall Ganz puts it, there is a real, probably intractable dilemma at play. "[UFW founder and leader] Cesar

Chavez thought that once you started to pay salaries, you lost your community, you became professionalized and bureaucratized. There's an element of truth to that. But on the other hand, how were we to stabilize the organization? Is there a point at which people need to be able to live whole lives?"[46]

The dilemma of paid or unpaid volunteer political work is nothing new. In his famous 1918 "Politics as a Vocation" lecture, German sociologist Max Weber drew a crucial distinction to make sense of this predicament. Weber argued that there were two ways of "making politics one's vocation": one can live "for" politics, enjoying exerting power or being rewarded by the symbolic gratifications of working for a noble cause, or one can live "off" it, turning it into a permanent source of income. And Weber added an important caveat: "Under the dominance of the private property order, some—if you wish—very trivial preconditions must exist in order for a person to be able to live 'for' politics. . . . Under normal conditions, the politician must be economically independent of the income politics can bring him. This means, quite simply, that the politician must be wealthy or must have a personal position in life which yields a sufficient income."[47] One hundred years later, Weber's observation is still highly relevant and resonates deeply with current debates.

In order to think beyond the professionalization = depoliticization dead end, it is necessary to properly engage with the contradictory dynamics of professionalization. Social scientists like Magali Sarfatti Larson and Andrew Abbott have developed critical tools to explore these contradictions. They argue that professionalization is about groups of workers seeking to establish an exclusive form of control over the work.[48] But to understand how that happens, it is important to look at the work people actually perform. Broadly speaking, professional work, a synonym for expertise, can be broken down into three phases: identifying and classifying a given problem, reasoning about it and considering possible solutions, and taking action to solve the problem.[49] These basic operations necessitate certain manual or cognitive skills that are "tied directly to a system of knowledge that formalizes the skills on which this work proceeds."[50] Professional work, therefore, is founded on a commitment to and belief in science, reason, and rationalization as ways toward solving concrete problems and advancing social progress. And since such work is about developing rational procedures to solve these individual cases, it requires a particular form of detachment on the part of the professional: they have no personal interest in the case at hand, yet they have an interest in solving it through the application of the body of knowledge they master.[51] In industrialized societies, professional work is endowed with positive qualities, connoting competence and trustworthiness, which makes it particularly appealing.

In the case of community organizing, the work that organizers perform consists in two broad sets of tasks: fostering the active civic participation of marginalized and oppressed groups whose voices and interests are not represented in public affairs, and identifying, training, and legitimating volunteer spokespeople for the mobilized group, called "leaders" in the community organizing lingo, who come from that group. The core principle binding these tasks together is a belief in people's ability to find collective solutions to their everyday problems through participation and engagement with existing institutions. And community organizers claim that they know how to identify people's immediate concerns (how to "meet them where they are at," as the expression goes) and turn these problems into broader issues without speaking in their names and becoming these groups' self-proclaimed spokespeople and representatives. They know how to step back and disappear behind people so that they speak and act for themselves.

If we look at such work as professional work, it means that some form of abstract knowledge is necessary. Now, abstracting a series of organization skills and principles that would guide organizers through the mess of people's divergent interests and hidden motivations, and help them reach their goal of producing new legitimate community representation, is exactly what Alinsky said he did during his career.

The replicability to a wide variety of situations of Alinsky's assertions and recommendations in *Reveille for Radicals* or *Rules for Radicals* is the reason why people still go to his books for instruction on how to organize. But in the process, Alinsky claimed that he discovered a science of organization to achieve social change that existed outside of politics and ideologies.

The formalization of abstract principles guiding how people perform their work implies attempts to seek forms of exclusive control over that work. If you believe that there are procedures that can effectively cure a disease or pass on knowledge to others and that you know how to apply these procedures, you develop a sense not only that you can solve other similar cases but also that you *should* do it, that your expertise works better than other ways of solving the problem. But in doing so, you bump against other people and groups who also place bids on the problems you are trying to control and who at first refuse to stand down. In the US, for instance, as the notion that there existed what Abbott calls "personal problems" emerged in the second half of the nineteenth century and gained significant ground in the first half of the twentieth, the clergy, neurologists, psychiatrists, social workers, and psychoanalysts competed with one another over how exactly to define the issue, identify and characterize it, and solve it, with the clergy failing to maintain the hitherto dominant idea that mental health issues were signs of God's intervention, and the psychotherapy model becoming hegemonic.[52]

To last in time such control must be recognized and legitimated by other institutions like public opinion, the state, and universities. Mechanisms like state-sanctioned licenses, academic degrees, and professional associations were used by emerging white-collar occupations like lawyers, teachers, and social workers in the late nineteenth century and first half of the twentieth to secure control over the work tasks they claimed as their own.[53] What I show in this book is that such mechanisms were used by community organizers to try to control the production of legitimate participation and representation at the community level. And that, in doing so, organizers tried to fend off other actors and collective entities who, like them, occupy intermediary positions in the complex social relation between the rulers and the ruled ("activists," elected officials, think tank policy experts, political consultants, and lobbyists).[54]

Once you look at professionalization in terms of professional work and struggles for control with other groups and entities, it becomes clear that the sole lenses of bureaucratization or nonprofitization cannot fully account for the advent of a group of full-time paid community organizers. When you think in terms of bureaucratization or the nonprofit-industrial complex, you think in terms of how organizational logics constrain and control activist work. You have two sets of entities, staffers and organizations (or a set of interdependent organizations and institutions, from the nonprofit-industrial complex perspective), where the latter constrain the former's work and their politics. But the actual content and meaning of that work remain elusive.

If you think in terms of professional work, a third entity comes in—the professional group—which is distinct from the other two, whose own logics are relatively autonomous from organizational ones.[55] Furthermore, thinking in those terms helps to clarify the nature and scope of the relationship between the organizers and the community leaders they select and train. As I said earlier, the organizer-leader relation is at the heart of the work. But it is an asymmetrical relation: organizers organize leaders, not the other way around. Of course, organizers can genuinely learn a lot through their daily engagement with leaders and build long-lasting bonds of friendship with them. But mutual learning and the existence of critical voices do not make that structural power imbalance go away. The distinction between the organizer and the community leader, a fundamental one to understand the entire historical arc of community organizing practices, is at its core a professional distinction.

Because of the nature of professional work, therefore, and because professions find their sources of legitimacy outside of the organizations for which they work, something happens at the profession's level that is analytically distinct from organizational constraints. When Patrick grabs the John Kotter book and tells me that he, "as an organizer," felt that Alinsky could have written it, what is going on is not just that he was a paid staffer for nonprofits stifling radical politics. What Patrick is saying is that he, who identifies as a professional, recognizes Kotter as a fellow professional because Kotter, like Alinsky, came up with useful abstract knowledge about how to more effectively perform the work.

Professional work should not be reduced to the use of abstract knowledge to solve particular problems, however. Learning how to perform the work does have an impact on people: it teaches them a particular language, a way of looking at the world, a way of acting that they internalize and practice on a daily basis. This ongoing, practical education leaves its mark on people even when they stop working in a paid organizer capacity. Not just in terms of conscious self-identification—people still calling themselves organizers years later after they left the community organizing world, like Patrick—but also at work or outside of work. The intentional focus on finding concrete ways to bring more people into whatever activity you are engaging in, the ever-present concern about the next steps, which are at the core of the work, stay with people who've worked as organizers when they pursue other careers as educators, labor union organizers, elected officials, yoga teachers, or management consultants.

Conversely, people's social attributes and backgrounds and biographies also have an impact on the work and professionalization dynamics more generally. This is one of the most essential takeaways from social science: the liberal-capitalist notion that people are free-floating, rational individuals who make decisions solely on the basis of their self-interest is completely inaccurate. As I show throughout the book, people's class, race, gender backgrounds, their prior educational and professional experiences, their religious upbringing or politics, which do not result from choices they made, shape and constrain how people perform their work and how they define it.

In order to assess the significance of Saul Alinsky's imprint on the professionalization dynamics that have driven community organizing's historical course, it is important to analyze how and why Alinsky came to endorse a professional project. A good starting point is to critically dissect Alinsky's biography—to relate his class background, his diverse and at times maybe conflicting educations (religious, academic, professional), and his cultural, economic, and social resources, the network of relations he was embedded into to broader social structures and contexts. Doing so is the only way we can avoid taking Alinsky's flamboyant rhetoric at face value and compare it with his social positions and status, institutional affiliations, and practices.

CHAPTER 2

ORIGINS

Saul Alinsky and the Chicago Reform Tradition

Throughout his career as a "professional radical," Alinsky stuck to the rags-to-riches story that he came from a working-class background. In the famous interview he gave to *Playboy* magazine in 1972, for instance, shortly before his death, he claimed that "we lived in one of the worst slums in Chicago; in fact, we lived in the slum district of the slum."[1] While he did grow up in a slum, it is inaccurate to say that he was born in utmost poverty. A Jewish immigrant fleeing the pogroms and misery he experienced in the Russian empire, Benjamin Alinsky, Saul's father, arrived in Chicago in 1897 after living for several years in New York City. A tailor by trade, Benjamin married one of his employees, Sarah Tannenbaum. Their son, Saul, was born in 1909 in the overcrowded, run-down Jewish neighborhood of Maxwell Street. But in 1915, the family's relative economic success allowed them to move out into the Lawndale neighborhood and buy a nine-apartment building. Lawndale was also predominantly Jewish but more upscale than Maxwell Street, and few households could own property like the one Benjamin Alinsky bought.

Saul grew up in a very religious environment. His parents were strict Orthodox Jews, the family lived nearby some of the largest synagogues in Chicago, and the dense institutional network of synagogues, businesses, charities, and mutual aid societies made Lawndale look like an eastern European shtetl.[2] In 1922, Sarah and Benjamin got divorced and the latter moved to Los Angeles. Saul Alinsky did not develop a close relationship with his father, but going to Los Angeles to visit him allowed him to travel outside the confines of Chicago and expand his immediate environment. It taught him how to move back and forth between two worlds, a know-how that he would put to good use during his undergraduate and professional years.[3] Like all other sons and daughters of Jewish immigrants, Alinsky grew up in a society where anti-Semitism was part of daily life. Until he graduated from high school in 1926, Saul Alinsky was an average student. But as the only child of first-generation immigrants, he was endowed with a mandate for upward mobility that could primarily be honored through academic success and social recognition. In the 1972 *Playboy* interview, he insisted, with his signature dry irony, on how his professional status was a symbol of achievement in the eyes of his mother: "To other people, I'm a professional radical; to her, the important thing is, I'm a professional. To Momma, it was all anticlimactic after I got that college degree."[4] The college degree was not just a sign that the kid from Maxwell Street had made it into the world, however: the social learning and experience it encapsulates largely shaped Alinsky's subsequent professional trajectory.

URBAN SOCIOLOGY, REFORM, AND THE COMMUNITY ORGANIZATION TRADITION

In 1926, thanks to his family's relative financial stability and his decent grades, Alinsky was admitted into the University of Chicago, at the time one of the most dynamic institutional places for the social sciences—sociology in particular.[5] Emerging in the second half of the nineteenth century in France, Britain, and the United States, sociology as a nascent scientific discipline was fueled by the social survey movement and its ambition to investigate the living conditions of the growing urban proletariats in order to reform them. In the early decades, the discipline's development was deeply interwoven with reform-minded, Progressive Era circles. Some proponents of the discipline were sympathetic to socialism or even committed socialists, like Émile Durkheim in France and W. E. B. Du Bois in the US. A more precise understanding of social realities, of the complexities of group processes and institutions, sociologists believed, would strengthen society and make the government of individuals more democratic, rational, and efficient.

The intellectual production and reflections coming out of the University of Chicago—the theoretical works and empirical studies of sociologists like Ernest W. Burgess, Robert E. Park, and Louis Wirth, as well as the pragmatic philosophy developed by John Dewey and George Herbert Mead—vindicated the Progressives' belief that the "social milieu" determined individual and collective behaviors, which could not be reduced to psychological factors and biological heredity.[6] If that was indeed the case, reformers' primary goal must be to change people's environments in order to solve social problems. Jane Addams, who developed close friendships with many members of the University of Chicago Department of Sociology, was the best-known reform-minded figure blending a theory of society and militant praxis, but there were countless others in Chicago and in other industrializing urban centers who followed her lead.

The University of Chicago played a pivotal role in the development of a broader reform movement at the turn of the century. Founded in 1890 by the American Baptist Education Society and oil tycoon John D. Rockefeller, the institution quickly became a hotbed of intellectual activity. Its sociology department was the first in the country. In the fall of 1928, Alinsky enrolled into several courses taught by Burgess and Park, two of the main architects of the department. The way they defined and practiced their science had a profound effect on Alinsky's worldview and the categories he used to perceive and make sense of the social world. For Park and Burgess, sociology was fundamentally an empirical science: the sociologist's goal was to describe social processes from firsthand data collected through original investigative methods, where ethnographic immersion went hand in hand with statistical analysis. Their primary object was the city of Chicago itself, "its ethnic and racial intermixture, its social problems, its urban form and its local communities."[7] They looked at those phenomena through what they called an "ecological" lens. The ecological structure of a given city could be broken down into various "natural areas," each having their specific modes of organization, traditions, and customs that sociologists could describe and make sense of. In that regard, the community was a crucial unit in their conceptual apparatus and worldview: it referred to "societies and social groups where they are considered from the point of view of the geographical distribution of the individuals and institutions of which they are composed."[8]

To capture how multilayered interactions between individuals and institutions generated consent to social norms and habits, Chicago sociologists used the concept of "community organization." "The community, including the family, with its wider interests, its larger purposes, and its more deliberate aims, surrounds us, encloses us, and compels us to conform; not by mere pressure from without, not merely by the fear of censure, but by the sense of our interest in, and responsibility to, certain interests not our own."[9] When institutions in a given community such as the family, schools, churches, or voluntary associations failed to produce such conformity to the set of common rules that held society together, the community suffered from processes of "social disorganization," which in turn generated the various social ills that reformers fought against.

Understanding the factors underlying such processes could not be dissociated from a broader reform agenda whose political horizon was the integration of immigrant groups into the mainstream of US society. In an article from 1916, Burgess argued that the sociologist's role was not just to survey the population of a given "community" but to give that community the means to survey itself—a necessary first step toward improving people's living conditions.[10]

Studying sociology with Park and Burgess profoundly affected how Alinsky saw and experienced the world.[11] He quickly developed a long-lasting taste for the discipline, engaging in empirical fieldwork, learning how to cross social boundaries, embedding himself in hitherto unknown social environments (dance halls, bars, gang hideouts), and building relationships with people who resisted the normative push of bourgeois conformity. Under the supervision of Burgess, Park, and their colleagues, Alinsky learned how to conduct informal interviews, collect people's "lifestories," as Park and Burgess called them, observe people's daily practices, and find and analyze various written documents, from the most personal (diaries) to the most public (census records, demographic data, and the like). Sanford Horwitt, Alinsky's biographer, insists on the profound effect that this experience had on Alinsky.

> Alinsky flourished in this environment on the edges of conventional culture because, at the simplest level, he looked and sounded as if he belonged. With a cigarette dangling from the corner of his mouth, he could speak easily in the language of the street and could strike a pose that, if it did not quite suggest toughness, effectively passed for surliness. Where the pose ended and the real Saul Alinsky began was not always clear. What was clear, however, was that he was finally attracted to an academic pursuit that allowed him to draw on his strengths. In the process, he was also beginning to develop a sociological perspective, a more sophisticated understanding of the relationships among Chicago's institutions and people.[12]

After graduating with a bachelor's degree in 1930, Alinsky received a fellowship for a graduate program in criminology. He specialized in the study of organized crime. For the next two years, he managed to talk his way into Al Capone's gang and to develop somewhat of a close relationship with Capone's second-in-command, Frank Nitti, as well as other prominent mobsters throughout the city. Alinsky enjoyed the fieldwork itself, but he was not particularly thrilled by the other courses required to complete his PhD, such as statistics and sociological theory. In 1932, he dropped out of the graduate program and gave up on academia as a potential career. Instead, he started working as a criminologist and social worker.

In December 1931, Alinsky started working as a full-time assistant sociologist for Clifford Shaw at the Institute for Juvenile Research (IJR), a research institute affiliated with the Illinois Division of Criminology, in the Department of Public Welfare. Going into social-work institutions like the IJR, which straddled the fine line between scientific research and clinical work, was very common for sociology graduates at the time. Like Alinsky, Shaw was a University of Chicago sociology graduate and a former protégé of Burgess's. In 1930 he became famous in national reform circles for the book *The Jack-Roller: A Delinquent Boy's Own Story*, a first-person lifestory reconstructing the delinquent career of the son of Polish immigrants from Chicago's South Side and shedding light on the effects of that environment on juvenile delinquency.[13]

Between 1932 and 1935, while still employed by the IJR, Alinsky was detailed to the largest state penitentiary, in Joliet, Illinois, forty miles southwest of Chicago, as a staff sociologist and a member of the parole classification board. The year 1932 was also the year he married Helene Simon, a University of Chicago graduate herself who came from a wealthy German Jewish family in Philadelphia. The marriage introduced Alinsky to reformist sectors of the local ruling classes. It allowed him to expand his social horizons, climb farther up the social ladder, and accumulate new forms of social capital. When he got out with Helene's relatives and friends in the circles of Chicago's reform-minded, educated bourgeoisie, Alinsky compensated his relative lack of financial resources with the substantial symbolic gratifications he received from the colorful—and somewhat embellished—stories he loved to tell to entertain his audience about prisons, the Chicago mobs, and organized crime. As a result, Alinsky consolidated his position as an intermediary between otherwise disconnected social worlds. He became a master in the art of code-switching, which his family background and formal schooling had already predisposed him to.

In 1935, Alinsky left Joliet and went back to the IJR, where he started working on a new project of Shaw's: the Chicago Area Project (CAP). Funded by public and private money (Rockefeller in particular), the CAP was an experimental program launched in 1934 to push the residents of a given so-called disorganized area to fight against delinquency through collective organization.[14] It was a direct application of the Progressive Era belief that social surveys could be used as a tool for social reform. Shaw would send out assistant sociologists and other staff, colloquially known as "curbstone counselors," into neighborhoods CAP had identified as particularly prone to socially disorganized behaviors.[15] There, curbstone counselors "were literally to 'hang out' with youth in the customary gang haunts, to spend as much time as possible with them during after-school and evening hours, when their potential for mischief was considered to be the greatest."[16]

Alinsky, for instance, was assigned two groups, a gang of Italian American youths on the West Side and a gang of young Poles in Russell Square, on the South Side. Putting his ethnographer's skills and his ability to cross social boundaries to use, he successfully reached out to numerous youths and developed trusting relationships with them. Like his colleagues, he "assisted youth in trouble with the law, provided advice on handling personal or family problems, encouraged adolescents to stay in school, and helped youths find work."[17]

The main focus of those efforts was not individual behavior but their ecological underpinnings. Because juvenile delinquency was seen as the product of social disorganization, strengthening informal social control exerted by the community would prove a far more effective solution. Ideally, the community should be "able to supplement, and to some extent supplant, the family and neighborhood as a means for the discipline and control of the individual."[18] Hence the CAP's insistence on active citizen participation as the real long-term solution to juvenile delinquency and other ecological social problems. The scope of such participation was to be very local in nature; it was not to spill over into the political arena.

One of the tools that Shaw developed consisted in creating "community committees" bringing together the so-called natural leaders from a given area; the committees would then design and implement a whole range of programs that both addressed local welfare issues and fostered people's participation. In a ten-year retrospective report he sent to the board of directors of the Chicago Area Project, Shaw summed up CAP's mission: "The method of the Project has been to encourage and aid the residents of these communities to organize themselves into cooperative self-help units and through these groupings to initiate, finance, and manage programs of social and educational activities."[19]

Although Alinsky would later part ways with Shaw and academic disciplines, sociology as it was defined and practiced at the University of Chicago had a formative impact on his worldview. His focus on natural leaders, who he insisted were not necessarily the ones who occupied public leadership positions, can be directly traced back to his education as a sociologist and his work with Shaw. Same goes for the way he defined the organizer's outside position: it closely mirrored the curbstone counselor's role, itself modeled after how University of Chicago sociologists had defined the sociologist's role and position.

In emphasizing self-help at the community level as a solution to juvenile delinquency, CAP built upon a reform tradition that rejected two competing visions of social policy writ large: on the one hand, the individualizing, psychoanalysis-inspired practice of "casework," which had become the dominant trend in professional social work since the 1910s; on the other, the monopolization of social intervention by the state, which would come to be symbolized by Roosevelt's New Deal in the mid-1930s.[20] This middle ground, which Alinsky and his fellow curbstone counselors learned and internalized, was called community organization.

At first, community organization was synonymous with demands for increased democratic cooperation formulated by various sectors of the ruling classes in the context of US intervention into World War I. In early 1918, the Council of National Defense, formed in 1916 to coordinate and improve resource allocation, developed state and local community councils under the slogan "every community a little democracy."[21] The federal government was not the only one interested in boosting ordinary people's participation to consolidate the overall organization of society, however. Numerous social reformers embraced this perspective too. In a book published in 1918 titled *The New State: Group Organization and the Solution of Popular Government*, for instance, reformer and former social worker Mary Parker Follett, a notable intellectual figure of the Progressive Era whose first book was acclaimed by Theodore Roosevelt, developed an ambitious theory of the links between government, democratic values, and local communities and between the individual, the group, and the state. Only at the local level, Follett argued, could a real civic life and full realization of democratic ideals come into existence. What Follett called "group organization" was the most reasonable, rational, and effective way to solve the failure of representative government; avoid the evils of "crowd philosophy, crowd government, crowd patriotism"; and bring about genuine democracy.[22]

From 1916 to 1929, community organization grew and consolidated into an institutional object that was argued for in books, academic journals, conferences, and public interventions. But most social workers doubted its legitimacy, in the context of intense battles over the meaning and status of their occupation. In 1915, Abraham Flexner, an educator who had made a name for himself by writing a famous report on medical education commissioned by the Carnegie Foundation, had thrown down a public gauntlet at social work during a national conference by claiming that social work was not a genuine profession, like law, preaching, and medicine were: like other legitimate professions, social work combined an intellectual and a practical dimension, but it lacked a distinct area of activity, a clear, transmittable method, and it was too entangled with politics and conflict.

Over the next years, social workers would strive to give the lie to Flexner's bomb and prove him wrong. Professionalism appeared as the best way to "secure the trust and respect of lower-class clients as well as convince the upper classes to fund their work as social control agents and determiners of who was fit or unfit for aid."[23] Borrowing from a psychiatric understanding of individual problems and mobilizing Freud's psychoanalysis as its foundational abstract knowledge, casework became the favored way to establish social work's credibility and effectiveness. Mimicking the mechanisms and procedures that characterized the prestigious medical profession, professional associations of social workers were founded in the 1920s to shape a distinct professional identity and build channels of representation. Codes of ethics and qualifications were also elaborated; university courses were designed; specialized journals were created and circulated. In 1929, there were twenty-five master's programs in the country.[24]

As a result of this aggressive professionalization strategy, and against the backdrop of a broader political backlash targeting radical social movements in general, reform positions were marginalized within professional social work. As two social-work specialists argue, "the prevailing definition of the community organization function in social work became agency service coordination, administration, community fund raising, and community integration. Community organization as social and political reform was de-legitimated."[25] Even the type of supervised, rationalized civic participation that Mary Follett had called for receded into the background. In Chicago, the Chicago Central Council of Social Agencies lost the radical, political edge that had been at the core of the settlement movement led a decade earlier by Jane Addams, Mary McDowell, and many other reformers.[26]

The social crisis triggered by the Great Depression fundamentally altered the material bases and categories undergirding social policy. Traditional private actors, such as ethnic welfare agencies, fraternal associations, religious charities, and philanthropic institutions, were now faced with new contenders, like the federal government and labor unions, who argued that they, too, could provide for the welfare and security of individuals and that they could do it better.[27] In this new context, the type of rejuvenating civic participation that marginalized community organization practices advocated for could take on a new meaning. Those were some of the larger structural forces at play when, in the fall of 1938, Clifford Shaw sent Alinsky to set up a new CAP-powered community committee in the working-class immigrant neighborhood of Back of the Yards.

THE BACK OF THE YARDS NEIGHBORHOOD COUNCIL: A "MIRACLE OF DEMOCRACY"?

At that time, the popular belief in Chicago was that it was impossible to build anything resembling a community committee in Back of the Yards because the neighborhood was so deeply fragmented and segmented along ethnic lines that its residents shared little in common. Located south of the stockyards, the neighborhood was the setting for Upton Sinclair's best-selling 1906 novel, *The Jungle*, which made infamous the gruesome living and working conditions of workers in the meatpacking industry—most of whom were eastern European immigrants or their descendants. By the early twentieth century, Chicago's South Side was "a patchwork quilt of vibrant ethnic neighborhoods" from various national backgrounds (Irish, German, Polish, Lithuanian, Bohemian) where elite-driven "Americanization"—such as English instruction and naturalization—met with growing "ethnic national consciousness."[28] Religious beliefs and observance heightened such fragmentation. While 70 percent of the residents were Catholics, there were eleven different churches in the neighborhood, whose boundaries overlapped the ethnic boundaries separating the various groups. Indeed, most parishes included a school where the nuns in charge of teaching belonged to the same ethnic group as the pupils and their parents, relatives, and neighbors. Classes were taught in their native tongue rather than in English, thus creating largely autonomous ethnic microcosms that barely interacted with one another.[29]

The Great Depression and its aftermath hit the neighborhood particularly hard. It wiped out most of the informal solidarity network and ethnic mutual aid institutions that had so far helped residents cope with daily hardship. Despite the nationwide movement of worker revolts that swept the country in the 1930s and led to the creation of a powerful industrial union movement, forcing the Roosevelt administration to pass social legislation that, by US standards, was unprecedented, living conditions for the Back of the Yards residents remained difficult. After a new economic recession in 1938, unemployment reached 20 percent. For many, there were numerous days and nights without enough food on the table.

A shrewd observer of neighborhood formal and informal networks, Alinsky applied his sociologist's skills to identifying the various individuals he could reach out to and rely on to fulfil his CAP assignment. The first person he decided to approach was Joseph Meegan, the young director of nearby Davis Square Park. They met on February 23, 1939, at a meeting of the Packingtown Youth Committee, a youth organization sponsored by the union representing meatpacking workers, the Packinghouse Workers Organizing Committee (PWOC), which had been "formed to help other youths by improving their recreational facilities and helping them find jobs."[30]

The son of an Irish immigrant who went from working in the stockyards to being a janitor in a Catholic parish, Meegan had become park director in March 1937 after working as a schoolteacher for a couple of years. Like many of the other parks in the city that opened in the early twentieth century, Davis Square was meant to provide recreational spaces and playgrounds for children and adults alike. Its field house also contained gymnasiums, meeting rooms, a public library, and a cafeteria. In the face of dire living conditions, Meegan broadened the park's activities and started to turn his office into a pivotal institution for the neighborhood, providing both direct services—such as lunch programs with surplus food from the federal Department of Agriculture and free Halloween and Christmas parties for youngsters—and standing out as a driving force in the fabric of neighborhood life.

Like Alinsky, however, Meegan was critical of public-aid programs because he felt they treated the end products of poverty rather than its causes. Besides, they blunted people's sense of independence, dignity, and responsibility. Democratic self-organization, on the other hand, could rely on people's firsthand knowledge of their needs to find collective solutions. Both Alinsky and Meegan shared a common frustration with traditional social action and felt that "direct action was needed."[31] During their numerous meetings and telephone conversations, they talked about creating not just a CAP-oriented community committee but a new kind of organization that would bring together all the existing institutions in the neighborhood to represent its collective interests.

Thanks to Meegan's connections, Alinsky was introduced to Bishop Bernard Sheil, who would become the second pillar in the creation of the Back of the Yards Neighborhood Council (BYNC). Sheil was a singular figure in the world of US Catholicism. After he abandoned his initial ambition to become a major-league baseball pitcher, Sheil followed a religious vocation and became auxiliary bishop to the Archdiocese of Chicago in 1928. A dedicated supporter of social Catholicism, Sheil founded the Catholic Youth Organization in 1930 to provide working-class kids with a recreational alternative to both youth gangs and competing communist youth organizations.[32] Sheil was one of the very few Catholic higher-ups with national standing who actively supported the labor movement, the New Deal, and the struggles against racism. Although he held controversial positions within Catholic institutions, Sheil had an intimate knowledge of the city's Catholic networks, which played a significant role in organizing people's social interactions in immigrant working-class neighborhoods like Back of the Yards. Sheil knew exactly which church might be interested in Alinsky and Meegan's project. In addition to Sheil, several younger priests in the Back of the Yards were willing to engage in reform efforts and break with the older generation's nationalistic factionalism. At the founding meeting of the BYNC, on July 14, 1939, Sheil, the main speaker, was elected honorary chairman.

The third key person whom Alinsky met as part of his work for CAP was Herbert March, the PWOC's district director. The son of socialist Jewish immigrants, March grew up in a working-class neighborhood in Brooklyn. A member of the Communist Party, he was very active in the unemployed workers' movement in the late twenties and early thirties, first in New York and then Kansas City, as a Young Communist League organizer. In 1933 he and his wife moved to Chicago; while Herb started working in packing at Armour and Company, his wife Jane worked with the nearby University of Chicago's settlement house. March became one of the core organizers of what would officially become the PWOC in October 1937 after it was established and chartered by the Committee of Industrial Organizations (CIO) to take on the meatpacking industry, Chicago's second-largest industry. Furthermore, the CIO's organizing campaign in packing was launched after several unfruitful unionizing attempts in the late 1910s and early 1920s to create lasting union organization to protect workers' rights, organize workers beyond the color line, and roll back the bosses and owners' offensive and the introduction of scientific management practices in the wake of World War I.[33] March identified racism and the division between Black and white workers as a major obstacle to building a powerful union and argued that unionizing Black workers should be a priority.[34] He also "realized the value of community support for a union organizing drive, especially when the employers were tough and anti-union companies like packers."[35]

Claiming the Liberal Democratic Tradition

On July 14, 1939, through the combined efforts of Meegan, March, Sheil, and Alinsky, more than 350 people representing 76 local organizations from various ethnic groups and nationalities attended the first public meeting of the BYNC, where they adopted a statement of popular self-government as their motto: "We the people will work out our own destiny." That several hundred people from a whole gamut of organizations—from parish clubs, nationalistic lodges, and ethnic charities to social-athletic clubs, other youth organizations, and women's organizations—should attend the July 14 meeting and come to formulate shared goals and interests belied the notion that ethnic divisions were impossible to bridge in Back of the Yards.

On that day, delegates agreed on concrete resolutions and programs addressing health, childcare, child nutrition, employment, and housing issues. Delegates called for the creation of a neighborhood recreational facility and the implementation of disease-prevention and daycare programs. Against the backdrop of protracted class tensions on the shop floor in Chicago and across the country, the BYNC also called on meatpacking giant Armour to negotiate a settlement with Herb March's PWOC to prevent workers from going on strike. Within days of coming into existence, the BYNC showed it had the potential to wield real power in local politics. On July 16, Armour finally caved in: the packers agreed to settle with the union, officially recognized it, and conceded (modest) wage increases. It was the first time that the bosses' power on the shop floor and in the neighborhood more broadly was successfully challenged. The victory ended two decades of attacks against labor by packers and their middlemen.

Although improving living conditions in the neighborhood certainly was a real concern cementing the organization, it was not the BYNC's primary objective. Rather, the council's official statement of purpose stressed its civic-democratic foundation and outlook: "This organization is founded for the purpose of uniting all of the organizations within that community known as the 'Back of the Yards' in order to promote the welfare of all residents of that community regardless of their race, color or creed, so that they may all have the opportunity to find health, happiness and security through the democratic way of life."[36] Posited as the ultimate horizon of the council's activity, the "democratic way of life" had the potential to bridge ethnic divisions in the name of common interests. In the process, first- and second-generation "new immigrants" claimed as their own the long-standing ideals of US liberal democracy.

In the summer of 1939 in Chicago, appealing to the "democratic way of life" was laden with several layers of political meaning. At the local level, it reiterated what Democratic candidate and Czech immigrant Anton Cermak had done in 1931 when he was elected to city hall, thus putting an end to decades of Republican hold over city politics: Cermak had built a multiethnic coalition despite interethnic rivalries and long-standing Irish dominance. Instead, he brought together "new immigrants" from eastern and southern Europe into a new political bloc, forcing the Irish social and political elites to share power. An independent "organization of organizations" like the BYNC, which fell outside the scope of local ward bosses and their political machines, had the potential to challenge the status quo. But it also exemplified the type of multiethnic pressure groups acting as intermediaries speaking on behalf of otherwise fragmented factions, which fit nicely within the pluralistic "house for all peoples" that Cermak had called for, where ethnic allegiances were key in shaping voting behaviors and political identifications.[37]

Such alliances, however, did not cross the color line. Despite the growing number of African Americans who migrated to the city from the South, they remained excluded from social and political power for decades.[38] The 1919 riots had shown that African Americans' oppression and active relegation to the bottom of the social and racial order were, in the words of the Chicago Commission on Race Relations' 1922 report, "Chicago's greatest problem."[39] The riots "left an indelible mark on the city: its sense of boundaries, of relationships between neighbors, of fear and mistrust were cemented for a century to come."[40] Although the meatpacking union was indeed interracial, and although there were Black residents near Back of the Yards, the thought of building an interracial "organization of organizations" was not on the agenda.

Nationally, the rejuvenation of class struggles led by workers in the automobile industry, the rubber industry, and also farmworkers in the West, the unemployed in Michigan, and African American tenants in cities like Chicago signaled the consolidation of class politics on and outside the shop floor.[41] The turmoil of the Great Depression and social upheavals prompted various attempts inside and outside the Roosevelt administration to redefine democracy and dominant political institutions in terms of genuinely popular politics. Internationally, liberal capitalist democracies like the United States, the United Kingdom, and France were threatened by both the rise of the USSR and fascist regimes in Europe. Warnings about a "crisis of democracy"—a fear as old as the word itself—gained momentum among different sectors of the elite, strengthening the belief that something must be done to "save" it.[42]

These were the different meanings that the defense of the "democratic way of life" resonated with in the summer of 1939. The council emphasized civic education and active citizen participation in public life as its fundamental goals. Social antagonisms must take a back seat in the name of "unity," the building of "community" transcending class divides, and the creation of an educated people, as the council's slogan and logo—a worker in overalls, a priest, and a businessman all smiling against the backdrop of smokestacks—would later make clear.

The opposition between an organized, educated people and dangerous, irrational crowds, as well as the underlying unwillingness to see the social world in terms of class antagonisms, had been at the heart of the populist imagination of the late nineteenth century. It was also a defining feature of the Progressive Era reform movements and modern liberalism.[43] Building on this liberal tradition, the BYNC was premised on the belief in the principles of representative institutions: representatives should be designated through electoral channels; rulers should enjoy a relative independence in taking decisions, but conversely their constituents should be able to freely express their opinions; and public decisions must be taken deliberatively. The council's aim was to bring together all existing organizations, beyond ethnic or class divides, through their representatives, through formal procedures mimicking the country's foundation in order to create a new territorialized entity whose own representatives could legitimately claim they stood and spoke for "the people" and its localized expression, "the community." The political claim made by Back of the Yards residents in forming the BYNC was that they had every right to be considered as genuine, active American citizens.[44] "Packingtown people, like most Americans whether they are of the first or fifth generation, are joiners," wrote one journalist at the time, using a category that echoed nineteenth-century French liberal thinker Alexis de Tocqueville's idea that the strength of American democracy was voluntary association and active popular participation in the political process.[45]

The Park Director, the Union Organizer, the Priest—and Saul Alinsky

Why did a park director, a Catholic auxiliary bishop, and a communist labor organizer—an unlikely combination indeed—agree to Alinsky's initial project? Beyond the real personal sympathies these men shared for one another, they arguably all saw in Alinsky's assignment an opportunity to further their own agendas and the interests of the institutions they worked for. For Meegan, the creation of the BYNC was a way to consolidate the type of self-help social action he had been advocating as the head of Davis Square for a couple of years. For Sheil, not only could the project open up new organizational opportunities for the Church's charity work, but it could also push further the Americanization policies that Cardinal Mundelein had advocated in Chicago since the 1920s by showing a shared desire on the part of "new immigrants" to fully endorse the political ideals and values of liberal democracy.[46] For March, the BYNC could mean strengthening the PWOC's foothold in the community and neutralizing the opposition from the Catholic churches—a valuable asset and source of legitimacy in its struggle for union recognition against Armour.[47]

From Alinsky's perspective, it made sense to reach out to Meegan and Sheil: both represented "natural leaders" representing institutions that corresponded to the University of Chicago definition of community organization that he had internalized. But labor unions were something else altogether. They were not really the type of institutions that CAP field-workers went to when they tried to build community committees. They did not hold a significant place in the mental world of Shaw and other like-minded social reformers, who were at least as intent on fending off class politics as they were on solving social problems. Class politics put to the fore social antagonisms that reformers hoped they could bridge. Besides, in the 1920s unions wielded extremely limited social power, which means that unless someone believed in their usefulness and necessity regardless of their particular situation at a given moment, they would be unlikely to look to them as potential allies.[48] And while their numbers skyrocketed in the wake of workers' rank-and-file revolts in the 1930s, they were still looked at with distrust by many social reformers. Unsurprisingly, therefore, Shaw did not support Alinsky's decision to reach out to March and the PWOC. Bringing in such a controversial player as a CIO-affiliated union was not the purpose CAP's community committees were to serve. Several CAP funders also rejected the BYNC publicly supporting workers' unrest.

So why did Alinsky turn to March? Should the explanation be found in the fact that he belonged to a generation who came of age politically in the 1930s, in the wake of the Great Depression and the rising menace of fascism in Europe? Thousands of young people, a large portion of whom were the children of eastern European Jewish immigrants, joined political organizations like the Communist Party or labor unions and saw collective struggle as a path toward individual and collective self-realization.[49] In interviews he gave in the 1960s, Alinsky argued that he "went in there [in Back of the Yards] to fight fascism; delinquency was just incidental, the real crime was fascism. If you had asked me then what my profession was, I would have told you that I was a professional anti-fascist."[50]

It is actually difficult to pinpoint Alinsky's political practice with accuracy. He was never an active member of any political organization, labor union, or civic association where he could have acquired predispositions toward collective tasks and dedication to a cause. Given that Alinsky built his entire career on talking others into building and joining collective efforts, this is no small irony. While some accounts claim he was a volunteer labor organizer for the CIO in the second half of the 1930s, his biographer makes no reference to this.[51] Neither does Alinsky himself in the various interviews where he talks about his early political education. As he was growing up, because of his religious background, his experience of the social hardships of the time, and his scattered involvement in collective action, he did develop a deep sense of injustice and the conviction that ordinary people need to organize collectively to fight it. During his last year as a University of Chicago undergraduate, for instance, he helped organize solidarity toward striking Southern Illinois miners. During the Spanish Civil War, which soon became the focal point in the fight against fascism after it started in July 1936, he participated in a fundraising effort for the International Brigades.[52] But it does not seem that his commitments went farther than that.

The crucial factor in the formation of his politics was his association with the CIO, which was undoubtedly initiated by his wife Helene. In the mid-1930s Helene was a social worker and the president of a social workers' union affiliated with the CIO; she was also a member of the American League for Peace and Democracy, a coalition of left organizations founded in 1933 to oppose war and fascism, which liberals and conservatives alike thought was controlled by communists. Existing archival material and books do not say clearly when Alinsky got in touch with CIO organizers and officials.[53] All we know for sure is that his growing politicization materialized in his fascination for the CIO's national leader John L. Lewis and his sympathy for the popular-front strategy against fascism endorsed by the Third International in 1935. Former Alinsky right-hand man Nicholas von Hoffman writes that Alinsky, through his work with the BYNC, "became a confidant of Lewis's and an adviser or as much of one as the man's dictatorial personality would tolerate."[54]

The BYNC's unexpected success forced Alinsky to choose between two options. He could either follow the professional track he was on and, like many other people with the same background and education, pursue a respectable career in social work or criminology.[55] Or he could take a more adventurous path and try to capitalize on the BYNC's success. Although the exact reasons remain unknown, on January 15, 1940, Alinsky quit the Chicago Area Project. A couple of weeks later, he created the Industrial Areas Foundation to support his nascent career as a political entrepreneur, someone who would live off and for spreading the good word about rejuvenating US democracy through community organization.

From this fledgling organizational setting, he started to publicize the work he had done in Chicago and reached out to journalists. Public recognition came in the summer of 1940, at a moment when a new world war loomed larger, with France's swift defeat against Nazi Germany in June and Philippe Pétain's subsequent ascent to power. In the local and national press, the creation of the BYNC was hailed as a "miracle of democracy," and Alinsky turned into a champion of liberal democratic values and active citizen participation.[56] A long op-ed published in the *New York Herald Tribune* on August 21, 1940, titled "Democracy in the 'Jungle,'" glorified "an exciting experiment in democracy" that stirred "a sense of joint responsibility for the common welfare." The journalist emphatically prophesized that "in these difficult times, it may well mean the salvation of our way of life."[57] Another journalist writing in the *Survey Graphic* magazine similarly emphasized how "civic unity," in stark contrast with the other "dramas" that had unfolded in the neighborhood in the previous decades, had come about against all social odds in "Packingtown" to solve the community's "problems":

> The impossible is happening. Back of the Yards in Chicago. In that neighborhood next to the slaughter houses representatives from the local Chamber of Commerce, the American Legion Post, the AFL, the CIO, the Catholic Church—Protestants, Jews,

Irish, Slovaks, Mexicans, Poles—are gathering together in a new kind of attempt to solve the problems of a community. The experiment may effect a pattern for democratic action in industrial areas throughout the country.[58]

The BYNC was again taken up as an example by the press as the world conflict was coming to an end in the spring of 1945. In the *Washington Post*, Agnes Meyer, the newspaper's co-owner (who would soon become an IAF board member), wrote a lengthy six-part series called "An Orderly Revolution," where she extoled the council's virtues and accomplishments. Meyer's series, which President Harry Truman reportedly ordered be reissued for his personal use, consolidated the BYNC's legitimacy and Alinsky's growing fame.[59]

The elites extoling localized civic engagement as the best way to reactivate the US's exceptional democratic institutions in the face of impending war was nothing new. During World War I already, the *New York Times* had praised community councils as "neighborhood democracy made efficient by organization, not an autocratic bureaucracy of the type against which this war is waged"; indeed, the councils established "a direct means of communication between the Government and the people in their respective localities."[60] But this time around, there were two main differences. First, the "organization of organizations" that Alinsky, Meegan, March, and Sheil created in Back of the Yards resulted from an original blend of liberal community organization reform efforts on the one hand and militant labor movement tactics on the other. Over the years, the social alliances underlying this hybrid would be somewhat altered, with labor exiting the scene with the advent of the Cold War, but the initial balance between self-help and direct action would remain a guiding thread of Alinsky's "procedures."

The other difference was that there was someone whose upbringing and education had predisposed him to embrace the meritocratic myth and harbor ambitions about climbing the social ladder, someone whose academic schooling and occupational experiences had taught him to see expert, professional work as the best channel to do so—someone who was both objectively ready and subjectively willing to try to turn the promises of producing professionally controlled, "orderly" citizen participation into a career.

CHAPTER 3

MANAGING THE DEMOCRATIC CRISIS IN THE AGE OF THE COLD WAR

I n late August 1959, John O'Grady wrote to Cardinal Secretary of State Domenico Tardini, one of the most powerful Catholic officers in the Vatican, to introduce him to a good friend of his: Saul Alinsky. A social reformer who served as the executive secretary of the National Conference of Catholic Charities, which supervised and coordinated Catholic philanthropic activities at the national level, O'Grady was a vocal proponent of the social dimension of Catholicism. He and Alinsky had met in Chicago several years before and had become friends. In his letter to Tardini, O'Grady insisted on Alinsky's credentials. Granted, he was not a Catholic, but he "really [had] given his life to applying the doctrines of the Church, the doctrines that Pope Pius XII used to call a 'universal brotherhood,' to the ordinary relations of life."[1] He had also worked very closely with Samuel Stritch, Chicago's archbishop between 1940 and 1958, who shared O'Grady's commitment to the Church's social mission. They had been discussing the possibility of applying Alinsky's "principles" in "missionary countries" like Ghana or Nigeria, and in "the older countries of Europe, more especially in Italy" through Church-funded projects. O'Grady concluded his letter by insisting that he "would like to have Mr. Alinsky involved in the setting up of these projects."

A week later, to substantiate the positive introduction to Tardini, Alinsky sent O'Grady a private memorandum pointing out "how successful the work has been in Chicago and in other parts of the United States." The best case for his work, he felt, was that "when we apply these principles and practices into a situation such as in Italy we know it will work."[2] The memo started with a general diagnosis of the lay of the land. A "rapidly growing climate of despair, frustration, demoralization and bitterness among ever-increasing great parts of our people," where people and their children "[resigned] to an apathy of surrender," provided "the essential dry tinder for the flame of organized Communism," an obvious threat to democracy and freedom.[3] The problem was that all existing approaches to "counter these conditions and the Communist Party" had proved ineffective. The reason, Alinsky went on, was that they did not address the underlying cause of despair. They did not fill the "vacuum in the power and social life of the community." The "organizational practices and principles" Alinsky had developed first through the Back of the Yards Neighborhood Council and then with the Industrial Areas Foundation (IAF), on the other hand, could fill this "vacuum." By creating "a responsible area of authority which possesses the loyalty of the people by virtue of its active representation and implementation of the people's hopes and desires," these practices and principles fought against apathy and the feeling to be left out through the active stimulation of social ties at the community level. As a result, they produced "an exciting experience which becomes a most potent weapon against the fundamentally dull, monotonous robot-like character of Communist operation." Such a "positive approach," which focused on "the basic conditions affecting the people," had rapidly undermined Communists "everywhere" the IAF had worked, Alinsky boasted. And he was confident that it could be applied effectively in any situation, "whether it took place in Rome or in Tokyo."[4] In April 1960, Alinsky flew to Rome to discuss the partnership project with Catholic officials.

The archives do not say whether the project came to fruition. But the anecdote sheds light on some of the ways in which Alinsky built his line of work and established his reputation. It shows, in particular, how much anti-communism was baked into Alinsky's professional project.

The Vatican was not the only institution whose anti-communist agenda resonated with Alinsky's "procedures."[5] In the aftermath of World War II, the partition of geopolitical alliances into two antagonistic blocs competing for world hegemony while European domination in its colonies was unraveling transformed anti-communism into a cornerstone of US politics abroad and at home. Red-baiting and the state-sanctioned repression of radicals of all stripes already had enjoyed a long history by then, but in the Cold War context they took on an even more urgent meaning. As historians have shown, the scope of anti-communism as a dominant cultural code was more structural than Wisconsin senator Joseph McCarthy's witch hunts or the House Un-American Activities Committee's hearings. It was built into the very fabric of the Cold War ideology.[6]

Anti-communism destroyed people's careers and personal lives, reorganized prevailing social norms, and redefined the contours of what was politically thinkable and doable. Similarly, the Cold War transformed the collective fate of African Americans into a geopolitical issue. Against the backdrop of the Great Migration from former Confederate states to northern and western metropolises, the successful "integration" of African Americans and other racial minorities into the mainstream of society would prove the validity and superiority of the "democratic way of life."[7] "Freedom" and "democracy" became redefined as absolute opposites of anything remotely associated with Soviet communism.[8] If freedom and democracy were core American values, and if communism was the exact opposite of them, it then followed that communism was "un-American" and represented the political threat par excellence.

What has been overlooked, however, is how these overarching political norms shaped and legitimized a growing professional sector dedicated to what President Harry Truman called "[correcting] the remaining imperfections"[9] of US democracy by encouraging active, neighborhood-based citizen participation. This "civic" imperative was taken up by several public and private institutions who perceived their activities in terms of professional expertise. Through their encouragement of citizen participation and voluntary association, these actors made a major contribution to cementing the Cold War dominant ideology and the belief in the intrinsic superiority of US political institutions.

Alinsky and the IAF occupied an original position within this emerging sector. Most existing analyses of his career and the development of the IAF tend to focus on their contribution to building active citizen participation and representation without articulating it with anti-communism. Sanford Horwitt, for instance, calls Alinsky an "Anti-Anti-Communist," insisting on his disdain for McCarthy's methods and worldview, the FBI's active surveillance of his activity, and his support to various friends who "had gotten caught in the web of anti-communism."[10] Mike Miller and Aaron Schutz rightfully point out that the all-out attacks against organized labor following the Taft-Hartley Act of 1947 undermined the relationships with labor unions, who had been a central pillar in building the BYNC but whose role in supporting the IAF rapidly vanished. And yet, as the Vatican anecdote makes crystal clear, Alinsky *did* conceive of his work and vision of democracy as the most effective way to positively combat communism.

To understand how and why Alinsky defined anti-communism through a professional logic and how it reverberated onto the work itself, three elements must be considered: Alinsky's nascent career as a political entrepreneur; what the organizers Alinsky hired did to implement his "organizational practices and principles"; and the ambiguous version of anti-communism that was subsequently developed.

A POLITICAL ENTREPRENEUR IN MILITANT LIBERALISM

Whatever their take on Alinsky's politics and legacy, most existing accounts emphasize his contribution to political ideas and political theory. While Miller and Schutz enthusiastically highlight his "core concepts" and values about democracy, Bardacke's critical perspective considers "Alinskyism" as a genuine political ideology that still holds a strong influence in American politics.[11] What these analyses partly miss in portraying him as a political theorist, though, is the professional dimension of his activity.

Political Crème Brûlée

Alinsky's contribution to political ideas was first synthesized into *Reveille for Radicals*. Published in 1946, the book reflected on his own experience in Back of the Yards and elsewhere and laid out Alinsky's conception of democracy, collective action, and civic education. But it also offered practical solutions to what he diagnosed as a "democratic crisis" through an idiosyncratic blend of different intellectual and political traditions. The book's bottom-line argument was pretty straightforward: only "people's organizations" following the blueprint laid out in Back of the Yards and bringing together existing local institutions on a cross-class, interethnic, and interracial basis could regenerate a democratic system that was undermined by industrialization, urban anonymity, and social isolation.

Alinsky's political imagination was deeply shaped, first, by the American liberal political tradition, as was suggested by an epigraph quoting Thomas Paine or by the frequent references to figures like Jefferson, Madison, or Hamilton. At heart, his conception of democracy is undergirded by a deep-seated belief in the value of compromise. It is pluralistic and representative. Borrowing directly and heavily from Alexis de Tocqueville's analyses of US democracy, Alinsky posits that the voluntary association of rational citizens, whose actions depend on their own self-interest, is the foundation upon which a pluralistic regime can rest and whose goal is to arbitrate between these individual interests and a broader, collective interest.

For Alinsky, while "the people" is the absolute source of political legitimacy and sovereignty, it only exists as a political entity insofar as it is organized and represented. Democratic life is made of organizations representing various groups who deliberate with one another and apply pressure on elected representatives to defend their members' interests. If the active engagement of citizens is the standard to assess a republic's health, then political participation becomes a political goal in itself, a form of democratic schooling in practice. Direct democracy, the notion that political representation constitutes an obstacle to people's active participation to political life, has no place in Alinsky's perspective: "The only way that people can express themselves is through their leaders. By their leaders we mean those persons whom the local people define and look up to as leaders.... These indigenous leaders are in a very true sense the real representatives of the people of the community."[12] In keeping with dominant tenets in social psychology at the time, the leadership qualities attributed to these individuals meant that changes in their behaviors would be followed by other members of their respective institutions.

This liberal-democratic imagination articulated with Alinsky's intellectual and professional training as a sociologist and social worker. His insistence on "community" as the basic unit and horizon for political interactions can be seen as the political application of Park and Burgess's sociological work, where the organization of urban life into semiautonomous, local communities appeared as a determining phenomenon in modern social life. Communities were not havens of harmony, however: conflict between individuals and social groups plays a cardinal, dynamic role in shaping them. Park argued, for instance, that conflict does not weaken social ties; quite the opposite: it strengthens people's sense of belonging and drives "acculturation" processes and assimilation into the organic whole of American society.[13] Alinsky's obsession with conflict and power is a direct application from the work of Park, Burgess, and their colleagues. In a language tinged with Hobbesian hues, he posits the conflictual defense of people's self-interests as the unavoidable condition of humankind. Rather than pretend this primordial reality can and should be papered over with moral principles, the "radicals" glorified in Alinsky's book should embrace "the world as it is" and harness people's self-interests toward a greater common good.

The blending together of these two intellectual threads is the reason why Alinsky calls for a hard-nosed, "radical" embrace of conflict and power while at the same time exalting the virtues of pluralism—a militant liberalism of sorts. To put it differently, Alinsky's idiosyncratic mix resembles a crème brûlée: a thin crust of broiled power politics on top of a smooth and creamy custard of negotiation and compromise. The trick is, of course, that if you don't crack the top with your spoon, the outside appearance of it all might fool you into thinking that the dessert is all about crisp, when it really is not.

It would be a mistake, nonetheless, to conclude that "the people" is *Reveille*'s main protagonist. The real subject in Alinsky's "procedures" is not the "democratically minded people." The hero is the one who kindles their active participation in public affairs, who identifies the "real leaders" in a given community, who wins victories showing "the people" that they must band together in the self-interest of all, who shapes "people's organizations" from behind the scenes before lonesomely moving on to another community, the eternal outsider who makes democracy happen—the organizer. In Alinsky's terminology, "organizer" is synonymous with "radical"; he uses both terms interchangeably. The radical is the real heir to the American democratic tradition: "America was begun by its radicals. America was built by its radicals. The hope and future of America lies with its radicals." Because of his vocation, the radical can foster conflict between "the people" and their representatives to fulfill his historic destiny: the actual realization of America's democratic genius.[14] As Alinsky wrote in the new introduction to the 1969 edition of *Reveille*, "Paradoxically the roots of the radical's irreverence toward his present society lie in his reverence for the values and promises of the democratic faith, of the free and open society."[15] Hence his unfaltering defense of US political institutions, whose antidemocratic nature he never calls into question.

Alinsky's definition of the organizer's role builds upon his professional training as a sociologist and a social worker, but it also borrows from the labor movements of the 1930s. Although his exposure to CIO organizing practices was arguably shallow, his fascination for and proximity with John Lewis led him to borrow many of its conflict tactics and adapt some of its organizational practices to a new setting—out of the workplace and into the community. Indeed, the "organizer" in *Reveille* bears many similarities with the paid organizers sent by labor unions and federations in the late nineteenth century to create unions in workplaces throughout the country. The Knights of Labor, the first national labor federation in the country, concluded their 1886 Declaration of Principles by offering their services in the following terms: "If you believe in organization, you are earnestly invited to join with us in securing these objects. All information on the subject of organization should be sent to the General Secretary-Treasurer of the Order, who will have an Organizer visit you and assist in furthering the good work."[16] In the 1930s, the CIO's national organizing drives were implemented by hundreds of paid organizers, many of whom, like Alinsky's friend Herb March in Chicago, were communists.

By shedding light in *Reveille* on the actual mechanics of organization building and the organizer's role, Alinsky echoed a widely read 1936 booklet by labor organizer and Communist Party leader William Z. Foster, *Organizing Methods in the Steel Industry*. But *Reveille* signaled a dramatic departure from this genealogy by turning its back on the labor movement and focusing on its bureaucratic structures. Ironically, the book came out right in the middle of a postwar strike wave spreading across the nation, with some five million strikers in 1946 alone—and not long before labor leaders started purging their ranks of communists, socialists, and other radicals.[17] To Alinsky, with collective bargaining integrating unions into the daily operation of the capitalist economy, labor unions had become "strong, wealthy, fat, and respectable"—they behaved very much like organized business.[18] As a result, union leaders had an interest in maintaining the status quo to keep their organizations running. The labor movement was not bound to behave like a corporation protecting its own interests: it could still play a progressive role if it freed itself from the bureaucratic shackles of collective bargaining and extended its strategic horizons beyond strict bread-and-butter workplace issues.

Of course, the critiques against labor's bureaucratization have a rich history on the left, and on the surface it might seem like they resonate with Alinsky's analysis. But they actually lead to different conclusions. Indeed, Alinsky prophesized that if labor unions failed to fight against bureaucratic trends, they would be superseded by cross-class people's organizations as a positive politicizing collective force because these organizations saw workers not just as workers but as "American citizens." In formulating such a line of criticism, Alinsky built upon a long-standing Progressive tradition of anti-union rhetoric, with thinkers like Louis Brandeis trying to formulate a balanced defense of industrial democracy, fully compatible with the liberal tradition, supporting workers' right to strike while warning unions against the threats a closed shop system posed to individual freedom.[19]

Diagnosing and Treating the Democratic Crisis

Reveille for Radicals was an immediate best-seller. It was praised throughout the mainstream press, from the liberal *New York Times* and *Time* magazine to conservative publications like the *New York Herald Tribune* and the *Chicago Tribune*. It firmly established Alinsky's reputation as an expert in citizen participation and civic voluntarism. But the importance of Alinsky's contribution did not reside in his theoretical arguments.

What is most significant in *Reveille*—and Alinsky's ideas more generally—is not their theoretical inconsistencies or "philosophical poverty"[20] but the claims that there were certain universal principles of organization and power that applied to any situation (so-called positives and negatives), which could be used to rejuvenate democratic institutions, and which he had discovered and knew how to use. More particularly, what was specific about these claims was that Alinsky formulated them in terms of a professional expertise that could solve any problem identified as such. And a deficit in citizen participation was a problem Alinsky could solve better than other existing professions, such as professional social workers, because he knew how to create representative, effective "power" organizations.

In resorting to the language of professional expertise, he tried to convince his audiences—the groups who were interested in using the Industrial Areas Foundation's services, such as the Vatican, but also the reform-minded fractions of the ruling class who were willing to give money to the IAF itself—that his ideas about citizen participation and political action were valid and, above all, effective. Alinsky's organizer did not come out of the rank and file, as had hitherto been the case for most union organizers, who were recruited by unions as part-time or full-time staff from their workplaces. The organizer described in *Reveille* and operationalized into IAF job positions was, from the start, a full-time professional. More specifically, the organizer's role resembled something like a sociologically trained social worker cum political agitator cum human relations management consultant.[21]

Indeed, the history of management practices in the first decades of the twentieth century is key to understanding the arc of Alinsky's career and the particular expertise he built, as Patrick's second pile of books intimated. At the time when Alinsky presented himself as an expert in innovative "voluntary community organizational procedures,"[22] the word "organization" resonated first with concerns that had little to do with social justice. The need for organization, for more effective ways to harness individual interests and motivations to collective goals and hierarchy, had been a prime concern for a whole range of business actors from the late nineteenth century on, which fueled the birth of white-collar supervisory professions like manager, engineer, and management consultant.[23] These new intermediary positions and roles were meant to control the production process in order to increase workers' productivity and profit. Frederick Winslow Taylor or Henri Fayol were the most prominent figures in this "managerial revolution," trying to codify these new roles and establish universal, scientific management principles.[24] In this perspective, "organizing" toward more effectiveness and efficiency was a central component in a manager's activity. In the first decades of the twentieth century, words like "efficiency," "engineering," and "organization" spread to other sectors of US society and entered the political lexicon, laden with rational, scientific legitimacy.[25]

The growing body of knowledge produced on management did not just rely on the principles of scientific management, however. Just as decisive was the focus on "human relations" as a pivotal element to improve organization efforts and industrial efficiency. In the late 1920s, sociologist Elton Mayo and his team conducted a series of experiments at the Hawthorne Works factory in Cicero, Illinois, and discovered the importance of emotional elements in workers' productivity. Contrary to what Taylor's principles suggested, meeting workers' social and psychological needs was a prerequisite for increased productivity. As a result, managers should look toward fostering workers' motivation and loyalty to their corporation by focusing on creating positive dynamics between workers and their hierarchy, but also among workers themselves. A wealth of experts came up with different ways of harnessing individual drives and concerns to an organization's own goals.

Ironically, at the time when Alinsky created the BYNC, business executive Chester Barnard had just published *The Functions of the Executive* (1938), a best-selling book where he presented "a theory of cooperation and organization," building upon Mayo's insights that resonated very much with Alinsky's work in Back of the Yards. For any organization to last, Barnard argued, it must be effective in accomplishing its stated goals, but it also needed to be efficient and satisfy the motives of its members. The executives, who occupy leadership positions in the organization, must therefore make sure they initiate, develop, and maintain cooperation among workers.

The focus on human relations as a key issue in managerial practice was brought to the fore when the United States entered World War II. The need to increase productivity in strategic industries became all the more urgent. Roosevelt created the War Manpower Commission in April 1942 to determine the needs for employment in key industries and make sure the entire workforce participated in the war effort without clashes and conflict among workers. Although the details remain unknown, Alinsky worked for that commission for several years. He "was involved in efforts to maintain worker morale and harmony in key industries, such as in defense plants," working alongside Black labor leader Hank Johnson to convince white workers to work alongside African Americans.[26] Because what people do for a living plays such an important role in shaping their worldviews, and because the war was so central in confirming Alinsky's deep-seated attachment to the genius of US political institutions, one can reasonably argue that such a stint at the War Manpower Commission left an important impact on Alinsky. It must have corroborated his belief in the virtues of "organization" and the importance of finding ways to bridge social and racial divides, which he had already internalized for years as a sociology student and criminologist.

It is unclear whether Alinsky read management theory or psycho-sociologists like Kurt Lewin, who started working on group dynamics in the 1940s. But in a certain way, when he emphasized the radical's organizational expertise and rationality, or the ability to identify "indigenous leaders" who would represent citizens' voices and interests more authentically, he extended some of the core tenets of management theory—about rationalization, efficiency, leadership, and productivity—to social relations in general. Producing legitimate, skilled community leaders whose seating at a wide range of negotiating tables would create a more stable, predictable system of interindividual and intergroup relations dovetailed with a lot of what management theorists advocated for. So when Alinsky set up shop to sell his nascent expertise to various clients under the banner of the Industrial Areas

Foundation, he established a consulting agency specializing in democratic apathy management.

SELLING SERVICES IN VOLUNTARY CITIZEN PARTICIPATION

When he founded the IAF in the early days of 1940, in the wake of the BYNC's unexpected success, Alinsky sought to "spread this work across the Midwest, particularly in places with sympathetic bishops and strong locals in the Packinghouse Workers union," thanks to his friendship with Bishop Sheil and PWOC officials.[27] Soon, other projects were launched in Kansas City, Missouri, and Saint Paul, Minnesota, in 1940–1941. But they were abruptly interrupted by the Japanese attack on Pearl Harbor on December 7, 1941, and the subsequent US military involvement into World War II. After Alinsky came back from the War Manpower Commission, he resumed building the IAF.

From the late 1940s on, the organization grew nationally, as new requests came in from across the country—from Los Angeles to New York City, Buffalo to Butte. Alinsky hired a full-time secretary, Dorothy Levin, to whom he delegated most of the administrative work he had overseen so far. This allowed him to focus on more gratifying and socially valued tasks as executive director: designing projects; fundraising; managing the IAF staff; developing his ties and relationships with members of the intellectual, political, and economic elites; and giving lectures and speeches. Though his fiery, bravado-inflicted rhetoric valued radicalism and conflict, his class position was determined by his large cultural capital, his elite-oriented social capital, and his growing economic resources. As early as 1942, the *Who's Who in Chicago*, a biographical dictionary cataloguing the local elites, included an entry with his name, where he was listed under the heading "sociologist." Despite his public scorn for professional social work throughout the 1940s and until the early 1950s, he kept close ties with this milieu, particularly the worlds of criminology and juvenile delinquency prevention.[28] Alinsky's burgeoning career meant that his standard of living was relatively comfortable. In 1947, after his wife Helene died, the board doubled his salary to $15,000 and started a $5,000 retirement plan (or $195,000 and $65,000 in 2021 dollars).[29]

As the IAF grew, a strict, hierarchical division of labor was established. Ironically, although Alinsky praised the work of building people's organizations as a key solution to the crisis of democracy, he quickly stopped performing the tedious, day-to-day tasks of organization building, which he delegated to his subordinates in the IAF hierarchy.

A Wide Array of Organizational Techniques

The actual building of people's organizations was performed by organizers, whom Alinsky recruited himself but who never stayed long.[30] Turnover was quite high. That bottom layer in the hierarchy was managed and monitored by supervisors—Fred Ross in California and, from 1953 on, Nicholas von Hoffman. When the IAF's "assistance" was contracted by an individual client or a group of organizations, one of the organizers on staff was dispatched to set up new "organizations of organizations."

Their work started with a careful, detailed study of the neighborhoods they were sent into. Borrowing from the ethnographic community surveys performed at the University of Chicago Department of Sociology, organizers would start by embedding themselves into local community life to find out the issues that could bring all the existing forces together, identifying local institutions, gathering places, and relationship networks that structured people's lives. "[John] Egan and I spent about five hours just walking around the area, up one street and down the other, making notes of churches, organizations, etc., that we saw in talking with people," Lester Hunt reported in September 1957.[31] The immersive inquiry was complemented with the study of official documents (census data, reports from municipal committees) and newspaper clippings. This prospective work was meant to identify two elements that were central in Alinsky's expertise: "Plot the power pattern of the community, and search out and evaluate the local leaders."[32]

Although the specifics of the work varied greatly from one context to another, it basically followed the same pattern. First, because there was no systematic match between official leadership titles and the "real," "natural," "indigenous" leaders who actually controlled an organization or a community, firsthand observation and research were needed to identify them. "Leaders are found by organizing, and leaders are developed through organization," stated von Hoffman in a speech he gave in 1963 at the second Students for a Democratic Society national conference. Organization and leadership being "inseparable," creating a new organization logically implied making new leaders and new leadership.[33]

Organizers then conducted individual interviews with people they had identified as local leaders in order to convince them that creating a new organization federating all existing institutions would serve their interests and reinforce their bargaining power. This required some convincing and sweet-talking since, as Alinsky, von Hoffman, and IAF organizer Lester Hunt put it, "it is not true . . . that just because people know what some of the problems in their community are that they will do anything about them. As a matter of fact, we are more correct to assume that they won't do anything about them." Finding ways to make people realize that "it is THEY who must do something about their own problems" was similar to being a labor "agitator."[34] Soon that word turned into a transitive verb of its own, to agitate, which became part of the IAF lingo. In IAF terminology, "to agitate someone" meant to make them do something about the local issues they had identified and not just complain about them.

After managing to recruit enough "indigenous leaders" and agitate them into action, organizers brought them together into a temporary committee that would then recruit other organizations. When enough organizations were on board and the newly formed group was representative of all preexisting voices, the classical tools and rituals of representative democracy came into play. A founding convention was set up, with democratically elected delegates who then drafted a constitution and bylaws, elected officers, created ad hoc or standing committees, and so on.

In California, the work developed by Fred Ross followed a slightly different pattern. Alinsky had hired Ross in 1947 after the two met through a mutual acquaintance, University of Chicago sociologist and prominent local reformer Louis Wirth, who regularly played poker with Alinsky in Hyde Park. When Ross joined the IAF, Alinsky immediately dispatched him to California to expand the IAF's community organization procedures. But rather than use the BYNC routine of setting up representative organizations of organizations, where individual institutions paid dues to the new organization, Ross decided to build direct-membership chapters.

The departure from the work patterns modeled after the BYNC had to do with the differences in community patterns in the Mexican American communities of California, where Ross concluded that it would be very difficult and counterproductive to work with the Catholic Church there. Instead, Ross identified informal or potential leaders whom he then talked into organizing "house meetings" to discuss daily issues and concerns with other relatives and neighbors. Those meetings represented a safer, more private place to meet and talk as well as a more effective recruitment tool: through a combination of informal social control, moral obligation, and pride, they forced the host to make sure that people would attend. A successful "house meeting" demonstrated that there was local interest in getting collectively involved in civic duties and could then lead to the organization of a new Community Service Organization (CSO) chapter. Similar chapters spread rapidly to the entire state of California and made some inroads in neighboring Arizona. Soon, the CSO became known as "Alinsky's most successful early project outside Chicago" and the organizational vehicle for Cesar Chavez's first foray into politics.[35]

Archival records do not really say how Alinsky reacted to Ross's changes in how the organization-building work was performed. But given Alinsky's pragmatism and opportunism, what probably happened is that he did not really care how exactly Ross did it as long as the work produced tangible results and led to the creation of new, powerful organizations. In any case, Alinsky always seemed pleased with Ross's work on the West Coast. For years in the annual IAF reports, the sections on the CSO chapters in California and Arizona were the most developed ones. In 1953, Alinsky appointed Ross as IAF West Coast director and raised his annual salary to $8,500 ($88,000 in 2021 dollars). But the CSO's house meetings and direct-membership style always remained a separate entity. In all his other endeavors, Alinsky still favored building IAF-supervised "organizations of organizations."

In the mid-1950s, the IAF grew in profile and prominence. Its activities diversified around three axes: consulting, staff training, and adult education programs. Aside from conducting surveys leading to the creation of new representative organizations, the IAF increasingly acted in a consulting capacity for other, preexisting organizations that already had their own staff. "With reference to methods of community organization and consolidation," it provided a number of services like "personnel selection, training of staff people, overall evaluation of community operations of outside organizations and recommendations for same, and consultation for solving specific organizational problems in the area of community organization."[36]

An example of this was the IAF's intervention in the Chelsea neighborhood of New York City. After receiving a three-year $120,000 grant (or $1.2 million today) from the New York Foundation, Alinsky started working with a settlement house called the Hudson Guild Neighborhood House to focus on the neighborhood's growing Puerto Rican population. His early doubts about the project's feasibility (he thought that professional social workers were incapable of building powerful organizations that did not shy away from the reality of power and conflict) offer a good illustration of the type of competitive relationship he maintained with professional social work. To him, social work was more about working "for" the people rather than "with" them, which meant standing in the way of ordinary people's becoming truly active citizens. Still, Alinsky decided to take that "calculated risk" and concluded that "certainly a partial projection of the ideas and concepts of the Industrial Areas Foundation into community organization is better than none at all."[37]

Second, the IAF started to act as a training ground for "key personnel of major institutions in the understanding of power patterns of community life, and in the acquiring of familiarity and competency in the various procedures, practices and principles of community organization."[38] These institutions were primarily religious ones. They included the Catholic Archdiocese in Chicago and the Protestant National Council of the Churches of Christ, which sent small groups of its clerics from almost every Protestant denomination to learn the IAF's work methods by being assigned as trainees to specific IAF-supervised organizations over an extended period of time. In a letter from May 1956 to Marshall Field III, the famous capitalist, banker, and president of the IAF board, Alinsky gloated,

> The Catholic Archdiocese in Chicago is desirous of our training some of their people in community organization for which the Archdiocese contributes their salary into the Industrial Areas Foundation. The same thing is beginning to develop in the West Coast where Presbyterian churches are requesting assignment of about six of their best people to work under the supervision of the Industrial Areas Foundation staff and be trained in our procedures.[39]

Alinsky was delighted about the prospects that these collaborations entailed in terms of disseminating his work. "The potentialities inherent in the churches opening up are enormous," he told his friend Robert Hutchins, a former University of Chicago president who would later become a senior executive at the Ford Foundation.[40]

Lastly, the IAF initiated "adult education programs" in California through local CSO chapters. In its early days, the CSO's "adult education" activities rested on two main pillars: citizenship classes—with classes on the US Constitution being taught in Spanish—and voter registration drives throughout the state. For instance, it registered fifteen thousand new voters to help elect Edward Roybal to the Los Angeles City Council in 1949, "the first time in the century that a Spanish-speaking Hispanic had been elected" there.[41] Over the years, CSO chapters provided direct services in areas like "health and housing, discrimination and civil liberties, delinquency prevention, citizenship education and naturalization, safety, integration with the larger community youth programs,"[42] which departed from other IAF-initiated projects. Despite the confirmation that the CSO worked in a relatively autonomous way, all its projects remained undergirded by the central claim Alinsky built his professional career upon: active citizen participation was necessary for people to come up with solutions to their own problems, but such participation must be fostered by outside experts.

Management Consultants in Disguise?

The expertise the IAF organizers used to "encourage voluntary citizenship participation"[43] can be broken down into two main skills, which closely resembled the type of work that management consultants performed. Management consultants performed two main work tasks: they brought new ideas to organizations, and they analyzed gaps and pitfalls in order to improve an organization's performance.[44]

First, organizers must be pragmatic, which meant they must have a sense of precision and detail, refrain from showing their own politics and ideological perspective, and be able to adapt to ever-changing situations. Indeed, encouraging new leadership to emerge meant recognizing that the organization's leadership figures could evolve over time. "At the beginning keep the organization very loose, spread the responsibilities and the conspicuous places around," von Hoffman warned. "This permits you and the new membership which you are supposed to be recruiting, to judge the talent, and it keeps things sufficiently porous so that new talent isn't blocked off." This pragmatic recognition necessitated what von Hoffman called a "calculating mentality," constantly evaluating the costs and benefits of any given situation and decision.

The injunction to pragmatism combined with another skill: reflexivity and self-criticism. "The calculating organizer is forever suspicious of himself, forever mistrusting his analysis of the situation, and his plan of action. He is always asking himself questions like what am I doing? Why am I doing it? What if I succeed in doing what I am trying to do, will we really have gained anything worth gaining. However the organizer with a calculating mentality shall assuredly fail if he is trying to do the undoable."[45] Reflecting on a failed action organized in Chicago by the Woodlawn Organization (TWO) against school segregation, von Hoffman insisted that the point of self-critical analysis was to identify mistakes in order to improve the organization's efficiency and accumulate victories against its adversaries: "All flops (and we have had them in the past) must be carefully dissected to learn their causes."[46] In order to learn from those mistakes, it was necessary to identify them and name them, to conduct a nuanced analysis of the situation and the balance of forces at play in order to infer more general principles for action, which could then be applied to new organizational situations.

The organizer's role was almost that of a technician, one that existed outside of political and ideological struggles. "The organizer's first job is to organize," von Hoffman wrote, "not right wrongs, not avenge injustice, not to win the battle for freedom. That is the task of people who will accomplish it through the organization if it ever gets built. When things are looked at through the glass of organizational calculation, they assume new shapes."[47] Von Hoffman's portrayal was disingenuous, however. It dissimulated the underlying power dynamics in the name of organizational effectiveness and neutrality. The arrival of an IAF organizer in a given neighborhood or locality introduced a very strict division of labor. Activating the "calculating mentality" meant that organizers controlled—or at least tried to establish control over—the course of events. In theory, they should "know what they are doing, why they are doing it, and the relationship of their specific act of the time to a general plan of action. They become deliberate and knowing in their activities."[48] Such cognitive superiority, which is so central to the distinction between professionals and "the laity," put them in a position where they could potentially manipulate the organization's members into doing things without their full knowledge or consent.[49]

But the relation of power at play was contradicted and dissimulated by the belief—what sociologists would call a well-founded illusion—that community organizers were "destined to be employees of the people."[50] They were "the servants of the people in the organization and the people in the community."[51] The paradox in their position was that they must disappear behind those they serve. They must "develop self-reliance and aggressiveness in people" without doing things for them, such as "[approaching] public officials and other so-called important persons and demand what they want."[52] Otherwise, people became dependent on the organizer's knowledge and know-how, which hampered the development of individual and collective leadership and self-determination. If organizers did not take a step back, they risked "dulling" people's civic enthusiasm. They constantly performed a balancing act: trying to gain the residents' trust to teach them how to overcome their feeling of social and political illegitimacy and "apathy" while refraining from speaking and acting for them.

As a result, the end goal for IAF organizers was to become superfluous. "The most successful staff man is one who has worked himself out of a job," von Hoffman wrote. "A perfect organizational job, I repeat, is one that will stand by itself without the need for any of us; since perfection is hard to come by, we will have to content ourselves with getting as close as possible to it."[53] While this statement was meant to embody the IAF's commitment to democratic self-government by the people, it also indicated that the organizer's departure was determined not by political goals but by standards of professional excellence ("a perfect organizational job") over which local leaders had little democratic control. A marker of professional detachment and evenhandedness, this outsider's status was reinforced by the fact that IAF organizers were never members of the new organization they set up. Their presence was temporary and bound to the realization of a particular mission. Among the founding principles Alinsky laid out when he created the IAF was the rule that every new project must be fully funded beforehand and must reach financial autonomy within three years.

In a very real way, therefore, IAF organizers acted as management consultants whose job was to kickstart or increase productivity in the budding domain of professionally powered civic participation. A marginal element in the 1930s, civic participation was now a central component in the postwar era and was taken up by institutions occupying central positions within the field of social action, in a parallel development to the IAF's course.[54] In the 1950s, for instance, the Welfare Council of Metropolitan Chicago (WCMC), which brought together all social-work agencies in Chicago, developed its own community organization programs. In 1957, its community organization service launched the "Citizen Participation Project" in order "to expand and strengthen the community council movement in Chicago," which had been supervised by the Association of Community Councils since 1949.[55] The project was meant to stimulate residents engaging in debates around the effects of large urban redevelopment programs on the South Side on access to schools, parks, and other neighborhood facilities. Dynamic local associations were crucial for the success of welfare planning: "A strong community council movement in urban communities is necessary to a strong democratic society, to good government and to sound welfare planning," participants to a meeting of the Citizen Participation Project noted.[56] Two years later, the WCMC issued a report on what it now called "the field of local community organization," which clearly indicated that beyond the wide range of issues—health, social planning, juvenile delinquency, urban renewal—all forms of community organization practice were united by "the mobilization of people through democratic organization for the prevention and solution of social problems. This participation of people is the most prominent characteristic of the community organization process."[57]

Staffers were called "area consultants" or "community consultants." Operating from an outside position, they were dedicated to strengthening organization and developing more effective local leadership, using a rhetoric like the IAF's:

> The development of an active articulate and devoted leadership core in a local community should not be diminished by the employment of paid staff. The role of paid staff should be to handle administrative detail, to recruit and assist voluntary leadership and to coordinate program activities—not to supplant the voluntary leader as spokesman for the community, as policy maker of the council or as presiding officer at council or committee meetings.[58]

This job description could fit what IAF organizers did if it weren't for one thing that established social-work agencies or settlement houses vigorously opposed: the IAF's emphasis on conflict to build power.[59]

Contrary to the management consulting sector, which flourished in the postwar era, with firms like McKinsey and Company and Booz Allen and Hamilton selling their services to large corporations, government agencies, and nonprofits in the US and abroad, but also contrary to social-work-oriented community organization, the expertise that IAF organizers put into practice failed to gain legitimacy and social recognition, for a number of reasons.

An Art, Not a Science: Obstacles to Professional Stabilization

First, there was a real lack of candidates for IAF jobs. Although the main symbolic incentive driving people to take IAF organizer positions was the belief that their intervention would help people realize their capacity for self-government, the arduous conditions IAF organizers worked in prevented them from keeping their jobs and stabilizing the material foundations for the IAF's expertise.

Their appointment as field organizers involved "a six-month tenure subject to re-appointment for another six months with final tenure dependent upon the working experience at the end of one year."[60] They received low wages compared to the long hours they worked and the college degrees they usually held. Many of the weekly reports that organizers had to send to their supervisors and to Alinsky highlight the low wages and the long hours but also the chronic lack of staff and the consequent work overload. Organizers could work in parts of the country they knew nothing about for several weeks or months, their only contact with IAF cadre being on the phone or through written correspondence. In contrast to business consulting agencies, they were not given a clear road map as to how exactly they were supposed to do their job.[61] They were often left to their own means and wits to figure out how to proceed. They had no standardized questionnaire to conduct their interviews, for instance. The lack of prior training combined with the strains of organizers' personal lives to create a sense of isolation.

As a result, Alinsky did not manage to retain the people he hired for a long time. In 1959, one of his "ace organizers," Cesar Chavez, left the IAF to work as full-time staff for the national CSO. While praising Chavez's commitment to the work and dedication toward "the ones below the bottom," Alinsky also lamented that "at no time has the Industrial Areas Foundation ever been able to afford the concentration of one full-time trained field representative to be in a particular area for at least a year, if not longer."[62] In 1963, Nicholas von Hoffman, who wanted to pursue a career in journalism, left the IAF too, which dealt another blow to the IAF's professionalization process.

A further obstacle hampering the IAF's professional project had to do with sexist biases and the deeply gendered nature of how the organizer's role was built and thought of. Tapping into the pool of women social workers who had been socialized to care work could have opened new hiring possibilities, but Alinsky's sexism made that all but impossible. "Alinsky's attitude toward women (which changed somewhat by the end of his life) was typical of the male world of Chicago politics and especially of the CIO subculture," Sanford Horwitt notes.[63] "Organizing, power, politics, and toughness were all related to manhood—and vice versa." In Alinsky's eyes, most of the organizer's credibility depended on posture, creativity, and stamina, which he felt were incompatible with women's temper and character. The case of Marjorie Buckholz offers a good example of this. A social worker by trade from Cleveland, Buckholz was hired as assistant director by the Hudson Guild, in the Chelsea neighborhood of New York City, which had hired the IAF for its consulting services and tried to organize the Puerto Rican population there. Buckholz was hired without Alinsky's knowledge, and he strongly disapproved of the decision. Horwitt writes that when Buckholz first met Alinsky in New York, "he treated her virtually as a nonperson."[64] Conversely, Buckholz had doubts about Alinsky's antagonizing tactics, his authoritarian management style, and his animosity toward social workers, but she did not know the extent to which he was involved in Chelsea. Had she known, it is probable that she would never have taken the position in the first place.

Unsurprisingly, the overwhelming majority of IAF organizers were men. Although not all their social attributes and backgrounds were similar, they belonged to two main categories. First, there were former social workers who felt their occupation did not provide adequate solutions to people's woes. Often working in community organization agencies, many of them also had received undergraduate or graduate training in social sciences. A case in point is Fred Ross. Born into a middle-class Methodist family in San Francisco in 1910, he graduated from the University of Southern California with a degree in teaching and social work. He worked his way up in the Farm Security Administration (FSA) in the 1930s and managed seventeen FSA camps housing displaced farmworkers in California and Arizona. During World War II he worked with the War Relocation Authority and managed a Japanese internment camp in Idaho, before landing a job with the American Council on Race Relations as a "field representative" in Southern

California. There, he worked with Mexican Americans to "[establish] community organizations devoted to the improvement of conditions in minority nieborhoods [*sic*] and of intergroup relations in general."[65]

The other main category comprised religious personnel or lay activists—particularly those who were involved in social Catholicism. When they started working for the IAF, von Hoffman, Hunt, and Edward Chambers were at first loaned by the National Conference of Catholic Charities. Although he never became a staff person, Catholic priest John Egan worked closely with IAF organizers. A dedicated proponent of the "see, judge, act" method of Catholic social action, which very much resembled the IAF's expertise and work practices, Egan was fully immersed in social struggles and well aware of the role religious institutions could play to tilt the scale in favor of the poor and the downtrodden. In the postwar era he headed the Young Christian Workers and the Young Christian Students.[66] In the late 1950s he founded the Interreligious Council on Urban Affairs to bring together religious denominations in a joint social action project by training clerics in the IAF procedures.[67] The council's goal was not to offer outside assistance, which ran the risk of being frowned upon by residents, but to fund the training of "skilled community organizers" who could then help them "generate their own social structures, strength, and direction."[68] The possibility to work directly with poor people and foster their participation and sense of individual responsibility is precisely what must have appealed to these would-be organizers: because they had a deeply religious upbringing, they were committed to religion's social justice mission and were predisposed to considering their work as a form of sacrifice for a higher cause.

A third obstacle to erecting solid professional boundaries around the group had to do with Alinsky's own trajectory and his ambiguous relationship with academia. While he very much resorted to the language of reason and abstract principles and fully embraced the Progressive Era promises that science and rationality would pave the way for human progress,[69] he also rejected the model of professionalism that at the time was embodied by occupations like law, medicine, and social work. And he did so with a dose of anti-academicism that verged on anti-intellectualism. He opposed the very idea that, in his line of work, "a body of techniques and full knowledge exist which can be taught and which endow an individual with the capacity to organize other people." The "ability to organize" could never be "transferred from one person to another by any known academic curriculum, even with the superficial accessory of 'field work.'" Academic titles or "professional qualifications" were not "necessary accomplishments for the good organizer" because organizing was not a science but an art.

> It is for these reasons that we cannot speak of an organizer being a member of a learned profession in the same sense that we can speak of a lawyer, a social worker, a surgeon or an engineer being a "professional." Our organizers . . . may be professionals in the sense that they are paid to do what they do; but in no other sense. When they are very good at their jobs we cannot refer to them as professionals, but perhaps we could use the description that certain sports reserve for their outstanding performers when they say that such-and-such a man is an "old pro." When the Industrial Areas Foundation looks for a potential staff man it looks for innate capacity.[70]

That Alinsky made efforts to discredit contemporary professions and academic learning to and embrace his occupation as a creative, unteachable "art" does not mean, however, that he and IAF organizers did not perform professional work—because they did. Had Alinsky drawn different conclusions from his bittersweet experience in the University of Chicago milieu and maintained a more instrumental attitude toward higher education institutions, he could probably have tried to integrate his "procedures" into academic curricula, the way management consultants disseminated their practices through business schools and graduate programs.[71] Furthermore, there is a great deal of hypocrisy (or self-delusion) in Alinsky's tirade about genius and "innate capacity." He might not have explicitly required college degrees to hire organizers, but the fact remains that IAF organizers were overwhelmingly college educated—and that overrepresentation has not fundamentally changed since. Whatever the group they work for, the vast majority of professional community organizers have received at least some college education.

THE DOUBLE-EDGED SWORD OF MILITANT LIBERALISM

The last reason why Alinsky's professional project did not translate into the birth of a self-reproducing group of trained specialists has to do with the confrontational nature of the work itself. Tactics such as demonstrations, picketing, and rent strikes targeting elected officials and unscrupulous landlords were indeed a distinctive tool in IAF organizers' toolbox. They were moments when the constituency got together to apply pressure on its "target" and demonstrate its social strength and legitimacy as the community's genuine representative channel. They were the militant layer of crust hiding the cream of compromise underneath. In a Cold War context, where "anticommunism was so pervasive that any type of protest was immediately vulnerable to red-baiting," displaying such militant liberalism was a double-edged sword.[72]

On the one hand, because they were ready to use confrontational tactics to build organization, Alinsky and IAF organizers exposed themselves to red-baiting, anti-communist suspicion, and political surveillance. Alinsky's political sympathies were often called into question. He was the object of close surveillance by the Federal Bureau of Investigation, which started investigating him in September 1940 after he caught the attention of federal agents in Kansas City. At first, the FBI thought Alinsky was a communist and that the "community center" he had established in Chicago was "reported to be communistically controlled."[73] Police institutions rapidly discovered that Alinsky was in no way "Communistically inclined," but the FBI kept tabs on him throughout the 1950s and 1960s.[74] In August 1967, he was added to the FBI's Rabble Rouser Index. The FBI also regularly received letters denouncing Alinsky, his books, and IAF-affiliated organizations as "subversive," "un-American" elements fostering hate. Contrary to many on the left at the time, however, Alinsky was never a direct target of state repression. While the FBI surveilled him, it never infiltrated his organization, brought him before the House Un-American Activities Committee (HUAC), or murdered IAF members.

Still, the suspicion surrounding the IAF's true nature did hamper its on-the-ground activities. On the southwest side of Chicago in the late 1950s, Alinsky and the three IAF organizers he had hired for the occasion wanted to build an "organization of organizations" to find compromise solutions in the face of residents' adamant refusal to accept Black families moving into the neighborhood. As in other instances of whites' "massive resistance" against integration, many whites found their violence to be justified, if not abetted, by institutions like real estate agencies, businesses, and Catholic parishes.[75] Despite having received the Catholic hierarchy's blessing, Alinsky and his subordinates were the targets of a violent red-baiting campaign in the spring and summer of 1959. In a letter to Carl Tjerandsen, the executive director of the Schwarzhaupt Foundation, a prominent funder of civic education and citizen participation in Chicago, Alinsky jokingly mentioned the various threats and verbal abuse he had received from neighborhood improvement associations. He was described as "(a) a dangerous Communist, (b) raping thirteen year old girls every day . . . , (c) having Negro blood, (d) of illegitimate parentage."[76] He took the situation with a pinch of salt in his private correspondence, but the fierceness of the backlash forced him to publicly announce that the IAF would no longer support the project—even if it kept supervising it from a distance.[77]

To use the culinary metaphor again, it appears the palate of the FBI and other rabid red-baiters was too coarse to appreciate Alinsky's political crème brûlée. They were too obsessed by the crisp layer to care about the mellow cream underneath: the defense of active, "orderly" citizen participation as the most effective way to improve democratic

institutions and include marginalized groups into the mainstream of political pluralism. As a result, the IAF played a real part in activating and
reactivating anti-communism as a core characteristic of the dominant
political culture by extending it to the loosely organized but politically
crucial sphere of civic engagement. Even if he worked with communists
in the late 1930s, over the course of the 1940s and the 1950s Alinsky
came to see them as a nuisance whose very existence undermined the
production of orderly civic participation and pluralistic representative
democratic institutions. As it developed and consolidated an original
expertise, the IAF carved out "an idiosyncratic non-Communist niche"
in the name of fighting communism's appeal to the marginalized and
the oppressed on its own turf.[78] Doing so meant two things: outorgan-
izing the communists and defending a form of liberal anti-communism.

Archival records suggest that IAF organizers, while they did not
lead red-baiting campaigns, saw their work as a way to outorganize the
communists, who were still active in protest movements at the local
level throughout the 1940s and 1950s.[79] In 1951, Fred Ross laid out the
CSO's position on communism and communists in a letter to Alinsky.
A couple of years before, the CSO membership had expressed its opposition to "all forms of totalitarianism," which in the Cold War context
meant Soviet communism and Soviet communism only. Instead, the
CSO's goal was "the safeguarding of the Civil Rights of all Americans
as guaranteed by our Constitution." The organization's membership
rules also mandated that members should refuse to "advocate the overthrow of our democratic form of government." While there had been
"a few people among the membership whose actions indicated they
adhered to extreme leftist ideology" when the organization was first
founded, they had since been marginalized by the rest of the membership. Ross was confident that members knew how to identify and
neutralize "extremist elements" and did not fear "future Communist
inroads" into the organization.[80]

A decade later, in one of his weekly reports, organizer Edgar
Jamison was even more explicit in his embrace of the anti-communist

rhetoric. Jamison was employed by the Woodlawn Organization, which was created in the late 1950s by the IAF in the predominantly Black neighborhood of Woodlawn on the South Side of Chicago. In his eyes, improving race relations was a direct way of fighting the Communist threat.

> I feel that the Industrial Areas program here in Woodlawn, T.W.O.'s program, actually undermines Communism, and I think Communism in itself would have a hard time with the Negro in Woodlawn because the Negro is becoming more cynical in that he asks questions. If there's no racial strife, then what could the Communists exploit? They begin to feel that the Communist Party don't intend to improve anything, that they want to make a lot of noise about it to cause friction between the various races and produce an Athens and Sparta-type situation here in the United States and that they will destroy us through internal weakness and if more people, white, would realize that when they go around and holler about Communism and bring in the House of Un-American Activities Committee that they themselves should be investigated because they are not American, they are un-American.[81]

The rhetoric is similar to the one Alinsky used in his discussions with the Vatican: the most effective way to "defend" and strengthen US democracy against the communist threat lay in multiplying representative institutions and decentralizing leadership at the local level.

Such a Tocquevillian possibility to outorganize the communists by active voluntary association appealed to a particular audience, with whom the IAF shared similar ideological commitments to what historian Ellen Schrecker calls "liberal anti-Communism."[82] Despite their disagreements, liberal anti-communists agreed with ultraconservatives and anti-Stalinists that communism was fundamentally evil, but they felt that the best weapons to combat communism were to be found in the liberal tradition: the heightened defense of the individual, pluralism, and achieving social progress through deliberation and reason.

This is where Alinsky portraying himself as an expert and a political entrepreneur was so important. To make up for his lack of professional credentials, he highlighted the organization's standing and respectability, renting office space in the Willoughby Tower—a majestic gothic building in Chicago's Loop—and calling his organization a "foundation" to suggest bearing and stateliness. More importantly, he surrounded himself with a board of trustees who could support his enterprise, in both senses of the word. The composition of the board, which met in a luxury hotel in Manhattan, exemplifies the type of social power Alinsky was trying to muster. Except for Bishop Sheil, the entirety of the IAF's first board comprised members from the reform establishments of Chicago, New York, and other large cities. Board members included Marshall Field III, heir to the multimillion-dollar Field fortune; prominent philanthropist Hermon Dunlap Smith, president and executive officer of a large international insurance company; Britton Budd, president of the Public Service Company of Northern Illinois and of Chicago Elevated Railways; Stuyvesant Peabody Jr., president and executive officer of Peabody Coal Company, which his grandfather founded in 1883; Assistant Secretary of State G. Howland Shaw; and Judge Theodore Rosen, from Philadelphia. Throughout the years, the new members who joined the board belonged to the same circles of power—business, philanthropy, law, medicine, Christian clergy, journalism, and academia.[83]

Board members' social attributes and networks bear witness to the close-knit liberal anti-communist circles that the IAF became a part of. G. Howland Shaw sat on the boards of the National Conference of Juvenile Agencies and Catholic Charities. Marshall Field III, who created his own philanthropic foundation to fund various reform efforts, was also a member of the American Council on Race Relations (ACRR). Founded in May 1944, the ACRR was meant "to bring about full democracy in race relations," "to serve as an instrument for the more effective utilization of the energies and resources which a considerable number of Americans were willing to devote to the perfection of our democracy."[84] Fred Ross had worked there for some time before Alinsky hired him. Attorney Leonard Rieser, another IAF trustee, also sat on the board of the ACRR.

An undated memorandum on an IAF grant application to the Fund for the Republic illustrates the way the IAF's definition of democracy resonated with liberal anti-communist positions. Quoting Tocqueville at length, as Alinsky often did, and identifying "urban anonymity" as the prime threat against democracy, the grant application is predicated on a stark opposition between democracy as a "way of life" and totalitarianism. While the former is characterized by pluralism and the recognition of "the worth of the individual human being and the multiple loyalties of that individual," the latter rests on "a single, unqualified, primary loyalty to the state" that smothers individuals' quests for self-actualization and realization. The memorandum, in return, praised the IAF's programs and underlying conception of democracy as a solution against "the fundamental factors giving rise to the element of repression, violation of civil rights and the current drive for conformity."[85]

The Fund for the Republic was established in 1952 by the Ford Foundation, at the time the largest philanthropic foundation in the country, with a $15 million grant (or around $157 million in 2021). The fund's goal was to finance projects defending public liberties on various fronts: race and civil rights, the excesses of the McCarthy purges, but also the ideological struggle against communism.[86] Several IAF board members also sat on the fund's board, such as Seniel Ostrow, a Los Angeles businessman and philanthropist, and George N. Shuster, the president of Hunter College, a prominent Catholic and race relations specialist and a crucial ally in Alinsky's professional career, who was one of the first board members of the fund. Shuster also participated in the influential Center for the Study of Democratic Institutions, a think tank affiliated with the Fund for the Republic.

Consolidating the IAF's niche but real position within liberal anti-communist sectors rested more particularly on long-term alliances with two institutional actors: philanthropic foundations and the Catholic Church. For the first ten years, IAF finances relied primarily on individual donations from board members. Its annual budget never exceeded $20,000 (or $237,000 in 2021). In the mid-1950s, however, philanthropic funders started to take an interest in the organization's activities. Chief among them was the Schwarzhaupt Foundation. A German Jewish immigrant who came to the US in 1910, Emil Schwarzhaupt became a prominent salesman for several Chicago distilling firms and a prominent national player in the liquor industry in the 1920s, during the Prohibition Era. When he died in 1950, he bequeathed a significant amount of his wealth to a philanthropic foundation bearing his name. Because Schwarzhaupt was a firm believer in economic and political liberalism who wanted to encourage upward mobility through hard work, the money would be dedicated to helping naturalization processes and promoting civic education among the foreign-born. The founding members of the foundation included close friends of Alinsky's like Leonard Rieser and Louis Wirth. Carl Tjerandsen, a graduate student at the University of Chicago when he was appointed to become the foundation's executive director, was also friends with Wirth and Alinsky.

Over ten years, the Schwarzhaupt Foundation granted more than $700,000 (or $6.7 million in 2021 dollars) to the IAF, about one-third of the total amount of Schwarzhaupt's funds.[87] As Bardacke points out, Alinsky lacked professional credentials to appear as a credible grantee to other philanthropic institutions. "He had already been turned down by a dozen potential funders, including the Rockefeller and Ford foundations. He was neither a social worker nor an academic, and in the early fifties, liberal, corporate foundation money primarily went to institutional intellectuals or charity operations."[88] Without his ties with liberal reform circles in Chicago, and without Schwarzhaupt's funds, Alinsky would have had a hard time finding the funds to stabilize the IAF, spread his expertise in civic participation, and live off his professional activity.

The other substantial source of revenues was the Catholic Church. In the face of declining religious observance and swift demographic changes in northern cities, the Church was intent on finding practical ways to prevent its "base" from leaving their neighborhoods, thereby undermining their local parishes.[89] People like O'Grady, Egan, and Cardinal Stritch, marginal but vocal proponents of Catholic social action, thought that Alinsky's militant liberalism provided practical solutions to these problems.[90] As a result of Alinsky's personal connections, the IAF developed close ties with the National Conference of Catholic Charities (NCCC). Alinsky and Fred Ross regularly spoke at the NCCC's annual conferences.[91] In the mid-1950s, von Hoffman, Hunt, and Chambers worked as IAF organizers on loan from the NCCC. In exchange, the IAF trained some Catholic clergy members in its procedures.

CONCLUSION

The advent of the Cold War, which shaped domestic politics in fundamental ways, was a double-edged sword for Alinsky's nascent career as a political entrepreneur. On the one hand, the communist threat was a specter that the IAF conjured up to bolster its claims to producing effective civic engagement, which, in a Cold War context, was a highly valued political commodity. Such a claim revolved around Alinsky's individual career as a political entrepreneur, thereby invisibilizing the tedious on-the-ground work that he delegated to his subordinates. From this standpoint, the rhetoric of expertise and effectiveness was key. Even if IAF organizers dismissed "professionals" and "professional qualifications," even if Alinsky's expertise was fundamentally "hardheaded, practical political art" rather than aloof professionalism, the IAF's project *was* professional—from its very inception.[92]

The standard to assess effectiveness was somewhat circular, however. If citizen apathy was posited as the fundamental problem in industrial democracies, any attempt to build local organizations could be pitched as a success by the people who claimed they were responsible for it. Because of the underlying assumption that organization was synonymous with effectiveness and performance, which were positive, desirable values, organizing people became an end in itself, regardless of the outcome. Alinsky shared with other social reform professionals (bureaucrats, academics, journalists, social workers) the belief that social progress would come from equalizing opportunity.[93]

But on the other hand, the ways in which Alinsky defined and practiced this expertise undermined the possibility of gaining social recognition. To distinguish himself from the other professionals who sought to encourage citizen participation, Alinsky overemphasized the contentious dimension of his "procedures," drawing stark boundaries between "radicals" like himself and "liberals" who were sold out to the "establishment." In a Cold War context, even the superficial valorization of conflict could backfire, obfuscating the unflinching commitment to liberal representative democracy. Although the IAF enjoyed institutional support among certain progressive liberals, the spectrum was far narrower than it had been for the community council movement in the late 1910s, for instance.[94] With the advent of the civil rights revolution, conflict, participation, and democracy took on new meanings, and the IAF had to find new ways to maintain its "militant liberal" position.

CHAPTER 4

THE PROFESSIONAL RADICAL

I n the opening months of 1967, there were talks between Stokely Carmichael and Alinsky about a possible partnership between the Industrial Areas Foundation and the Student Nonviolent Coordinating Committee, one of the leading and most radical organizations in the civil rights struggles. A short dispatch in *Newsweek* about the "Alinsky-Carmichael poverty team" indicated that "Saul Alinsky, the veteran professional agitator who shows the poor how to fight City Hall, has agreed to train Stokeley [*sic*] Carmichael's organizers in the Student Nonviolent Coordinating Committee (SNCC). The SNCC members will join Alinsky projects in slum areas of Chicago, Buffalo, Kansas City and Rochester. SNCC's object: to give its amateurs a touch of professionalism."[1]

Carmichael had been catapulted to national prominence in June 1966 after his "Black power speech" outside of a police precinct in Greenwood, Mississippi. At age twenty-four, he had recently and unexpectedly replaced John Lewis as SNCC chairman, soon becoming "the first SNCC person to rival King as a media sensation."[2] He was now at the top of the FBI's Rabble Rouser Index. Alinsky was not as famous as Carmichael, but by then he had enjoyed a controversial national reputation as a "professional slum organizer" for several years.[3] The collaboration project between SNCC and the IAF was built on shaky grounds from the start, however. In early 1967 SNCC was experiencing several organizational woes, with a dwindling local base, diminishing fundraising opportunities, and growing internal ideological divergences.[4] Right when the partnership conversation started in earnest, Carmichael announced he would not seek reelection as chairman.

This tentative collaboration has not made it into the standard narratives about the civil rights or Black power movements. In his acclaimed biography of Carmichael, historian Peniel Joseph never mentions it, for instance. But what is significant in this forgotten anecdote is not so much that the so-called poverty team never materialized but that it was perceived by participants and journalists alike through the lens of professionalism and the distinction between amateurs and professionals. It concentrates the general arc and direction of Alinsky's career as a political entrepreneur in the 1960s: seeking to bring "a touch of professionalism" to the nationwide groundswell of protest and collective action.

The 1960s were a decade of deep, multifaceted struggles against the established social order. The wave of Black insurgency that had been taking shape since the 1930s and swept through southern states in the mid-1950s extended to numerous groups nationally—students, women, welfare recipients, and racial minorities like Puerto Ricans, Chicanos and Chicanas, and Asian Americans—who recognized a community of interests with Black people in the South. Domestic insurgencies were fueled by anticolonial liberation struggles in former European colonies and the imperialist war in Vietnam. By the end of the decade, the politicization of large swaths of US society and radicalization of tools and discourses had fundamentally altered everyday routines. To contemporaries, it definitely felt like revolution was "in the air."[5]

At the same time, the advent of Lyndon Johnson's Great Society and the implementation of the Community Action Program (CAP) in 1964, with its notorious call for "maximum feasible participation," redefined the scope and nature of public social policy. Relatively new networks of social scientists and intellectuals working in federal government, academic institutions, and think tanks tried to find expert solutions to fight poverty.[6] In this context, the multiple symbolic boundaries that had been erected around citizen participation as a nascent locus of professional expertise crumbled. Protest movements were not couched in the detached, cool-headed horizon of professional intervention, to say the least. By recognizing nonprofessionally trained outsiders' experiential credentials, CAP pushed to deprofessionalize social work.[7]

In the face of spreading and radicalizing challenges to the racial foundations of the social order, Alinsky's expert militant liberalism, which he renamed "mass organization," now appeared particularly appealing to a new configuration of actors.[8] Some had supported the IAF since the beginning (religious institutions, private foundations), but others were newcomers (mainstream media outlets). In the process, Alinsky's procedures came to be redefined as a realistic way to achieve social change, an ill-defined, catchall category that became a rallying cry for a motley array of groups and social forces. The mainstream media played a central role in constructing the romanticized view that Alinsky was an effective professional organizer of the poor. But what was the factual basis of this narrative? What exactly did the "touch of professionalism" consist of? And what did "professional" and "organizer" actually mean?

CLAIMING EFFECTIVENESS AT BRINGING ABOUT SOCIAL CHANGE

In the late 1950s and early 1960s, the social environment where the arc of Alinsky's career unfolded underwent important changes. His political entrepreneurship became increasingly embedded within the field of race-relations experts. In many ways, the story of postwar race relations is fairly well known. With the advent of the Cold War, the reframing of domestic race relations as a geopolitical issue, and the effects of the Great Migration on the sociodemographic makeup of northern urban neighborhoods, solving the "Negro problem"—as Swedish economist Gunnar Myrdal put it in the best-selling *American*

Dilemma in 1944—became a national public policy imperative. Throughout the country, a myriad of working groups, councils, research institutes, social-work agencies, charities, and municipal, state, and federal committees held meetings, organized panels and conferences, and wrote minutes, reports, and charters about race relations to come up with plans and solutions to put an end to tensions and violence without addressing the underlying and overarching structures of racist oppression. "Race relations" referred to a wide variety of social phenomena, including the whole gamut of violence perpetrated by white people against racial minorities. Among other things, acts of collective violence targeted Black families moving into all-white neighborhoods—verbal or physical intimidation, harassment, if not mob violence, arson, and bombings.[9]

What is often overlooked in this story is that the social construction of race relations as a public policy issue was framed in terms of professional expertise: rational, comprehensive, treating all situations alike. As a lawyer acknowledged in 1944 in a letter to the director of the National Association for the Advancement of Colored People (NAACP), then the oldest and largest national civil rights organization, "race-relations has become a profession."[10] Civil rights lawyers, but also social workers, urban planners, academics, psychologists, ministers, and public officials competed with one another to come up with the best solution to the "race problem." In 1946, for instance, the Great Lakes Institute, a national Wisconsin-based research center, issued a report urging social workers and reformers to recognize that "the problem of racial and minority tensions is one of the most challenging frontiers in social welfare. It is essential for the preservation of a democratic society and our individual self respect that this problem be solved. It offers a field of experimentation in which the fundamental principles of social work are uniquely applicable."[11]

In the context of heightened interprofessional competition, Alinsky and the IAF used several arguments to distinguish themselves from their competitors and convince potential funders to provide financial support. Because his procedures were grounded in universal principles about group behavior and organization building, they could be applied to any group, including African Americans, whom many social scientists as well as civic and political actors believed were structurally disorganized and lacking genuine representative leaders. Alinsky felt that issues of integration, particularly when it came to African Americans moving into predominantly white neighborhoods, could be addressed through a cost-benefit analysis showing whites they had a self-interest in endorsing integration even if they disliked it. And because his procedures targeted people's civic apathy through decentralized participatory decision-making processes, the creation of representative, accountable local leadership also appeared less costly than something like service-based social programs. Three main elements contributed to legitimating the IAF's new position.

Creating Authentic Leadership in Woodlawn

The Woodlawn Organization (TWO), as the project came to be called, was the first turning point in installing Alinsky as a nationally recognized expert in creating organized representation in Black ghettos.

In January 1961, two Presbyterian pastors and a Catholic priest from Chicago who had taken a deep interest in Alinsky's work met with him and von Hoffman. On behalf of the Woodlawn Pastors' Alliance they had just formed, they wanted to foster racial integration as a response to the rapid demographic transformations at play in Woodlawn, just south of Hyde Park and the University of Chicago. While Woodlawn's population was 60 percent white in the early 1950s, a decade later it was more than 95 percent Black.[12] The clergymen also wanted to prevent a land-grabbing effort on the part of Alinsky's alma mater to annex part of the neighborhood.

Ever since he had founded the BYNC, Alinsky claimed he had launched forty-four IAF-sponsored community organizations in northern industrial centers. But he had never worked with African Americans before. In *Reveille* he had denounced in no uncertain terms the labor unions who refused to organize Black workers, but in practice he had hitherto never crossed the color line. Beyond the social and geographical facts of racial segregation, or the possibility that Alinsky was not identified by African American groups in northern cities as someone they could (should?) turn to, professional factors also definitely played a role. The IAF's invitation policy, whereby an organizer never went into a community to organize it unless it had been explicitly asked to do so by a group of people who wanted to build or renew community leadership and representation, meant that Alinsky responded to outside solicitations but never initiated organizing drives among groups or in locales that he deemed had strategic importance for his work. Alinsky also harbored a deep-seated belief that his organizational procedures did not work with everyone. They required a minimal amount of organizational and economic resources, which the overwhelming majority of the Black population lacked.

The fact that the Woodlawn Pastors' Alliance reached out to him forced him to rethink his position. Although he was initially skeptical of the Woodlawn project's feasibility and outcomes, he figured that working in Woodlawn might be a good opportunity to prove the universal validity of his procedures and their ability to produce local legitimate, representative organizations. Incidentally, this might also help him shed the anti-integrationist, racist image associated with the BYNC, which over the years had become a staunch opponent to Black families moving into the neighborhood. The conversations between the Woodlawn Pastors' Alliance, Alinsky, and von Hoffman resulted in the creation of the Temporary Woodlawn Organization.

In many ways, TWO was a classic IAF project. It was grounded in local social networks. It praised the virtues of social cohesion and tangible reforms through negotiations with officials. The money came from the IAF's established funding channels: a $60,000 grant ($560,000 in 2021 dollars) from the Schwarzhaupt Foundation and a $150,000 grant (or $1.4 million in 2021) from the Catholic archdiocese. TWO used innovative tactics to create conflict and catch its opponents off guard. Its first campaigns targeted local merchants who overcharged their customers and slumlords who refused to repair their dilapidated properties by organizing boycotts and rent strikes. TWO members also used white residents' racism to their advantage: members picketed the slumlords' own homes, located in well-off neighborhoods, and distributed leaflets to the slumlords' neighbors to shame them and expose their illegal and immoral practices.

The organization also departed from previous IAF projects in significant ways. So far Alinsky had always steered clear of associating with protest movements or left-wing organizations. But after von Hoffman attended a packed meeting with Freedom Riders, who had ridden buses from the North into the South to test new federal legislation banning segregation in interstate transportation, he and Alinsky decided that borrowing from the civil rights movement's tactics might be the best way to galvanize Woodlawn's African American population and advance their cause. Taking their cues from SNCC's own campaigns, TWO leaders and organizers bused 2,500 Woodlawn residents to city hall to register to vote. The move showed Chicago mayor Richard J. Daley that TWO was an independent force to be reckoned with and became one of the main civil rights organizations in Chicago.[13] Arthur Brazier, TWO's African American president and a Protestant minister, also became the main spokesperson for the Coordinating Council of Community Organizations (CCCO), the coalition of civil rights organizations that, in tandem with Martin Luther King Jr.'s Southern Christian Leadership Conference (SCLC), tried to expand the civil rights struggle into northern cities.[14] In an April 1962 interview with the *Chicago Daily News*, Brazier laid out his ambitions: "If our hopes are realized, TWO will be the first big solid Negro community organization in Chicago and in the United States. We'd like to prove that Negro communities can organize themselves effectively, not only for their personal well-being but for the betterment of the entire city."[15]

Second, for the first time in the IAF's history, Alinsky bypassed the rule of exteriority that he had established in hiring organizers and decided to hire an African American man, Bob Squires, whom von Hoffman had introduced him to. In an interview with Horwitt in the 1980s, Squires recounted the encounter with Alinsky, who made it clear that he hired him for opportunistic reasons: "I don't know who you are, I've never had a black organizer before, and I would never hire you if I didn't need a black organizer." "Well, we've got something in common. I've never heard of you either," Squires snapped back.[16] In the context of deep-seated structural racism, a Black organizer, Alinsky believed, would be a more effective organizational tool since he was more likely than whites to bond with Black residents, earn their trust, and move them to commit to the organization. Recruiting Squires was motivated by instrumental goals only. Looked at from a different angle, such a break with the organizer's outsider status was not as radical as it seemed. Not only did it illustrate Alinsky's real adaptability to changing circumstances, but it also vindicated the fact that the IAF, despite its lack of formalized recruitment procedures, always tapped into the same pools of candidates. True enough, Squires was Black, but he had also had years of experience in social Catholic institutions. Alinsky and von Hoffman had met him through John Egan, who knew him from Marillac House, a settlement house on Chicago's West Side run by the Catholic Daughters of Charity, where Squires worked at the time. (Lester Hunt, another IAF organizer, had also worked there before.)

If the BYNC had launched Alinsky's career, TWO represented the real stepping stone to national fame. For journalists, movement activists, academics, and the general public, it soon became the major point of reference in assessing Alinsky's approach. It also rekindled the FBI's interest in Alinsky. A good example of this newfound national attention is *Crisis in Black and White*, published in 1964 by Charles Silberman. A journalist and editor at *Fortune* magazine, the hegemonic business weekly in the country, Silberman argued that the deep feelings of frustration and anger in Black ghettos would inexorably lead to violent uprisings. Contrary to what other race-relations specialists argued, however, the emphasis on civil rights addressed only one part of the problem: it treated it as a white problem, rather than a white and Black one, "because of what white prejudice and discrimination have done to the Negro's personality and self-esteem."[17] But for Silberman there existed a solution to the problem thus redefined: the Woodlawn Organization.

Silberman waxed lyrical when he talked about the organization, "the first successful attempt anywhere in the United States to mobilize the residents of a Negro slum into a large and effective organization," "the most important and the most impressive experiment affecting Negroes anywhere in the United States."[18] In this perspective, TWO overturned the main obstacle keeping African Americans in a state of inferiority by building power. The importance of the organization lay primarily in demonstrating the virtues and superiority of self-help as opposed to the welfare system, which encouraged dependency and apathy (the final chapter, where TWO was described in detail, is tellingly titled "The Revolt against Welfare Colonialism"). "What all this means is that Negroes, like every other group, can really be helped in only one way: by giving them the means with which to help themselves."[19] Self-help was defined along classic liberal-philanthropic lines, which is not surprising given where Silberman spoke from. The laudatory picture was made all the more convincing since Woodlawn was presented as "almost a prototype of the disorganized anomic neighborhoods into which Negroes have been moving . . . the sort of obsolescent, decaying, crowded neighborhood which social workers and city planners assume can never help itself."[20] The conclusion to Silberman's line of argument was that since TWO could emerge against such odds, it followed that Alinsky's approach could indeed succeed where others failed.

Three weeks after *Crisis in Black and White* came out, riots broke out in Harlem, turning the book immediately into a prophecy of sorts and a must-read for whoever was interested in race relations. It remained on the *New York Times* best-seller list for nine weeks. This serendipitous release also highlighted another important component in legitimating the IAF's claims to effective expertise in organizing citizen participation: riot prevention.

All You Need Is Leaders: The IAF and Riot Prevention

The specter of urban riots loomed large from the mid-1960s on and was the second element that cemented Alinsky's national reputation and standing. IAF procedures appeared capable of creating local neighborhood leadership—identifiable, stable, partially predictable interlocutors with whom local and national rulers could negotiate and thus (so the thinking went) stave off violent explosions.

As the Civil Rights Act of 1964 and Voting Rights Act of 1965 seemed to put an end to Jim Crow and guarantee equality for all, urban unrest in the summers of 1963, 1964, and 1965 showed that legislative changes would not dramatically alter African Americans' material conditions, their second-class citizen status, or their experience of daily dehumanization in the northern ghettos. The failure of federal legislation to address the problem opened new professional prospects for several actors, including Alinsky. There were, of course, people who, taking Alinsky's fiery rhetoric at face value, blamed him for igniting the flames of discontent in the Watts neighborhood of Los Angeles and elsewhere. Dick Harter, a Los Angeles businessman, told the Governor's Commission on the Los Angeles Riots investigating the events in Watts that Alinsky was a "disrupter . . . [who] teaches people how to disrupt society by street action," someone who had given an "extremely provocative" speech that "excited the Watts riot."[21] But those who understood Alinsky's approach and did not focus on the brûlée part of the dessert knew that his expertise could offer a pragmatic alternative to unpredictable rioting by channeling unrest through a number of delineated, controllable steps: shaping identifiable leaders, formulating demands, and negotiating reforms through the creation of local representative entities. As a result, such indigenous leadership extended new chains of accountability and informal social control into areas where consent to institutional authorities could barely be obtained. In its report, the Governor's Commission on the Los Angeles Riots, headed by former CIA director John McCone, used language similar to Alinsky's when it emphatically concluded that

> the constructive assistance of all Negro leaders is absolutely essential. No amount of money, no amount of effort, no amount of training will raise the disadvantaged Negro to the position he seeks and should have within this community—a position of equality—unless he himself shoulders a full share of responsibility for his own well being. The efforts of the Negro leaders, and there are many able and dedicated ones among us, should be directed toward urging and exhorting their followers to this end.[22]

While such a political context was conducive to the IAF gaining in credibility, the most immediate prospects for legitimation manifested themselves through the creation of new IAF-managed organizations. A few months after the 1964 riots in Rochester, New York, Alinsky was invited by an interreligious committee to help create an organization representing the city's African American population. As they had already secured funding for three years, Alinsky responded positively to the invitation in March 1965. The organization was called FIGHT, for Freedom, Integration, God, Honor, Today. Its main leader, Franklin Florence, was a thirty-one-year-old Black minister close to Malcolm X. One of the first campaigns FIGHT organized targeted the Rochester-based Kodak company, demanding the hiring of a few hundred unemployed Black workers, positing itself as the sole legitimate representative with whom the company must bargain. In those years, similar ecumenical groups in Buffalo, San Francisco, Oakland, and Detroit approached Alinsky because they needed his help. In Detroit, an interreligious, interracial group wrote that "we know that we do *not* have the experience or 'know how' to build a tough organization of the people which can get many of these things done." Therefore, they needed Alinsky's "professional experience."[23] This was a first in Alinsky's career.

In FIGHT's early days, members mostly tried to prevent new rioting by patrolling the streets and "[cooling] hot tempers" where there were rumors "about an incident involving the police or a clash between rival gangs."[24] But soon FIGHT expanded its activity and challenged Kodak directly. The struggle lasted for several years, creating a lively controversy among the city's elites. But after three years, FIGHT leaders and Kodak officials came to an agreement, recognizing FIGHT as a legitimate interlocutor. Kodak further pledged to work with FIGHT to hire and train unemployed Black workers. The IAF officially withdrew from Rochester in the spring of 1968, with Alinsky emerging strengthened in his position as a capable intermediary between northern Black ghettos and the dominant classes.

In trying to establish representative organizations, Alinsky and IAF organizers on the ground potentially had to contend with other preestablished groups who were not necessarily willing to join an Alinsky project. In the wake of the 1963 riots in Lawndale, on Chicago's West Side, John Egan and the Interreligious Council on Urban Affairs tried to push for the application of Alinsky's procedures. Debates in the neighborhood focused on Alinsky's abrasive rhetoric and conflict tactics and polarized around two opposed sides, for or against Alinsky.[25] The Jewish Council on Urban Affairs (JCUA) also pushed for a "self-determination" approach adopting Alinsky's philosophy. But several Protestant groups disagreed with his call to "rub raw the sores of discontent" and favored instead the morality-centered efforts of Martin Luther King and the SCLC.[26] The urban riots that erupted between 1963 and 1965 also contributed to convincing King that the civil rights movement must shift its focus to northern ghettos and that nonviolent direct action was the best approach to achieve structural change. "After the urban rebellion of Watts, King came to realize that in addition to voting, true citizenship included a good job, living wage, decent housing, quality education, health care, and nourishment."[27]

In January 1966, the CCCO and the SCLC created a joint organization, the Chicago Freedom Movement (CFM), to spearhead King's northern campaign. Soon the campaign was confronted with brutal violence from white racist mobs and Mayor Daley's more insidious neutralizing strategy. As a riot broke out on Chicago's Near West Side in July, which King was unable to quell, King and the CFM were criticized from all sides, including by Alinsky, who told the *Washington Post* that "I think King is finished. He's trapped. He can't get out of [Chicago] in less than ten months to a year and he doesn't know what to do if he stays."[28] Two years later, Alinsky reiterated his criticisms with a vengeance in the *Chicago Daily News*, blaming King's marches demanding open housing in the all-white bastions of Marquette Park and Gage Park for "[building] white power in this town. They rallied the white supremacists the way Southern sheriffs rallied the civil rights forces in the South."[29]

The Conundrum of CAP

The third element that created positive conditions for Alinsky's professional expertise to be solicited, recognized, and legitimated was the Community Action Program and its call to "maximum feasible participation" on the part of the urban poor. Such a contribution was highly paradoxical, however.

The paradox lay in the fact that, on the one hand, CAP vindicated the community organization tradition of Alinsky's origin and the need to integrate citizen participation and encourage the poor to formulate their own solutions to fight poverty. Enhanced democratic participation was operationalized into an antipoverty policy instrument, even if the integration of participatory imperatives into policy making in domains like urban renewal actually predated the war on poverty.[30] CAP's intellectual origins could be traced back to a small, tightly knit group of dedicated philanthropists (the Ford Foundation and its Gray Areas Program); public officials sitting on the President's Committee on Juvenile Delinquency; and liberal social scientists like Richard Cloward and Lloyd Ohlin, from the prestigious Columbia School of

Social Work in New York City, whose work on juvenile delinquency rejuvenated the "social disorganization" approach at the heart of Clifford Shaw's earlier Chicago Area Project.[31]

But at the same time, vindication also implied recuperation. CAP posed an imminent threat to the existence of the IAF because it could potentially drive Alinsky out of business. The unexpected arrival of this new competitor of the growing market of citizen participation is probably what explains the vigorousness of Alinsky's attacks against the federal program. In an article published in 1965, he denounced what "may well become the worst political blunder and boomerang of the present Administration." Pointing to the collusion between the federal government, business, and the "welfare industry," he saw in CAP a tool in the hands of local officials and bureaucrats "to suffocate militant independent leadership and action organizations which have been arising to arm the poor with their share of power." Reveling in dropping provocative, antagonizing sound bites that kept the caramelized layer of radicalism nice and crisp, Alinsky concluded, "The poverty program is a macabre masquerade, and the mask is growing to fit the face, and the face is one of political pornography."[32] Furthermore, Alinsky's one-upmanship was probably driven by the fact that the monumental stir caused by the "maximum feasible participation" call took attention-grabbing scandal away from him. Calling CAP the "face of political pornography" was a good way to try to direct media attention back onto him—an effort that ultimately bore fruit, with the media happily building up the mythology of Alinsky as the "professional radical."

THE PROFESSIONAL RADICAL

Silberman's *Crisis in Black and White* participated in legitimizing TWO as a credible player in local politics and a blueprint to solve race relations through a mix of liberal self-help and conflict, but the book also gave additional weight to Alinsky's public image not only as "a specialist in creating mass organizations on a democratic basis" but also as a controversial figure whom you either loved or hated.[33] The *Fortune* journalist, a close friend of Alinsky's, was far from the only one who participated in the collective endeavor to personalize IAF practices around Alinsky and to paint him as the deeply polarizing and mysterious figure of the "professional radical." Two main actors were involved in the twin mythification and personalization process: the mainstream media, and Alinsky himself.

Mediatization and Personalization

In the wake of Silberman's book, a whole range of magazines, national newspapers, and bulletins from across the political spectrum published articles about Alinsky that invariably portrayed him as a "troublemaker," a "professional organizer of the poor," and a "tough-talking, hard-bitten organizer who calls himself a 'professional radical'" who was all the more fascinating since he was believed to be so good at his job.[34]

What is striking in these documents is how superlative and hyperbolic the language is. A featured portrait of "the middle-aged *deus ex machina* of American slum agitation" in a special issue of the *New York Times Magazine* published in October 1966 asserted that "Alinsky does one job—building effective slum organizations—better than anyone else in sight."[35] Conservative publications also used the "professional slum organizer" moniker but lamented his activity, often accusing him of communist sympathies or of being a dupe of the Catholic Church. A January 1968 editorial from the *Chicago Sun-Times* picked apart the "*hit-and-run salesman of agitation*" and concluded that "Chicago Doesn't Need Alinsky."[36] More astute right-wing pundits like William F. Buckley, however, understood that Alinsky's attacks against "welfare colonialism" could resonate with the right's defense of individual responsibility. The founder of *National Review* and a prominent voice in the conservative movement, Buckley seemed to take a genuine interest in Alinsky's work. In the fall of 1966, he wrote a short portrait of a "fashionable" man who was "twice formidable. For one thing, he is very close to being an organizational genious [*sic*]. For another, he has a way of making practical idealists feel sort of foolish—by pushing aside their efforts to help the poor or the racial minorities as ventures in fertility [*sic*]."[37] In December 1967, Buckley invited Alinsky on his famous PBS show, *Firing Line*. They kept writing letters to each other after the show, with Buckley suggesting that they should meet off the record to talk more in depth. The IAF archives do not say whether that ever happened.

Alinsky's flamboyant image in the media was fueled by his regular provocative statements, which were bound to attract journalists' attention and generate coverage. In the spring of 1967, for instance, in the middle of the campaign against Kodak in Rochester, he sneered that "the only contribution the Eastman Kodak company has ever made to race relations is the invention of color film. They run the town of Rochester like a Southern plantation."[38] Comparing King's action in Chicago with southern segregationist sheriffs or calling CAP "political pornography" followed the same pattern. He also agreed to several lengthy interviews that complemented his public image with deeper, reflective takes on his private life and character. In the summer of 1965, Alinsky conducted a series of interviews with Marion Sanders, a journalist at the liberal *Harper's Magazine*. "The Saul Alinsky who emerged from the *Harper's* interviews," Sanford Horwitt writes, "was a swashbuckling Renaissance man of independent thought and action, fearless, engagingly blunt, passionate but without sentimentality."[39] The interviews were compiled into a short book titled *The Professional Radical*. But the most famous and widely read interview is undoubtedly the one Alinsky gave to *Playboy* magazine in 1972. The notorious men's magazine, which reached its peak in the early 1970s, was also famous for publishing lengthy interviews with a wide range of celebrities (such as Miles Davis, Martin Luther King Jr., Vladimir Nabokov, Malcolm X, and Walter Cronkite).[40]

In those interviews, Alinsky embellished and exaggerated certain elements of his class background or his connections to Chicago organized crime, which cultivated the aura surrounding him. In the *Harper's* interviews, for instance, he fabricated a story about how he had been incarcerated in the late 1940s "in a Middle Western city where [he] was organizing people living in a miserable slum." He even went so far as to claim that this nondescript jail was where he wrote *Reveille for Radicals* ("sometimes the jailers would tell me to get out when I was in the middle of the chapter"[41]). Alinsky's biographer, who cannot be suspected of slanderous intentions toward a man he admired, convincingly shows that the jail experience never happened. In a context where civil rights leaders' use of civil disobedience to protest Jim Crow directly challenged Alinsky's claims to rationalize and control civic engagement, repeated jailings became not only a moral badge of honor but also a credentializing experience. Since Alinsky was increasingly described in the media as one of the prominent figures in the movement, he needed to show his credentials, going so far as to replicate the context in which King wrote his "Letter from Birmingham Jail" in 1963.[42]

The mix of rags-to-riches success story, provocative ruthlessness, and mysterious behind-the-scenes occupation, a material that fit perfectly within the mainstream media's codes and standards and constant search for exclusivity and scoops, provided the background against which Alinsky's most curious characteristic stood out: that he made a living off being "a radical." In the eyes of the mainstream media, Alinsky's distinctiveness and appeal lay in his distanced professionalism, his neutral, cold, technical rationality. As the *New York Times Magazine* feature explained, Alinsky

> is not a civil rights leader; he would just as soon organize poor whites or Mexicans or Indians as Negroes. Nor is he, like some youthful members of the New Left, the would-be leader of a national coalition of the poor; he wants to organize slums so they can make their own decisions; he does not want to make the decisions for them. "We're not trying to lead anything," he said recently. "We're just technicians trying to organize the people."[43]

Similarly, in an article published by the *Economist* in May 1967 titled "Plato on the Barricades," the leading voice upholding political and economic liberalism provocatively concluded that Alinsky's approach was actually more effective in organizing African Americans than Stokely Carmichael's or Martin Luther King's, the two African American activists and spokespeople at the time whom the ruling classes were most obsessed with.

> Mr. Alinsky seems to be the only radical who has succeeded in organizing the Negro communities. For, when he and his staff have left, the organization continues functioning with its own leaders while, by and large, the Negro civil rights groups have failed to create this staying power. When Mr. Stokely Carmichael or Dr. Martin Luther King and their aides have pulled out of communities in Alabama and Mississippi, the people have quickly fallen back into apathy and servitude.[44]

In the eyes of the *Economist*, Alinsky's superiority resided in his ability to create "staying power," wielded by durable local "leaders" who could keep "the people" in areas swept by waves of civil rights protests from "falling back into apathy and servitude." In other words, Alinsky and IAF organizers built enduring, permanent intermediary bodies that reinforced "civil society," disseminated a diffuse sense of individual responsibility, and increased the likelihood that unrest would happen in an orderly, controlled way. There was of course a great deal of cynicism in the assessment: it is quite unlikely that durable communist organizations would have received similar praise.

Alinsky's access to prominent media outlets was not a new phenomenon. Agnes Meyer, co-owner of the *Washington Post*, sat on the IAF board between 1945 and 1954, for instance. But the growing interest for his work on the part of mainstream outlets like *Newsweek*, the *New York Times*, the *Economist*, and William F. Buckley's PBS show was different in scope and nature. It was not the result of Alinsky intentionally building his social capital. Rather, the media's positive portrayal of Alinsky must be understood within the context of the evolution and radicalization of movement politics in the second half of the 1960s. In terms of covering the Black liberation movement, the mainstream media selected and emphasized the moderate alternatives as more "reasonable" than more structural critiques of integration and the two-party system. "In the second half of the 1960s, the press was often more critical of Black impatience than of white intransigence, and it portrayed understandable efforts to overcome white opposition . . . as betrayals of American ideals."[45] A month before the *Economist* piece on Alinsky, Martin Luther King delivered his famous Riverside Church speech, where he took a strong public stance against the war in Vietnam and connected the civil rights movement with a broader fight against US imperialism. The *New York Times*, the *Washington Post*, and other dominant newspapers all lambasted King's speech. Instead, Alinsky's "radicalism," which contained no anti-imperialist element, no support for the anticolonial revolutions underway in the third world, and defined politics in technical terms ("we're just technicians trying to organize the people"), was a much more suitable candidate for the media's patriotic defense of the social order and the status quo.[46]

Rules for Radicals

The media's portrayal of Alinsky as a professional radical took up an image that he himself actively promoted in his public interventions and interviews, but not so much in his writings. Apart from his unauthorized biography of John L. Lewis, which he had published in 1949, throughout the 1950s and well into the 1960s he complained that the IAF needed updated editorial material that reflected the evolution in work practices and theoretical conclusions about mass organization and power. While he originally conceived of his work as an art that was antithetical to codification, in the early 1970s he made an unexpected volte-face and now argued that there was such a thing as a science of revolution.

Published in 1971, *Rules for Radicals* had been years in the making, and many Alinsky enthusiasts waited anxiously for its release. As Hillary Rodham (later Rodham Clinton)—a recent graduate from Yale Law School who had written her senior thesis at Wellesley College on the

"Alinsky model" two years earlier (while she had doubts about the personalization around him and his insistence on conflict, she still admired him)—wrote in July 1971, "When is that new book coming out—or has it come and I somehow missed the fulfillment of Revelation? I have just had my one-thousandth conversation about *Reveille* and need some new material to throw at people."[47] Its working titles (*The Morality of Power* and *Rules for Revolution*) showed the type of position Alinsky was trying to occupy: that of a hard-nosed, Machiavellian strategist and political thinker. Writing for the younger generations who had been politicized through the movements of the time, Alinsky's "pragmatic primer for realistic radicals" was a justification for a "pragmatic revolution," where "working inside the system" was defined as the most effective avenue for social change.[48] This pragmatic argument had not fundamentally changed since Agnes Meyer praised the BYNC's "orderly revolution" in 1945. Neither had the underlying mystique surrounding the professional organizer, who, as in Alinsky's previous book, was still the real subject of the book.

Rules built on ideas and arguments Alinsky had advocated for years. It downplayed certain aspects of his work, such as the techniques and steps to identify real "indigenous leaders." But it also introduced new elements that reasserted his creativity as a tactician and a proponent of "mass political jujitsu."[49] More fundamentally, it bolstered his professional claims and clarified his politics. Although Alinsky did not disagree with the use of the term "revolution" and the need for one, he insisted that there existed a number of universal rules "pertaining to the ethics of means and ends" that radicals must follow if they wanted to change the world. The knowledge of these rules distinguished the serious, pragmatic, realistic radicals from the "rhetorical one," who could talk for hours but could not get anything done. The eleven rules identified by Alinsky laid the theoretical foundation for his science of revolution. One of these rules was the "great law of change": "Change means movement. Movement means friction. Only in the frictionless vacuum of a nonexistent abstract world can movement or change occur without that abrasive friction of conflict."[50] As Alinsky had kept hammering in his lectures, speeches, and one-on-one conversations, the basic requirement to achieve any change at all was to start from "the world as it is" rather than "the world as it should be," which was precisely what too many young "idealists" did—usually without realizing it.

If *Rules* presented itself as a modern equivalent to Machiavelli's *Prince* couched in pseudo-philosophical generalizations, it was also an anti–*Communist Manifesto*. Alinsky refused to let communists monopolize the language of revolution. The connection between the two must be severed and "revolution" reclaimed: "This is a major reason for my attempt to provide a revolutionary handbook not cast in a communist *or* capitalist mold, but as a manual for the Have-Nots of the world regardless of the color of their skins or their politics. My aim here is to suggest how to organize for power: how to get it and to use it." As Alinsky had done for years now in his public interventions, he defined power as "the ability to act," drawing from a commonsense dictionary definition. Power was the ultimate raison d'être for any collective endeavor. And it was the organizer's job to "communicate the means or tactics whereby the people can feel that they have the power to do this and that and on."[51]

The other novelty in *Rules* was that Alinsky spelled out his vision of class relations and articulated his political opportunism. The fundamental problem was that power was not equally distributed in society. Human societies had always been divided into three parts: the Haves; the Have-Nots; and the Have-a-Little, Want-Mores—the latter stood for the "middle class." But to Alinsky the real driving force behind any "realistic" social change project was not the Have-Nots (third world nations, the industrial proletariat, and certain sectors of the urban poor); it was the Have-a-Little, Want-Mores. Alinsky justified the argument by explaining that, although "thermopolitically [the middle classes] are tepid and rooted in inertia," their subjective experience of declining living standards and downward mobility made them potentially more revolutionary than workers who had been fully integrated into the capitalist system.

The argument about moving toward the middle classes because their subjective fear—a fear that is allegedly greater than the subalterns'—of *déclassement* could be more potently turned into a collective will to act was of course not original at the time. In the late 1960s, one of the debates raging in Students for a Democratic Society, the main embodiment of the New Left, with around one hundred thousand members in 1968, was over the political potential of a "new working class," a concept borrowed from French philosopher André Gorz that encompassed people with "technical, clerical and professional jobs that require educational backgrounds."[52] But Alinsky's inflection was not rooted in a broader reflection on class alliances. Nor was it meant to revitalize the US left, a task that never interested Alinsky. The prime goal was simply to "search out the leaders in [PTAs to League of Women Voters, consumer groups, churches, and clubs], find areas of common agreement, and excite their imagination with tactics that can introduce drama and adventure into the tedium of middle-class life."[53] This assessment dovetailed with the IAF's defense of liberal pluralism. As the 1966 annual report made perfectly clear, "It was to this end that [the founding fathers of the US] struggled to try to diffuse as much property (property then because it was an agricultural society, and today in an urban society we would call it economic opportunity) and power throughout the general body of our citizenry."[54]

The mainstream media and Alinsky himself were therefore the two main actors driving the twin processes of romanticizing Alinsky's role as a professional organizer and personalizing IAF practices around him. But such a narrative distorted the reality of Alinsky's work practices and social position.

THE PROFESSIONAL ORGANIZER OF THE POWERFUL

Although Alinsky liked to think of and present himself as a radical who despised the status quo and threatened the establishment, he was definitely a member of these ill-defined entities. Not only did he occupy the position of an intermediary between the ruling class and the oppressed and exploited, but he was also now willing to serve the powerful in addition to the poor. He had become a real power broker whose very legitimacy depended on his "ability to assume different stances in dealing with the constituents above and below [him]."[55] And in the process, he always took a cut.

In 1965 Alinsky's salary was raised to $25,000 (or $219,000 in 2021), and the IAF board approved that he could "take whatever lecture fees" he needed.[56] At the time, median household income was $6,900 ($60,000 in 2021), and only 8 percent of US households earned more than $15,000 ($130,000 in 2021).[57] His cultural tastes were definitely bourgeois, which he knew and seemed to enjoy. In early 1960, as he was on his way to meet with the pope in Rome, he sent a long letter to Cardinal Burke asking for his ecclesiastical advice on luxury automobiles. He hesitated between two models, a Mercedes and a Jaguar, which he wanted shipped to the US directly.[58]

The nature and structure of his personal friendships and professional acquaintances, which are good proxies to pin down someone's social position, also locate him firmly within the establishment. He spent more time among elite circles than in the slums of Chicago and other "industrial areas" or in movement spheres. In the IAF archives, there is no sign that he was ever in touch with revolutionary leaders from third world countries, radical thinkers, on-the-ground trade unionists, or civil rights fighters. Instead, he kept up a rich correspondence with philanthropists, Catholic higher-ups, government officials, journalists working in mainstream outlets, academics, and businessmen.[59]

Alinsky's social position and social capital confirm that his professed radicalism did not translate into radical personal politics. It was a facade. If he was a "professional," it was also in the sense of belonging to a prestigious group firmly grounded in the defense of the order of things. What about his work as an organizer? Despite his image, Alinsky's work routine was not exactly one where he would, as one newspaper report had it, "sit down with the Canadian Indians on

Monday night, help the Chicanos in the Southwest on Tuesday, be in a blue-collar suburb in Chicago on Wednesday, spend Thursday with white steelworkers in Pittsburgh, move Friday to a black ghetto, and be perfectly happy rolling, organizing."[60] Aside from managing and supervising on-the-ground IAF organizers from a distance, most of his professional activity in the 1960s can be broken down into two broad categories: public speaking and consulting. Like other academics and lecturers, Alinsky was paid to give lectures or speeches at various places: college campuses, social workers' conventions, religious congregations, and talk shows. In 1968, for instance, he spoke at fifty different venues throughout the country—once at the Saint Stephen parish in Grand Rapids, Michigan, twice at the University of Toronto, and four times at Harvard.[61]

In his consulting work during the 1950s, he mostly advised community organizations and religious institutions. But in the 1960s he also increasingly consulted with large corporations. Alinsky did assure his close friends that he would "not be corrupted by all the growing attention coming this way from our major corporations," but it is doubtful that in such spaces he advanced any "radical" cause but his own.[62] In corporate rooms and retreats, he was not a social justice fighter but an insightful and colorful character whose expertise could help large corporations develop their "social responsibility," a trend that became more and more dominant in the 1950s and 1960s in the wake of management consultant Peter Drucker's landmark *Concept of the Corporation* (1946).[63] Alinsky's no-nonsense language of self-interest and organizational power dynamics echoed with the significant changes management thought and practice underwent in the 1960s. As several authors have shown, the discourse of innovation and creativity promoted by countercultural radicals was recuperated by businesses and managers in the name of breaking all established hierarchies and embracing "change" instead. "Change" was not meant to liberate individuals from oppressive norms but to optimize economic productivity. The emergence of new fields like organizational development and the growing emphasis on participation and creativity against impersonal, stifling hierarchy and bureaucracy departed from scientific management tenets and brought to the fore instead some aspects of the human relations tradition associated with Elton Mayo and Chester Barnard. The best example of these transformations is Douglas McGregor's *The Human Side of Enterprise* (1960), one of the most widely read business texts of the time.[64]

Two examples in particular reveal the reasons for Alinsky's corporate appeal. In December 1967, for a $1,000 fee ($8,200 in 2021), he was invited by AT&T, at the time the largest telecommunications company in the world, ranked eleventh in Fortune 500 in 1966,[65] to share his professional experience and personal insights to an audience of "around 100 people, all involved in public relations, advertising or related work for the Bell system." The company's top officials had invited Alinsky after hearing him speak at a two-day seminar at Harvard. "Pick your own subject," consultant Walter Cannon wrote, "your philosophy of organizing the poor, the work of your organization, your views concerning the place of the corporation in social reform, or what have you."[66] Cannon later wrote to "thank [Alinsky] again for talking with us last week. From comments I've heard, I think you made a very good impression on the people here and gave them some new insight on the problems we face."[67] Nothing in the archives indicates what problems Alinsky talked about specifically, but the fact that he made a good impression on an audience of corporate executives speaks volumes in itself.

In early 1972, Alinsky was invited by a Chicago-based "management consulting firm specializing in labor relations" called John Sheridan Associates to be the guest speaker at a weekend retreat in the spring in northern Wisconsin. The annual retreat gathered "a select group of key executives from our client firms." Alinsky was asked to "give these people something to think about—and hopefully to act upon."[68] The guest list included senior partners from several law firms, people from the insurance sector, top banking executives working for large banking institutions like Chemical Bank in New York or Chicago's Northern Trust, and managers from manufacturing companies (Wisconsin-based Connor Forest Industries, Black and Decker). John Sheridan and Alinsky had lunch together in mid-April. "It was very delightful lunching with you the other day and needless to say, I could have spent the afternoon and on into the evening just trading anecdotes," Sheridan wrote a couple of days later.[69] They probably did not just talk shop but might have also lamented hippies' idealism and inability to stand up for the little guy or exchanged veteran's stories about Depression-era labor unrest and the general fate of labor. Indeed, Sheridan had had a brief stint as a union organizer in the late 1950s after studying English literature in graduate school at the University of Chicago. But since then he had crossed over to the other side and used his organizing know-how to go into the thriving antilabor consulting business.[70]

In terms of the overall balance in Alinsky's work, it is true that corporate consulting never became a major revenue channel. If we assume that corporate consultations were filed under "consultation fees" in the IAF's annual balance sheets, the picture that emerges from the period 1965–1971 is that, at their highest, consultation revenues reached only 12.8 percent of total revenues ($12,000 in 1965, $99,000 in 2021). Furthermore, in most cases, they amounted to 2 percent or so.[71] This is a big assumptive leap since the available evidence does not say whether consultation fees comprised only advice sold to corporate entities. Regardless of the amount of money the IAF made through corporate management consulting fees, or the amount of time Alinsky actually spent on those missions, that he did not object to consulting with large corporations bears witness to the gap between his public image and his actual deeds.

How can we account for Alinsky's professional collaboration with people who clearly belonged to the Haves he seemed to take to task in *Rules*? A mix of personal ambition, political opportunism, the conviction that corporations, like labor unions, were just another power group, might all be at play. But another possible explanation can be found in the way the IAF had come to define, frame, and perform the very work tasks it sought to control. The procedures of "mass organization" were primarily defined on a technical basis, as problem-solving tools that could be abstracted from political cleavages and antagonistic material and symbolic interests. By fueling conflict on a superficial level but deliberately leaving out broader ideological concerns, they could be pitched to basically any group that sought to implement "change," as long as the clients adhered to core Judeo-Christian moral values, as Alinsky emphatically underlined when he told William F. Buckley on *Firing Line* he would never consult for southern white segregationists. Such values were entirely compatible with a capitalist economy: throughout his career he never objected to working with reform-minded capitalists like Marshall Field or Julius Rosenwald.

The redefinition of Alinsky's occupation as that of a self-serving power broker, an expert who sold his advice to whoever was interested in improving its organization, regardless of the nature of the work they performed, was a notable development in the general arc of his career. It had long-term effects on the meaning of the "organizer" label, as the bewildering interaction I had with Patrick makes clear. But in the late 1960s there was another turn of events that further institutionalized the IAF's professional project: the creation of a training institute for organizers.

TOWARD A GROUP OF "TRAINED COMPETENT, POLITICALLY LITERATE, PROFESSIONAL ORGANIZERS"?

Creating mechanisms to recruit and train individuals into a particular professional activity is a key element in professionalization dynamics because, as sociologists have argued, it shapes a distinct group of individuals who master a common language, a specific corpus of knowledge, skills, and social technologies, that set them apart from nonprofessionals. Throughout the 1950s and 1960s, however, such mechanisms did not really exist at the IAF.

It is true that the IAF's training other staff, especially those who came from the progressive sectors of Christian religious institutions, was an important tool in disseminating IAF expertise. The partnerships set up in the 1950s kept up a steady pace throughout the 1960s, as a growing number of churches decided to reinterpret their social action role and get more involved in urban issues such as substandard housing, residential segregation, or work discrimination. In the summer 1970, for instance, a group of thirty Jesuit priests from all over the country were trained in Alinsky-style community organization by Tom Gaudette under the auspices of the Jesuit Community Organizers Institute. A former IAF staffer in Chicago, Gaudette had quit in 1966 after refusing to move to Kansas City, Missouri, to direct the IAF's project there, but he did not renounce Alinsky's approach. After the nine-week training, twenty-four "enthusiastic" Jesuits wrote to their fellow "brothers in Christ" to tell them about the good news they had just heard and learned and "urge" them to "see to it that the Summer Institute continues in Chicago. Encourage other Jesuits to profit from it. Allow novices and regents especially to include a summer or several years of community organization as part of their training. . . . If we are serious about the Christian renewal of social structures, such training should be mandatory."[72]

But training other staff did not solve the IAF's chronic staff shortages. Year after year, Alinsky complained in annual reports that there were not enough skilled organizers on the payroll. He also had to contend with retention problems at the supervisory level. When he signed the contract with FIGHT in 1964, von Hoffman had recently quit, and Fred Ross was still in California. In keeping with his "'have gun, will travel' rule for organizers," Alinsky decided to transfer Ed Chambers from Woodlawn to Rochester—without prior notice to the African American organizations in Rochester that Chambers was white.[73] Chambers also began to supervise other IAF projects. Despite the hierarchical division of labor within the organization, Alinsky still handled organizers' recruitment. Most of the process happened through interpersonal relationships, after Alinsky had sat down with potential recruits and talked them into working for him. There were no formal procedures or job descriptions.

Alinsky's growing national reputation somewhat altered that dire situation and increased the number of people who were willing to apply for organizer positions. Applicants still came from the two recruitment channels the IAF had tapped into since its inception, college students trained in social sciences or social work and religious personnel, but there were now more of them. A good indication of this can be found in the seventeen job applications the IAF received between May 1966 and March 1967. Archival evidence does not say whether it was common for the IAF to receive spontaneous applications like these, or whether other applications existed but never made it into the archives. Significantly, though, several applicants indicated they had read in the *New York Times* in October 1966 that the IAF lacked trained organizers. Most were young men, undergraduate students or graduate students from state universities as well as private elite institutions (the University of Chicago, Harvard), or college-educated social workers living in large urban areas in the Midwest and Northeast (Chicago, Cleveland, New York, Boston). A handful also came from a background in business, management, and market research.

Most applications emphasized selflessness and devotion to helping the powerless as their main professional motivations. But several letters also highlighted a deep dissatisfaction toward existing professional approaches in terms of fighting poverty or fostering civic engagement. One applicant, for instance, wrote that he had deliberately moved into the Black ghetto of Roxbury, in Boston, to "share that powerlessness, frustration and rage in order to help develop a sense of Community and Community Power, in this case Black Power." Indeed, he felt he had "an aptitude for Community Organization and a need to help the disenfranchised to enfranchise themselves."[74] The applicants also said what they hoped could boost their candidacy—they appropriated the prevailing public image that the IAF was indeed effective, that it was "doing what needs to be done and not merely proposing solutions."[75] Although most could not get into the specifics of what attracted them in the IAF's work, the language they used shows that the IAF was identified as an organization providing solutions that worked.

Despite the positive effects of Alinsky's national fame on the IAF's professional project, it did not remedy its inability to retain its staff. Part of the problem had to do with the precarious employment conditions the organization offered but also with the lack of sustained socialization for new recruits. Indeed, formal and informal peer socialization processes, the development of strong interpersonal ties, are key in the structuration of organizations in general. They play an important role in shaping people's commitments, their identification to the group, and the likeliness that these commitments will endure over time.[76] At the IAF, training happened on the job. There was no workplace where organizers could talk shop, exchange ideas and advice, and develop lasting bonds. Alinsky and von Hoffman did talk on the phone with organizers about their weekly reports, but such conversations happened on an individual, vertical basis rather than horizontally. So when people felt that the symbolic rewards they received from the work were dwindling (contributing to a worthy cause, helping people out) and considered leaving, there were no group mechanisms enforcing informal social control to convince—or push—them to stay.

In early August 1968, Alinsky set out to solve the staff shortage problem, and the IAF drafted a new project to start formalizing the production of competent organizers. Using the media once again to achieve his goals, Alinsky announced in a press conference the creation of an IAF training institute.[77] Tellingly, Alinsky spoke from the offices of Midas International Corporation, in Chicago. With its $400,000 donation ($3.2 million in 2021) in two installments, the corporation was one of the main sources of funding for the institute, the other one being the Rockefeller Foundation, which granted $225,000 (or $1.8 million in 2021).[78] The amount of money and the places it came from, again, speak to Alinsky's aura in corporate sectors.

The rhetoric used to justify the project to potential funders, the press, and direct competitors, rested on classic legitimating arguments about professionalizing tools and professionalism. The notion of a training institute tapped into commonly held beliefs about the benefits of competence and knowledge. "Lacking these trained competent, politically literate, professional organizers," the grant application to the Rockefeller Foundation read, "the entire world of community organization becomes one-tenth fact and nine-tenths mixed militant and academic verbiage in a context of wishful thinking." IAF-trained organizers would not just cut the wishful thinking. They would also optimize "all funds whether in private foundation grants or public government appropriations targeted for 'community action,' 'citizen participation' or 'community organization'" and prevent them from "[ending] up down the rat hole." In contradistinction to the myriad movement "training centers" that had developed in previous years and that the Rockefeller application deemed ineffective (without ever naming them), the IAF training institute would train versatile specialists who were "prepared to engage in effective organization in almost any sector of the society."[79]

Such a project signaled an important shift in Alinsky's attitude toward professional standards. A decade earlier, he had sworn that "the ability to organize" could never be formalized into "a body of techniques and full knowledge" that could be taught.[80] Now, because of the observation that the staff shortage problem was still unresolved, and probably because more philanthropic actors were willing to invest into institutions that would channel political radicalization,[81] Alinsky changed his mind. His customary hyperboles aside, the arguments about competency, cost effectiveness, impact, and technical replicability played into philanthropic actors' willingness to promote professional models of organization through their patronage.[82]

The training curriculum was composed of two parts. The first started with a ten-day seminar based on a reading list developed by Alinsky. "It was an eclectic mix that included *Federalist No. 10, Alice in Wonderland, Democracy in America*, Alinsky's *Reveille for Radicals* and *John L. Lewis*, and selections from the Bible, Mao, and Lenin." In addition to the seminar, the trainers would engage in individual conversations with the student organizers to "probe deeply into what made each of them tick and the source of their commitment, as well as their hang-ups and whatever else might impede success in the demanding job of community organizer."[83] Direct fieldwork observation complemented these readings and discussions. As one participant recalled, "For fieldwork observation, we immersed ourselves in a Chicago neighborhood and made written and oral reports on what we were learning. I was assigned to a part of Division Street that was in transition to becoming Puerto Rican. I spent three weeks there interviewing people, doing other research, and making observations."[84]

The second part of the curriculum consisted in a field placement, which was consistent with Alinsky's deep-seated conviction that real learning came through first-person experience. Trainees were either placed in existing organizations or requested by their supervisors to create new neighborhood organizations. Press accounts emphasized the fact that the training institute would focus on training "representatives of the white middle class to be social revolutionaries in their city neighborhoods or suburbs."[85] With the rapid spread of the Black power movement's rhetoric of racial authenticity and self-determination, by the late 1960s interracial organizing had receded into the background. Alinsky therefore pitched to the press the IAF training institute as an institute for white organizers only.

Field placements followed Alinsky's organizational practices and principles. For two of the trainers who supervised the second phase of the organizing school, Ed Chambers and Dick Harmon, this was not a problem, since they had already been IAF organizers for several years. But the third trainer, Staughton Lynd, came out of a very different political culture.

Lynd was a famous movement figure. He had served as director of the Mississippi Freedom Schools, and his anti–Vietnam War activity had caused him to be blacklisted from academia. The moment when Lynd was asked to join the training staff testifies to Lynd's radical commitments: "I was arrested during the protests at the 1968 Democratic Party convention. When I got out of jail and came home, I got into a hot bath. The phone rang. It was Alinsky, offering me a job at the newly formed IAF Training Institute."[86] Although he was highly critical of Alinsky's politics, he needed a job at the time. Besides, as a radical historian who was interested in alternative, emancipatory pedagogy, the proposition offered possibilities for new teaching experiences. Lynd started teaching courses on US workers' history but also on contemporary forms of collective action to the dozen or so individuals.

Things got more complicated when the field placements came. Lynd had been working on a campaign in Gary and other industrial locations in northern Indiana targeting the fact that US Steel, which had one of its biggest steelmaking sites in Indiana, paid almost no taxes. Since Alinsky had asked Lynd to supervise a placement in Gary, Lynd saw this as an opportunity to develop the demand around taxing US Steel, which had started to attract local newspapers' attention as well as the support of Ralph Nader. But Alinsky and the organizer Lynd was supervising had different plans. Instead, the trainee "tried to organize around the existence of a pornographic bookstore in Indiana, just next to Gary. It was quite a dramatic transition! The tax issue would be too divisive, whereas the pornographic issue would unite all groups in the community."[87] The IAF's systematic avoidance of "divisive" issues, the fact that Alinsky, the training institute, and IAF-supervised organizations had never publicly denounced the Vietnam War or US foreign policy in general, was fundamentally at odds with Lynd's own socialization and worldview. In May 1970, he requested a leave of absence to go back to his research in oral history. The next year, he left the IAF Training Institute altogether. The movement had been going through a rough couple of years, and Lynd's personal life had been complicated too. But in the letter where he announced his decision, he also emphasized a more structural factor: "[Saul and I] come out of quite different political and organizing backgrounds, and it is not surprising that sooner or later our paths would diverge."[88]

CONCLUSION

The mass protest movements challenging the racial and social order of the 1960s repositioned the IAF's claims to exerting some form of professional control over the production of citizen participation in significant ways. In the 1940s and 1950s, Alinsky and his staff had actively pitched their work as a form of militant liberalism that was best equipped to fight communism. But now, the IAF's work overlapped with movements and organizations led by volunteers and "amateurs," as the *Newsweek* report about the "Alinsky-Carmichael poverty team" put it. In this context, the IAF's professional project took on a new meaning. The myth that Alinsky was a "professional organizer of the poor" was still supported in the background by the IAF's traditional allies (philanthropic funders, religious institutions), but the mainstream media played a crucial role in elaborating, disseminating, and validating this image. In the process, it redefined Alinsky's expertise along the lines of a technicalized approach to collective organization, one which Alinsky himself happily promoted.

Alinsky was both the main artisan of and the main obstacle to the establishment of a self-reproducing group of professional organizers. His national reputation heightened the organization's standing and legitimacy. But he showed little interest in finding ways to sustain the organization and socialize the symbolic capital he had accumulated. Although he extolled people's collective genius, he did not attempt to push for collective—let alone democratic—procedures and work practices in his own workplace. The work was conceived of in a strict entrepreneurial, individualistic fashion. Hence the foray into the management consulting market in the late 1960s, which started to align his intermediary position with the ruling classes and not just "the people."

The contradictions between Alinsky's rhetoric and his actual work matter because they were baked into the institutional path that his career built. They were not just individual contradictions that would disappear with their bearer. Rather, Alinsky's unexpected death in June 1972 confirmed the original professional trajectory he had built for decades. In keeping with Max Weber's classic analysis on charismatic authority, now that the charismatic leader was gone, the routinization of his authority could start and a fully fledged, self-conscious body of professional community organizers come into existence.[89] Several months later, indeed, as he took over the IAF, Ed Chambers circulated a thirteen-page document where he took stock of the IAF's history, its recent transformations, and future prospects. He laid out a list of the most urgent needs the IAF must address to create new "volunteer citizens groups." According to him, the first, most important piece of "develop[ing] the citizen organizations, and eventually regional coalitions across the country" was "the paid, full-time, competent professional organizer. Generally one, or at the most two people, are needed to get the operation going and to sustain it. These people will have to be trained in the Alinsky method, and new methods developing."[90] Chambers's notion that there was such a thing as an "Alinsky method," which his boss and mentor had never put in those terms, signaled a full embrace of institutionalization and professionalization. Living off the work was now the top priority on the agenda.

Just as the organizer's role was being redefined by Alinsky and his staff as that of a "professional radical," an alternative definition emerged in movement circles, one that challenged the IAF's technical take on collective action and its lowering of the political horizon through avoiding so-called divisive issues. But contrary to what the *Newsweek* dispatch about the "Alinsky-Carmichael poverty team" argued, the "amateur" label was a misnomer.[91]

CHAPTER 5

SPADEWORK

The Radical Community Organizing Tradition of the 1960s

On January 20, 1967, the Student Nonviolent Coordinating Committee's central committee met to discuss several topics, including the prospect of collaborating with Saul Alinsky. Disagreements soon came to the surface. Cleveland Sellers, a close friend of Carmichael's from Howard University who had become program director in 1965, explained that when Carmichael and Alinsky met at a conference in Detroit in 1966, they "talked about the possibility of people working with him, organizers working with him, to develop certain skills and being able to relate and remain in those communities after he has been there and gone." Because many SNCC members saw building all-Black, independent, powerful organizations, like the Lowndes County Freedom Organization that Carmichael had helped build in Alabama in 1965–1966, as the way forward, a collaboration with Alinsky could provide a good opportunity to train capable, skilled organizers. At that point, Sellers went on, there was "a minute number of organizers left, if there were any, still around." As Carmichael pointed out, "Here is a guy who has [a training program] whether you agree with his politics or not, he is the only cat in the country who has been doing that."

Not everyone agreed on what Carmichael and Sellers meant by "organizer," however. Some participants were dubious that a partnership with Alinsky would prove fruitful. Others questioned the foundations of Alinsky's expertise. "Perhaps we're missing each other in terms of that phrase 'basic skills in developing an organizer,'" field secretary Charles Cobb ventured. "Do you mean like the use of a mimeograph machine, public speaking, the art of moving in a community, canvassing and that kind of thing and is it possible to isolate that kind of thing out say, within a lengthy thing, so somehow people we would encourage into this thing would get these kinds of various mechanical things, as to our political orientation or something like that?" Cobb was in favor of SNCC developing its own training, in-house, without reaching out to Alinsky, because teaching "basic skills" and "these kinds of various mechanical skills" could not and should not be dissociated from the organization's politics and programs. Learning how to become a SNCC organizer could not be transmitted through outsourced training programs and codified skills and techniques.

Raising the issue of Alinsky's fees and the potential need to raise extra money, executive secretary James Forman came up with a tentative synthesis. SNCC as a collective entity had not "made a real serious attempt to put down certain guidelines and principles for organizing" or intentionally trained people to become "good organizers," but he was willing to spell out what the core principles of organizing were ("creativity, follow-through, and initiative") and codify them into a training material, a "kit for organizing" that could be used by staff as well as new recruits. "People who feel they can [train an organizer] should sit down around the first week of April and submit your ideas," Forman concluded. The meeting then moved on to other matters.[1]

Not only does this conversation confirm Alinsky's reputation of professionalism and show that it raised serious doubts for some movement participants, but it also points to competing visions of what "organizing" and "organizer" meant in practice. As several academics have highlighted, over the course of the 1960s there emerged and developed a particular form of radical organizing at the local level that embedded itself in local community networks.[2] Rejecting Alinsky's militant liberalism and its underlying professional claims, it favored instead the development of oppressed people's collective leadership to achieve emancipatory structural change. There was no set name for such work. Initially called "community organization," in the mid-1960s it was increasingly referred to as "community organizing," probably to draw distinctions with categories like "community organization" and "community action" that had been taken up by institutional actors like the federal government, community action agencies, or the IAF.[3]

This form of collective organization departed from the dominant forms of the time. Its temporality was not driven by the short-term search for publicity; it did not manifest itself through rhetorical finesse, eloquence, and refined political analysis. Such political work was about being able to connect with people beyond the socially constructed boundaries of race, class, gender, age, and space. It required patience and dedication. The most valued skills were not about speaking (rhetorical finesse, oratorical eloquence, analytical sharpness) but listening and asking questions in order to help ordinary folks realize their individual and collective potential as human beings. The most important symbolic commodity was not ideas but relationships with people. As the participants to the 1967 SNCC meeting and their comrades in other cities and organizations were well aware, this radical-democratic perspective did not happen spontaneously. It required the catalyzing presence of an organizer. The organizer's skills, so several voices in SNCC's central committee believed, could be formalized, abstracted, and codified into training material, but contrary to Alinsky's IAF the organization was not there yet.

Using a phrase that has gained currency on the left in recent years, I suggest we see this particular form of organizing as "spadework." In a letter to NAACP executive secretary Walter White from 1943, Ella Baker, in her capacity as assistant field secretary for the organization in the South, wrote that "[she] must leave now for one of those small church meetings which are usually more exhausting than the immediate returns seem to warrant but it's part of the spade work, so let it be."[4] Such work was backbreaking, tedious, but in the long run it was the necessary thing to do to prepare the ground for significant action to bloom. Although it originated in SNCC, the conception of organizing as spadework was not patented by SNCC alone; it was taken up by other groups in other localities throughout the Long Sixties. Contrary to Charles Payne's argument that the "organizing tradition as a political and intellectual legacy of Black activists" developed by SNCC was eventually lost in the late 1960s and replaced by ideological posturing and in-fighting,[5] this chapter shows that such a conception did outlive individual organizations through the molding of a new role in the social division of political labor: the community organizer as spadeworker.

Spadeworkers can be seen as relational politicizers, who found ways not only to connect people's immediate lives with more structural issues of inequality, power, and oppression but also to help them make these connections themselves. They did not claim any professional control over their work, as was the case at the IAF, nor were they particularly interested in living off organizing (they couldn't anyway)—they were living for it, dedicating themselves fully to the cause. The development of this radical vocation was fraught with contradictions, however. Paradoxically, as the role emerged and people took it up and incorporated it, attempts were made to codify and formalize it, as the 1967 SNCC meeting indicates, thereby setting the conditions for the experiential know-how to coalesce into a social entity that drew a distinction between these full-time radical cadre and the oppressed groups they tried to connect with—a distinction that resembled the divide between professionals and "the laity."

Four major moments illustrate the way the spadeworker vocation was constructed, how it differed from Alinsky's work practices, but also how it came to resemble it in certain ways: SNCC's activity in the Deep South; the attempt by Students for a Democratic Society (SDS) to build an "interracial movement of the poor"; the creation of politicizing positions and vehicles by war on poverty legislation; and the Black power movement's emphasis on organizing at the local level.

SNCC'S MILITANT, IMMERSIVE ORGANIZING

SNCC provided the initial impetus that set the whole development in motion. Galvanized by the sit-in movement against racial segregation started in February 1960 in North Carolina that "now surpassed the militancy [Martin Luther King Jr.] had injected into the Montgomery protest,"[6] civil rights activists like Ella Baker wanted to build a collective vehicle that would harness the political energies unleashed by the student activists. SNCC, which was created in April, soon became the most militant group within the "Big Six" civil rights organizations—the NAACP, the Urban League, King's Southern Christian Leadership Conference (SCLC), the Congress of Racial Equality (CORE), and A. Philip Randolph's Brotherhood of Sleeping Car Porters (BSCP).

SNCC's politics were molded by a specific context: the segregated rural areas in the Deep South, where the other major civil rights organizations did not venture and where most of the Black population was illiterate and poor and worked underpaid, overexploited jobs as sharecroppers or farmworkers. The organizing practices that developed in that organizational crucible crystallized into a specific set of skills whose roots in radical pedagogy (rather than social work) distinguished it from IAF-style community organization.

Spadework

The most famous and most distinctive element in SNCC's own style of organizing is its defense and practice of "organizing," what Ella Baker called spadework in the 1940s, in opposition to Martin Luther King and the SCLC's "mobilizing." SNCC's conception of political work was molded by the organization's circumstances. As the name suggests, nonviolence was a core component in the group's approach to collective action. Yet there existed two competing tendencies within the organization that understood the concept differently.[7] Its first large campaign, organized in July 1961 in McComb County, Mississippi, solved the bitter internal debate between nonviolent direct action and voter registration by blending the two together.

Although the campaign's immediate goal was to exert moral pressure on the federal government to force it to side with the civil rights movement against segregationist states, the voter registration process itself was seen as a collective experiment in popular education and collective empowerment, where Black southerners shed in practice the skin of second-class citizenship, learning how to recognize their own skills, talent, and worth. The work was "tedious, dangerous, and unacknowledged."[8] In McComb, a handful of young field-workers (Bob Moses, Reggie Robinson, and John Hardy) canvassed the entire territory, knocked on doors to convince residents to register, and held voter registration workshops. Although they soon discovered that the chances of actually registering people were slim, and that it could unleash white supremacist violence ranging from physical intimidation to job loss and murder, the very act of standing up to white terror and state repression to do what had been forbidden them for so long and seemed utterly unimaginable planted the seeds of individual and collective emancipation. In the Deep South, voter registration *was* direct action.

SNCC members did not see themselves as potential leaders and spokespeople. Rather, they considered their role as a catalyst for southern Black self-organization. Indeed, the type of leadership that field-workers strove to build departed from mainstream, dominant conceptions: it was fundamentally horizontal, antihierarchical, and collective. Leadership was a collective attribute belonging to the people in the community and to them alone. Hence the idea that SNCC defined leadership as being "group-centered."[9] Because the legacy of slavery, the failure of Reconstruction, and the implementation of Jim Crow had cemented social and psychological constraints thwarting African Americans' recognition of their own worth and dignity, SNCC believed that its role was precisely to help people remove or bypass the objective and subjective obstacles to emancipation.

Doing so necessitated winning people's trust through the development of respectful interpersonal relationships. As a result, SNCC workers moved into the local communities when they could, living with Black families the organization had contacts with. These families helped them navigate local realities and sometimes protected them against white segregationists. They spent several months meeting up with people, working alongside them, chopping wood, picking cotton, and using literal spades, drawing their attention and becoming familiar figures. Such ethnographic immersion was largely determined by the lay of the land: the social networks undergirding forms of resistance and solidarity against racism were not as readily identifiable as they might have been in urban contexts. It also hinged upon the central role played by African American women in producing and reproducing local community relations. Furthermore, the ever-present threat of white supremacist violence forced SNCC workers to overcome fear and adopt low-profile approaches, as older generations of political radicals in the South had done before them.[10]

Genuine interpersonal relationships came to be defined as the bedrock of collective action, a fundamental condition of possibility and felicity of any mobilization of the oppressed. Charles Sherrod, who supervised SNCC's work in southwest Georgia, "commented that the whole key to organizing is finding one person other than yourself. One of his coworkers described organizing as slow work, respectful work."[11] The skills that were needed (and symbolically valued) to accomplish such work were not oratory talents or ideological articulation, but relational skills—the ability to cross social boundaries, talk to strangers and listen to their personal stories, to develop lasting relationships. "Organizers had to be morale boosters, teachers, welfare agents, transportation coordinators, canvassers, public speakers, negotiators, lawyers, all while communicating with people ranging from illiterate sharecroppers to well-off professionals and while enduring harassment from the agents of the law and listening with one ear for the threats of violence."[12] As a result, SNCC workers learned how to step back in order not to hamper the experiments in collective leadership at play.

The experiential knowledge and know-how collectively accumulated over the course of the struggle—how to "enter" a community,
make contact and identify people's needs, talk less and listen more,
bring people together, register new voters, and use nonviolence in case
of white reprisals—were articulated into a loose set of advice, recommendations, and warnings that were discussed and debated among
SNCC members. It was formalized through field reports, position papers, brochures, guidebooks, and training programs. It was passed on
to new recruits.

Radical Democracy and Popular Education

The second main pillar to SNCC's militant identity, which distinguished it from other mainstream civil rights organizations, has to do
with its connections with Black radical politics and the tradition of
emancipatory popular education.

The most immediate influence on the organization's style and politics was Ella Baker, whose role in transmitting what Barbara Ransby
calls a "radical democratic vision" cannot be overstated. Her own background, professional experiences, and politics shaped the organization's
later course in decisive ways. The daughter of a sailor and a schoolteacher, she was born in 1903 and raised in Norfolk, Virginia. From
a very young age, she was exposed to collective activities and imbued
with a deep sense of social justice in the Baptist church her mother went
to. A brilliant student, Baker attended Shaw University in Raleigh, the
first historically Black institution of higher education in the South and
one of the few across the country that were not closed to Black students
at the time of her graduation as valedictorian in 1927—a time when
educational opportunities for women were scarce, and even more so
for Black women. She then moved to Harlem and immersed herself in
militant circles. In the 1920s and 1930s, while occupying various positions within educational institutions, she was involved in intellectual
and cooperative projects designed by Black radicals of all stripes. As a

trainer for the Worker Education Project, a federal program educating workers on consumption practices, she further developed pedagogical skills and "the belief that education and the exchange and dissemination of ideas could make a difference in people's lives."[13]

Between 1941 and 1946, she worked as assistant field secretary at the NAACP and then became national director of branches—the only woman occupying such a position in the organization. In that capacity, she traveled throughout the South to raise money, set up and organize new local branches, and help jump-start the dormant ones. In that capacity, Baker accumulated a wealth of contacts throughout the South that were later critical in anchoring SNCC to local communities— this is the spadework she complained about to White in the 1940s. Although the countless meetings in local churches, beauty parlors, and grocery stores constantly rekindled the flame of her radical humanism, the NAACP's "class snobbery" did not sit well with her. In the end, it led her to resign from the organization in 1946.[14]

In 1958 she was hired by King's nascent SCLC, first to supervise voter registration efforts, then to head up the entire organization. She soon clashed with the SCLC's leadership of young Baptist ministers over King's charismatic authority; instead of the SCLC's hierarchical structure, she favored a group-centered leadership that would both consolidate the organization while leaving room for individual initiative and creativity. Because of her political experience in Harlem, "she thought that one of the most sensible structures for change-oriented organizations would have small groups of people maintaining effective working relationships among themselves but also retaining contact in some form with other such cells, so that coordinated action would be possible whenever large numbers really were necessary."[15] Her subaltern position as a Black woman within a male-centered, sexist organization further heightened political and intellectual divergences. She and King disagreed over the organization's nature and direction. While the young preacher hoped the sit-in leaders would affiliate with the SCLC as its youth wing, Baker urged them to set up a separate, autonomous, permanent organization, one that could sustain the sit-in demonstrations' impetus and militancy and "take the civil rights movement in a new direction."[16] Baker was also intent on building "a grassroots leadership that wasn't enmeshed with middle-class preachers" like King.[17]

In her mentorship and advisory capacity, Baker transmitted her own experiences in Black radical politics and her vision of pedagogy to the first generations who built SNCC. The organization's roots in education and pedagogy were enhanced by its ties with the Highlander Folk School, one of the rare left-wing institutions in the US that survived Cold War anti-communism, where Baker, alongside prominent civil rights figures like Fannie Lou Hamer, Rosa Parks, and James Bevel, had received training. The school was founded in 1932 in Tennessee by Social Gospel proponent and socialist educator Myles Horton. Horton's conception of education was both collective and emancipatory: "It isn't a matter of each one teach one. It's a matter of having a concept of education that is yeasty, one that will multiply itself. You have to think in terms of which small groups have the potential to multiply themselves and fundamentally change society."[18] In its early years, to put into practice that "yeasty education," Highlander focused on organizing unemployed and working people while also training CIO organizers and leaders.[19] In the 1940s and 1950s, it was one of the few counterinstitutions defending racial integration, social justice, and solidarity that survived Cold War anti-communism and repeated harassment and bomb threats.

Highlander served as what sociologist Aldon Morris called a "movement halfway house," where civil rights leaders from all stripes met to share experiences and learn new techniques and skills, which they then passed on to other people. This is where Rosa Parks and many other African American women who took part in the Montgomery bus boycott met to discuss and plan their action.[20] Highlander also provided literacy courses and citizenship classes for adults. Stressing the need to reclaim one's citizenship rights through learning how to read and write echoed with IAF-supervised CSOs in California, as is illustrated by the Emil Schwarzhaupt Foundation's interest in Highlander's activities.[21] But

Highlander was more firmly grounded in radical politics and civil rights activism than the IAF, which had its mooring in the tradition of community-organization-oriented social work. As Mie Inouye sums up, "the Citizenship Schools, like Highlander's other programs, aimed to give students skills but, more importantly, to change their self-understanding."[22]

The social properties, trajectories, and political experiences of Baker and people at Highlander are important to understand the type of organizing that SNCC practiced because they "espoused a non-bureaucratic style of work, focused on local problems, sensitive to the social structure of local communities, appreciative to the culture of those communities." Their contribution laid out "a developmental style of politics, one in which the important thing was the development of efficacy in those most affected by a problem. Over the long term, whether a community achieved this or that tactical objective was likely to matter less than whether the people in it came to see themselves as having the right and the capacity to have some say-so in their own lives."[23] The focus was on the people and the articulation between their individual lives and their collective power and potential. Contrary to the IAF's perspective, the goal was not to build a new, representative organization. Organization was not an entity to be built from the outside but a process that bound people together—including the organizer, despite the fact that many of them were strangers in the rural communities they immersed themselves in.

And yet, SNCC *was* a formal organization, which existed beyond the individuals who embodied it. And what was most original with SNCC—what was its most fundamental contradiction, too—was that its radical-democratic political style was developed through an organization that never tried to become a mass organization.

An Organization of Organizers

Despite its commitment to catalyze the self-organization of Black southerners, SNCC was built as and remained an organization of dedicated, full-time cadre. It functioned as an organizing group with a tightly knit core of dedicated members, where paid staffers and volunteers worked alongside one another. The McComb campaign of 1961 marked a turning point in this regard, as it drove rapid organizational growth. In August 1962, there were 20 or so permanent staff working in the field; a year later, there were 12 administrative staffers, 60 field secretaries, and 121 full-time volunteers. Although this did not result in a massive increase in voter registration rolls, from then on SNCC members "assumed full-time roles as a radical cadre," fully dedicating themselves to the struggle.[24]

The increase in the number of full-time staff was fueled by a number of complementary factors such as the national prominence gained through the Freedom Rides, an efficient new fundraising initiative implemented by executive secretary James Forman, and the organization's growing activity. Staffers were recruited from two main pools. SNCC's "field secretary" positions, as they were dubbed, offered opportunities "on the part of students already engaged in protest activity to take the further step of breaking previous social ties and becoming revolutionaries."[25] Trying to find a balance between school and activism, as some of the first sit-in leaders had done in the organization's early years, was no longer a dilemma for new student recruits, most of whom never completed their studies. Another recruitment channel was established by SNCC's presence in the field. Its campaigns in Mississippi, for instance, proved particularly appealing to local young people, who often felt that Freedom Riders or Martin Luther King himself were bringing to their town the movement they had heard about. Some of them were drawn into the organization and then became field secretaries themselves.

Field secretary positions were partly shaped by the social properties and trajectories of people who occupied them. The large majority of staffers were Black, but their social backgrounds, although diverse, set them somewhat apart from the Black southerners they worked with. In his 1964 study of SNCC, Howard Zinn drew an interesting portrait of Mississippi SNCC workers.[26] The forty-one staff represented a third of the total number of people SNCC sent into the Deep South. Thirty-five of them were Black; twenty-seven came from the Deep South—two of them white—and fourteen came from the North. While the white field secretaries and most northern Blacks had grown up in lower-middle-class families with large cultural capital—their parents were ministers, teachers, or civil servants—southern field secretaries came from overwhelmingly working-class backgrounds. Their parents held subordinate jobs in domestic service, agriculture, and manufacturing. Most SNCC workers had a college degree or had received some college education, and some of them were the first in their families who went to college. Writing about the campaign launched in the summer of 1962 in Greenwood, a cotton processing center in the Mississippi Delta, Charles Payne notes that "none of the early Greenwood organizers came from the most oppressed strata of Mississippi Blacks, but none of them came from backgrounds that could reasonably be called middle-class. Indeed, they came from backgrounds very much like those of the people they were trying to organize."[27]

Until the summer of 1963, Bob Moses emphasized the need to hire Black southerners rather than white northerners as field secretaries. A high school math teacher by trade, Moses was one of Baker's protégés and an influential voice in the organization. Not only was the intentional recruitment of Black people a more pragmatic way for to the organization to root itself into a community and gain the trust of local residents, but it also showed people that SNCC was dedicated to defending their interests and representing them, giving them back a sense of pride and dignity. As the federal government was stalling in addressing racial segregation head-on, however, Moses came to the conclusion that the massive recruitment of northern whites on college campuses could help the organization reach a critical mass to organize popular education work, conduct voter registration drives, and expose to the whole nation Mississippi's white terrorism and the blatant injustice Black Mississippians experienced—something the intentional, bottom-up recruitment strategy had only partially accomplished.

What was at stake was not the capabilities of the majority Black field secretaries, whose courage and painstaking efforts in the face of tremendous adversity gave SNCC its unique brand of radicalism. But sending a contingent of northern white college students to the Deep South and across the color line could trigger northern white liberals' and the media's dormant racism and shock them out of their indifference in a way that southern Black field secretaries could not. This decision gave birth to the Freedom Summer program of 1964, where one thousand northern white volunteers flocked to Mississippi to register Black voters, in an innovative experiment in collective action, mass popular education, and democracy that shaped participants' trajectories for the rest of their lives.

Opening the organization to white volunteers and staff was a testament to the widespread belief in the possibility of building interracial organizations and working toward the "beloved community" that King had posited as the end goal of nonviolent direct action in the late 1950s. But it also exposed the organization to heightened white supremacist violence, as the murders of James Chaney, Andrew Goodman, and Michael Schwerner in June 1964 demonstrated. The experience crystallized tensions between struggle-hardened SNCC veterans and idealistic, naive volunteers along race, class, gender, and ideological lines. It also paved the way for future disputes among SNCC staffers themselves—between those who, on the one hand, rejected organizational discipline and leadership, responded to whatever needs the local community put to the fore, and embraced nonviolence and interracialism as core philosophical tenets and those who, on the other hand, felt that "SNCC needed to move beyond the improvisational politics of moral suasion to mobilize political power through an increasingly structured organizational program" and who felt that the large presence of whites might inhibit the development of collective Black leadership and power.[28]

The emergence and consolidation of full-time positions fueled and was fueled by an all-encompassing commitment to a cause lived as an enduring vocation. Such a calling was characterized by the intertwined mastery of relational skills and a commitment to radical politics. SNCC organizers did not encourage people to give public speeches, hold civic debates about community issues, and register to vote to correct the short-comings of existing political institutions, as was the case with IAF organizers and other "community consultants." The initial SNCC goal to push for reforms dismantling Jim Crow was gradually superseded by more far-reaching demands taking on the material and symbolic structures undergirding white supremacy. From April 1962 on, as anticolonial revolutions swept the world and became a focal point of reference for Black liberation fighters and other radicals, a majority of SNCC workers saw themselves as "professionals" but also as "revolutionaries," which suggested "an increased willingness among [them] to associate themselves with a broad movement, spearheaded by young people, to achieve radical social change."[29] According to one member of SNCC's research division, the organization's goal was to "unstructure the power structure."[30]

Through this period, there always seemed to be lingering doubts about what an organizer was and did, a situation that SNCC's radicalization did not alter. Year after year SNCC members regularly tried to formulate their own definitions of the label and role. In a paper he wrote for a SNCC staff meeting in late 1963 or early 1964, white field secretary Mike Miller acknowledged that "there's been a great deal of discussion of what an organizer is, what he does, who he is—both in SNCC and among people interested in SNCC's work" and ventured "some brief thoughts on this topic." Miller had become a field secretary at the end of 1962 and worked in the Mississippi Delta in the summer and fall of 1963. Starting with the premise that an organizer must believe in people's democratic ability to know their own needs and decide for themselves, he insisted on the importance of liking and enjoying talking to "all kinds of people," of knowing how to constantly raise questions and how to raise them so that, in the end, "people in the communities get the knack of asking questions" and no longer need the organizer's catalyzing presence.[31]

Miller's emphasis on relational skills and empathy was shared by many, but it did not fully represent the centrifugal dynamics at play. For years SNCC's full-time cadre had become increasingly politically aware and self-conscious of their avant-garde position. Such collective awareness was produced by two interwoven developments: First, strategic and ideological divergences with other civil rights organizations, particularly with the SCLC, which many SNCC members believed garnered most of the attention while doing little actual groundwork; second, shared experiences during voter registration campaigns contributed to knitting the group tightly together and imbuing SNCC members with the moral authority and legitimacy such direct action entailed. "Though they had just begun to articulate radical or revolutionary ideas, they saw their methods of achieving social change as differing dramatically from those of any other reform organization." At the same time, staff members' ever-increasing, all-consuming dedication to the cause and the work widened the structural gap with local leaders while undermining the opportunities to reach out to potential new recruits. By 1964, SNCC appeared as "too radical, too professional, too full-time revolutionary to recruit large numbers of idealistic college students."[32]

At that point, such contradictions did not lead to full-blown organizational crises, as would be the case several years later. More importantly, SNCC's distinctive style and radicalism turned the organization into a militant training ground where hundreds of young people— Black and white, men and women—gained their political education and learned how to act and think as spadeworkers.

CATALYZING AN "INTERRACIAL MOVEMENT OF THE POOR"

The second main moment in the circulation and crystallization both of spadework as an alternative form of collective organization and the spadeworker's role was the Economic Research and Action Project

(ERAP) launched by Students for a Democratic Society in 1964. While most former SDSers and academics seem to agree that ERAP was a failure, the program's significance does not lie so much in its political impact (or lack thereof) as in the imprint it left on the people who participated in it, both in terms of practical know-how and political horizon and where and how the people applied such a formative experience later in their lives.

Founded in 1960 as the student branch of the League for Industrial Democracy, which came out of the early twentieth-century US socialist tradition, SDS rapidly broke free from its parent organization and became one of the main pillars of the burgeoning, overwhelmingly white New Left. SDS's early views and political vision were formulated after the group's first national convention in the 1962 "Port Huron Statement." Rejecting both America's Cold War domestic order and Soviet communism, the text offered a broad criticism of the monopolization of power by what sociologist C. Wright Mills called the "power elite" (the two-party system, the military, and big business); the mirage of the so-called abundance society and the ongoing presence of poverty and unemployment; the ongoing systemic racism against Black people and other minorities; and the generalized sense of alienation and political dispossession experienced by all US citizens in making decisions over their lives. What was needed to "challenge the Cold War status quo and other social evils"[33] was not just a shift in public spending away from the military and into social programs, as moderate leftists and liberals argued, or more federal dedication to push for civil rights legislation. The real political solution was "participatory democracy," a notion and a set of practices that had been at the heart of SNCC's campaigns and that the "Port Huron Statement" put to the fore. Participatory democracy, which stemmed from a bottom-up catalysis "transforming powerlessness into shared competence and responsibility," meant the equal participation of all citizens in the decisions affecting their lives.[34] Without ordinary people's direct participation, no radical social change could be achieved.

Although there were echoes of Alinsky's diagnosis in those pages, SDS called for bypassing traditional, hierarchical forms of organization and leadership. Because many of SDS's core leaders had worked as SNCC field secretaries or had been lastingly impressed by the group's aura and moral authority, the student organization was intent on applying SNCC's practices to northern urban neighborhoods in order to stimulate an "interracial movement of the poor," as a pamphlet written by SDS national leaders Tom Hayden and Carl Wittman argued in 1963, in order to end poverty, dismantle racial inequality, and remedy the democratic crisis. In the wake of the August 1963 March on Washington, and thanks to a $5,000 grant (or $45,000 in 2021) from the United Auto Workers "to emphasize economic issues on campuses and communities," ERAP was launched by SDS and designed "to organize poor people in the north against racism (although it turned out that most of the projects were in Black neighborhoods) and economic exploitation, with the goals of attaining significant power in the cities and ultimately of linking with the southern civil rights movement."[35]

ERAP was the product of a vivid debate that raged between 1963 and 1965 over the organization's orientation and strategy. Should it seek to develop as a national left student organization and maintain its focus on university campuses and politicizing students, or should it, as Hayden put it, "leave all that academic crap behind it" and "break out of intellectuality into contact with the grass roots of the nation"?[36] The second option prevailed as a result of a combination of factors: a growing desire to reject their predictable, professional futures on the part of students who mostly came from middle- to upper-class backgrounds; a romanticization of the poor and the ghettoes, to whom privileged, self-conscious students attached more moral authenticity; an interest in "immediate political activity and commitment"[37] spurred by the civil rights movement; and an underlying vision of postwar capitalist society where "the residential community, not the workplace, had become the main site of anti-capitalist protest and rebellion."[38] The poor and the unemployed (Black and white), rather than co-opted and hopelessly reformist blue-collar workers, were the potential agents of change SDS must try to organize into action.

ERAP was national in scope but local in implementation. In total, thirteen autonomous projects were established. Building upon a long tradition of university-educated and reform-minded members from the dominant classes crossing class and race boundaries to "go to the people" and know them firsthand, some 120 organizers interrupted their student lives in the summer of 1964 to immerse themselves in the poor neighborhoods of Chicago, Baltimore, Cleveland, Boston, and Newark to gain direct understanding of people's living conditions and, from there, galvanize them into taking collective action. ERAP's watchword was to "let the people decide." Bill Ayers, who worked in Cleveland at the time and went on to become a prominent advocate for SDS's turn to armed struggle at the end of the 1960s, explained that the intention was that "we would live with the poor, cast our lot with the poor, and that the wisdom of the people themselves would lead to whatever political direction we took."[39]

To do so, ERAP organizers worked in ways that were very similar to what SNCC field secretaries and IAF organizers did. Renting cheap apartments or small houses where they lived communally, they started immersing themselves in a neighborhood's daily life, networks, and institutions. Although many took up low-paying jobs to anchor their immersion and get by, most of their work consisted of knocking on people's doors or reaching out to them in the street, outside of welfare agencies, or in bars to determine people's priorities and discover specific grievances around which a local organization could then be created. Usually with no preestablished plan.[40] Such systematic canvassing was complemented with more formal surveys when more specific data was needed, a research tool that many had learned to use in their social science undergraduate classes. As Andrew Kopkind, a journalist sympathetic to the movement, accurately noted at the time, "it is more than the Fabian idea of 'getting to know the poor,' and much less than the old communist idea of infiltrating the proletariat."[41] When

ERAPers managed to get a conversation started with a local resident—women, most of the time—they tried to recruit them to the project and "convince most residents of the power and positive outcomes of working together, of the efficacy of solidarity and organization."[42] The attempts to set up committees for tenants, workers, and welfare beneficiaries were often met with the hostility of local administrations but also the distrust of residents themselves.

When the convincing did work, ERAP organizers then supervised the creation of a new organization, which, by addressing the issues identified by community members (inadequacy of welfare payments, lack of recreational facilities for children, building repairs, and so on), would connect specific reform goals to broader, structural issues of power. In the socially and racially diverse neighborhood of Uptown, located in the north of Chicago, the local project was called Jobs or Income Now (JOIN). One of the more famous ERAP projects, which lasted longer than most, it focused on slum housing, urban renewal, welfare rights, and access to employment. After a few years it renamed itself JOIN Community Union, to indicate its willingness to address potentially all issues that were relevant to Uptown residents. "JOIN Community Union is over 2000 poor and working people in Uptown," a pamphlet claimed. "JOIN is people like yourself, people who want decent treatment from the welfare and police, fairer prices from stores, decent pay at day labor, and good schools. JOIN is people fighting to give the 'little guy' a voice in how Uptown, the city and country are run."[43]

To become a visible and credible presence in the neighborhood, and to gain acceptance, organizers often created an office "where people felt comfortable and where they might go to discuss neighborhood problems."[44] Although they refused to take on any leadership position, they "introduced into the neighborhood projects a decentralized, nonhierarchical structure and shared leadership with decision making by consensus," in keeping with SDS's rejection of bureaucratic, top-down hierarchical structures and its conception of what direct democracy should look like. Like SNCC, ERAP started from the notion that everyone could be a leader and take on responsibilities, but that such qualities needed to be recognized by the people themselves and developed. Organizers then coached residents on various fronts: "Training varied from learning how to run meetings and how to research and write about topics relevant to organizing, like the War on Poverty and urban renewal, to developing personal confidence."[45]

The organizer's role was defined both nationally, at the outset of the project, and by people when they went into communities, and it was defined as a catalyst, explicitly modeled after SNCC's field secretary positions. In his "President's Report" from December 1963, SDS president Todd Gitlin hoped that "a new variety of 'radical vocation,' of off-campus work, will be created: one that requires full-time dedication similar to that of SNCC field secretaries."[46] Bearing strong resonance with a long tradition of voluntary poverty, such "vocations" could offer meaning to students who questioned their position within the class structure and who were willing to "give away" their social power in the (radical) service of the poor. Again, Kopkind captured ERAP's fundamental impulse and significance when he wrote,

> [The SDS kids] are part of the slums, a kind of lay-brotherhood, or worker-priests, except that they have no dogma to sell. They get no salary; they live on a subsistence allowance that the project as a whole uses for rent and food. Most of the time they are broke. In the dining room of the Cleveland "project house" last week was a sign: "Panic point. Bank balance $4.09." Newark project workers have to call "friends in the suburbs" every so often for $5 or $10, so the necessities of life can continue. The kids are the very antithesis of paid organizers the unions or political parties have to hire. Most of them have committed their lives to "the movement"; no matter if in a few years they change their minds. It is important that they now have the expectation of remaining.[47]

Even if several local projects tried to hire residents to legitimize their position further and opened up new possibilities and opportunities for several working-class men and women, there was a fundamental contradiction in the organizer's outsider position that no voluntaristic impulse could push away.[48] Although they wanted to "let the people decide" on their own terms, without organizers playing a directive, avant-gardist role, they were still "outsiders who entered unfamiliar communities with a definite purpose and their own agenda,"[49] which residents were usually not cognizant of when they talked with them.

Barriers of class, race, and gender between SDS organizers and residents often hampered the process of politicizing from the bottom up. Even when it succeeded, "getting to know the poor" was in itself not enough to kick-start a local contentious dynamic—let alone a movement. Although such structural difficulties were far from unique, they were compounded by several factors specific to SDS. First, probably due to SDS's own structure and limited institutionalization, ERAP organizers received no training or briefing before going into the field, which meant that "many had no idea what they were supposed to be doing, felt 'scared' and 'inadequate,' and ended up leaving the ERAP projects."[50] Second, the structure of postwar US social sciences, dominated by Paul Lazarsfeld's quantitative survey research at Columbia University and Talcott Parsons's and Robert Merton's grand theoretical models at Harvard, meant that students were very unlikely to have been exposed to the type of ethnographic surveys Alinsky and others on his staff had undertaken in the 1920s and 1930s, which could have offered them skills and know-how that ERAP would have then reactivated—or at least given them a sense of what they were doing.[51]

Finally, ERAP organizers also turned down the opportunity for SDS members to be trained in Alinsky's procedures. In an effort to build bridges between the IAF and the New Left, labor leader Ralph Helstein, an IAF board member, convened an informal meeting between his boss and several SDS leaders in the summer of 1964. By then, Alinsky already enjoyed a national reputation for professionalism, and he shared many similarities with the students in terms of class background and trajectory. But the meeting proved a failure: Alinsky dismissed the whole project as naive and idealistic, while SDS leaders rejected Alinsky's approach and procedures, which they deemed "too apolitical" and "liberal" because they did not fundamentally challenge the dominant culture.[52] For all these reasons, ERAP organizers started from scratch and, in many ways, reinvented the wheel of social surveys as political instruments.[53]

Organizing difficulties were not equally experienced by men and women, however. Although male organizers probably outnumbered women, several studies point out that women very often had an easier time than men in canvassing efforts. This was the result of early gendered socialization to care work but also because, when organizers knocked on people's doors, neighborhood women were more frequently home than men were.[54] As Cathy Wilkerson, an ERAP organizer in Chester, Pennsylvania, remarked, women "feel more at ease in the wash-tub situation or in small-talk over coffee which is useful just to get to know and establish a friendship with the women."[55] Hence sociologist Wini Breines's conclusion that "the female organizers were more successful than the men in generating political consciousness and activity that acknowledged their own politics but was neither manipulative nor directed from above."[56] The "radical vocations" ERAP carved out also appealed differently to men and women. While many male organizers experienced it more as a "rejection of the professional career track that was clearly in their futures," for many women these vocations opened up an alternative to the family track and trap; it held "greater appeal than the distinctly unsatisfactory future of marriage and motherhood, poor jobs, and low pay."[57] And while the adventurous, frontier-like imaginary of the organizer moving into unknown territory tapped into traditional representations of American masculinity, for female organizers to embrace such a role implied a real transgression of assigned gender norms and roles.[58]

ERAP was short-lived. As local projects hardly delivered on the hoped-for "interracial movement of the poor," over the course of several months in 1965 the escalation of US imperialistic intervention in Vietnam triggered the creation of a mass antiwar movement, leading SDS's national leadership to come back to college campuses as the main locus for the organization's activity. In the spring of 1965,

ERAP was disbanded as a national project. Therefore, most former organizers and scholars alike argue that the project was a failure as most local organizations collapsed after a couple of years without achieving meaningful local victories.

The importance of ERAP's legacy lies elsewhere, however. Historian Jennifer Frost, for instance, analyzes the project as a mix of "large defeats and small victories," pointing out that ERAP organizers did introduce several working-class people—mostly women—to professional and political possibilities they had hitherto never even thought of. More significantly, the project left a particular imprint on the organizers who performed such politicization work at the local level. As Frost emphasizes, "A core group of radical activists not only gained training and experience as organizers but also an irreplaceable perspective and lasting understanding on poverty,"[59] which they used and activated in other movement spaces (the antiwar movement, women's liberation, labor organizing, and more).[60] To ERAP, participating did not determine once and for all people's later commitments, but it did shape their own definition and conception of political work as well as their attachment to organization as a necessary road to build collective power. As the next chapter shows in detail, several ERAP organizers, like Steve Max and Richard Rothstein, were instrumental in institutionalizing community organizing as a lifelong career and profession.

SNCC and ERAP organizers were not calling for the self-organization of the oppressed and participatory democracy in an ideological vacuum. Despite obvious divergences, their radical politics were embedded within a broader political context that paradoxically legitimated them.

FEDERALLY POWERED POLITICIZATION FROM BELOW?

A crucial legitimating push in the process that molded radical community organizing came from the federal government and its framing of poor people's active participation as a solution to end poverty through the Economic Opportunity Act (EOA) of 1964, one of the main pieces of legislation in President Johnson's war on poverty.

The EOA created institutional mechanisms and used a language that had a long-lasting effect on the trajectory of community organizing practices. First, it established the Volunteers in Service to America program (VISTA). A domestic parallel to the international Peace Corps, tapping into the ideology of volunteer civic engagement and its value for democratic life, the program was initially meant to provide a (cheap) workforce to wage the war on poverty, with over four thousand volunteers in the field in 1970. But the program's seemingly consensual horizon rapidly slipped out of its designers' hands. As two sociologists pointed out at the time, "The positions are often turned into activists' adjuncts," serving as "a training ground for those who would make social movement activity a life career, while at the same time suggesting the possibility of such careers."[61] While the positions were volunteer ones, VISTA became one of the institutionalized routes traveled by activists and organizers in their careers, paving the way for subsequent professionalization dynamics.

The most famous creation of the EOA was of course the Community Action Program (CAP). To receive federal funding, local programs "had to foster 'maximum feasible participation' to planning, development, and administration from the communities they served."[62] CAP immediately opened unprecedented avenues for the active politicization of the urban, racialized working class. As soon as the program was set up, thousands of applications were sent in by local elected officials, social workers, and moderate as well as radical activist groups, who immediately seized this window of opportunity to force the authorities to take concrete measures in waging the so-called war on poverty promised by the Johnson administration. "Poor people went from conducting surveys about neighborhood needs to fielding candidates who promised to address those needs and registering voters to try to elect those candidates."[63] The Baltimore chapter of the Black Panther Party obtained funding for a self-managed public housing project; Chicano activists in

Milwaukee received funding to provide social benefits for immigrant workers; and activists in New York's Chinatown filed an application to build and manage a public housing project. By December 1964, nearly a thousand federally funded Community Action Agencies (CAAs) had been established. By 1968, four out of five agencies were private nonprofit organizations.[64] Federal funds were allocated through a grant-application system. Grantees were as diverse as the rehabilitation of abandoned buildings; the opening of neighborhood clinics, nursery schools, and community centers; the cleaning of public gardens; the renovation of municipal swimming pools; and also the publication of local newspapers and the fight against drug trafficking.

The program also anchored political struggles over poor people's representation within the CAA governing bodies, turning the racial makeup of institutions into a controversial yet legitimate object of public debate. Indeed, for many activists and politicians, the injunction to maximum feasible participation shifted the terms of the debate from the nature of the services and programs to the evaluation of the CAAs' democratic representativeness, in a context where calls for community control were highly publicized and polarized public debate.[65] "If community control meant 'the people' controlling their own fate," concludes historian Thomas Sugrue, "the legitimacy of social welfare agencies and community development organizations depended on having black faces dealing with black constituents."[66] This space of politicization was soon shut down as a result of intense lobbying and pressure on the part of local officials, who resented the fact that funding channels operated outside of their reach and felt that CAPs were ill suited to respond to recurrent urban unrest. In December 1967, an amendment to the Economic Opportunity Act made the attribution of federal funds for a CAA conditional on its official authorization by local and city governments.

Whether or not CAP was effective in its goals to reduce poverty, it did allow thousands of laypeople to gain expertise in grassroots organizing, to expose them to the world of public affairs and politics, which might never have happened otherwise due to the articulation of race, class, and gender oppression.[67] A case in point is Bobby Seale. Before becoming the cofounder of the Black Panther Party (BPP), he was hired in the summer of 1966 to run a CAP-funded youth employment program at the North Oakland Neighborhood Anti-Poverty Center. This position played an essential role in Seale's political trajectory because "he came to understand even more clearly the economic and social needs of black youth" and acquired knowledge, know-how, and ways of looking at things and thinking through issues that he later reinvested in his political activism: "Rather than merely guiding young blacks into a government-prescribed path, he used his authority to help them stand up against oppressive authority, particularly against police brutality."[68] In early 1967, Seale successfully talked his managers into hiring BPP cofounder Huey P. Newton. They used part of their salary to rent an office in North Oakland, where their fledgling organization operated from.

But this dynamic of politicization had the largest impact on women.

> Across the country, untold numbers of poor mothers became politicized during the 1960s and 1970s in pursuit of better food, schools, and health care for their children. Unwilling to remain passive clients of social welfare and health professionals, they came to see themselves as the true experts on poverty and to believe that they could run poverty and community health and education programs more effectively than the supposed experts.[69]

While working-class women had long performed unpaid domestic labor to reproduce the workforce as a whole, the fact that parts of this work could be done for compensation—wages—not only opened up possibilities to alleviate poverty, but it also credentialized their expertise, which upended the traditional boundaries professional poverty experts and social workers had erected for decades between themselves and the general laity. A preliminary report on CAP written by Office of Economic Opportunity officials noted a stark evolution in the professional assessment of excellence and efficiency in service provision and of the legitimate skills to perform the work. "Staff chosen from the indigenous community possess certain attributes which can improve the services offered by agencies working with the disadvantaged. They are often more effective than professionals especially in those roles that require staff to 'reach out.' They are skilled in dealing with their own environment and can communicate effectively with local people."[70]

Despite all its shortcomings, in turning the call for active popular participation both into a public policy instrument and a political goal, CAP drove a wedge into the boundaries separating social action professionals and beneficiaries, experts and nonexperts, giving weight to the notion that matters of civic participation need not be monopolized and controlled through professional means. Ultimately, CAP's fate and legacy became deeply intertwined with the Black power movement, as the multifaceted movement redefined the nature, direction, and scope of urban politics and protest and had a dramatic impact on the parameters of organizing.

BLACK POWER AND THE REDEFINITION OF LOCAL ORGANIZING

In the middle of the 1960s, heightened internal dissensions within the civil rights movement and the radicalization of the movement's repertoires of collective action, combined with increased state repression and white supremacist violence against protesters broke against the lack of any firm federal commitment to real racial equality.[71] This impasse weakened the belief in the possibility of achieving structural change through nonviolent direct action and "more suasion," undermining in the process the relational bases and prestige of the interracial "beloved community" and interracial organizing more generally. Nonviolence as the bedrock and guiding principle of tactical and strategic choices had been effective at winning groundbreaking psychological, legislative, and symbolic victories against segregation in the South, but it proved less adapted to the social fabric and political and socioeconomic structures and mechanisms that prevailed in ghettos in the North. In its place a competing, loose set of practices, repertoires, norms, and discourses took center stage in movement circles and beyond following Stokely Carmichael's June 1966 Black power speech, in which he reactivated Malcolm X's call for Black political self-determination.[72] For historian Jeffrey Helgeson, it was a landmark moment in establishing a collective identity for African Americans, revolving around a sense of pride and solidarity: "Black Power changed forever how African Americans approached everything from employment activism and community development to higher education and electoral politics."[73]

Contrary to what is often believed, however, the favored scale for Black power activity was the local level. Its international, anticolonial outlook notwithstanding, it primarily manifested itself "in a series of community-based struggles that found beachheads in urban cities, rural hamlets, neighborhoods, and universities," focusing on issues as diverse as education, jobs, university curricula, welfare and tenants' rights, and freedom of expression.[74] The concept of Black power itself also had "extraordinary plasticity." It was a political and cultural rallying cry that "meant everything from revolution to electing African American school board members to wearing a dashiki" and whose polysemy was precisely the reason it was so attractive.[75] But even if one subscribes to historian Peniel Joseph's argument about "the movement's intense local character, commitment to grassroots organizing, and political pragmatism," which challenges "prevailing wisdom that black militancy represented a retreat from organizing and that black nationalism inspired an emotional racial separatism that triggered the end of interracial alliances and the demise of core organizations (most notably SNCC and Congress of Racial Equality)," what impact did it have on grassroots organizing and on the way the figure of the organizer as spadeworker was taken up and redefined?[76]

From Interracial Organizing to Black Self-Determination

The first, most visible and publicized impact of Black power's prominence was to challenge the validity and legitimacy of interracial organizing. Contrary to Martin Luther King's beloved community, Black liberation struggles were redefined along self-determination lines. The defiance toward white involvement was symbolized by a vote to expel white staff and volunteers from SNCC in December 1966.[77] Although most white staff and volunteers had left the organization and only seven white members were still active in SNCC by then, the narrow-margin decision was still symbolically important, all the more since it was immediately taken up and blown out of proportion by a national press all too willing to vilify calls for Black self-determination.[78]

SNCC's decision brought to the fore and into writing a tacit norm that had spread in recent years in activist circles: in the struggle for liberation and true equality, only Black people could organize or speak on behalf of other Black people, both in the sense of having the right set of skills, abilities, and social and cultural know-how and of possessing the authority and legitimacy to do so. Racism was so deeply ingrained in white people's behaviors and psyches that they were bound to reproduce it when they worked alongside people of color. If white radicals wanted to play a productive role in the movement, they must "work with poor white and working class youth, overcoming racism, and have them join the movement, join the struggle along with Black people and Latinos to overthrow the racist-capitalist-imperialists who were running the show," as former JOIN Community Union organizer and Rainbow Coalition participant Mike James later remembered.[79] Achieving such racial representation was not a goal in itself, however. It was a means for oppressed groups to come together and dismantle what Carmichael and coauthor Charles Hamilton had dubbed "institutional racism" in their widely read *Black Power: The Politics of Liberation* (1967).

There were countless interactions and moments when challenges to white direct participation in Black liberation struggles were mounted in the name of Black self-determination. For the purposes of my argument about the historical arc of professionalization dynamics that shaped community organizing, I want to focus on one example in particular. It involved Alinsky and Black nationalist leader Ron Karenga.

Born in 1941, Karenga was the son of a tenant farmer and Baptist minister from Maryland. He moved to Los Angeles in 1959 and got involved in CORE and SNCC while obtaining bachelor's and master's degrees in political science from University of California, Los Angeles. While there, he cofounded the powerful Organization Us in California ("Us, not them, the whites") in the aftermath of Malcolm X's assassination and the Watts riots in 1965, becoming a prominent voice in the Black power movement. Claiming Malcolm X's political legacy, he "preached that Black liberation required a reconstitution of Black identity that purged white influences and reclaimed African roots: cultural revolution, in his view, must precede sociopolitical revolution."[80]

In June 1968, Karenga spoke at a meeting in Dayton, Ohio, sponsored by the Interfaith Foundation for Community Organization (IFCO), a nonprofit created in 1966 by a civic foundation and a number of interreligious institutions to promote "community organization, community development, and ghetto economic development" through funding, fundraising, coordination, training, and research.[81] In his speech, Karenga took issue with a grant application for the creation of a national training institute for organizers that IFCO had received and that he had learned about. He forcefully voiced his opposition to the project—its author, he later disclosed, was Alinsky, who was looking for funds to set up the IAF Institute. Karenga insisted that whites could not teach Black people anything about community organization because Blacks had their own culture; the very fact of applying for funding was an attempt by white outsiders to get control in the Black community. During a panel discussion afterward, another participant, who chaired the Los Angeles Black Congress, called Alinsky an "economic exploiter who gets money that should go to the black community" and argued that "a training program must project an image of blackness."[82]

At first, Alinsky had reacted favorably to the Black power slogan, explaining in the fall of 1966 that "we've always called it community power, and if the community is black, it's black power."[83] But by 1967 he had become more critical of what he perceived as empty rhetoric

backed by no actual on-the-ground organizing. In a seven-page letter to IFCO's director, which he brought to the attention of the press
in retaliation for Karenga's disclosing his identity as the incriminated
applicant, he announced that the IAF board would withdraw its application for a $225,000 grant (around $1.8 million in 2021 dollars). He
objected to Karenga's statement that "Blacks are a country and if you
support America then you're against my community." Instead, he went
into a patriotic, equal-opportunity rant.[84]

What stands out in this conflict about formalizing community
organization trainings is the opposition between two logics of legitimation. On the one hand, the IAF's professional bid for the formalization and institutionalization of training was grounded in
instrumental rationality and professional detachment. On the other,
Karenga's rhetoric conceived training programs as sites where the racial representation pushed forward by the Black power movement
applied as well. Several weeks later, when he publicly announced
the creation of the IAF Institute, Alinsky presented it as a school for
white organizers.

Coalition Building, Pragmatism, and Community Services

The second main addition to the alternative definition of organizing practices and the organizer's role had to do with a broadening of
scope to include coalition building and service provision. As Peniel
Joseph notes, Black power's call for Black self-determination was not
"one that consistently advocated racial separatism."[85] It was also a
broad tent for several attempts at building interracial coalitions. The
most famous organization that combined radical self-determination
and coalition building across racial divides was the Black Panther
Party, but it was not the only one that developed an expanded practical definition of what "organizing" meant, integrating direct service
programs into its day-to-day activities and giving them an explicitly
political dimension.

Armed self-defense had been the Black Panthers' hallmark since it was founded in October 1966 in Oakland, California, by Seale and Newton, one that immediately attracted the attention of white elites and the state apparatus (J. Edgar Hoover's FBI, in particular) and resulted in constant police harassment. By the fall of 1968, with membership and influence growing steadily, "the Party sought meaningful activities for members that would serve the community, strengthen the Party, and improve its image in the public relations battle with the state. In this context, community programs quickly became a cornerstone of Party activity nationwide." The Panthers' first Free Breakfast for Children Program was launched in Oakland in late January 1969. "At the height of the effort, between 1969 and 1971, at least thirty-six breakfast programs were operating nationwide with larger chapters running multiple sites." Other "community service programs" included free health clinics, daycare centers, food distribution, free emergency ambulance services, free shoe and clothing programs, and liberation schools building on the radical pedagogy of Ella Baker, the Highlander Folk School, and SNCC's Freedom Summer. Presented as "revolutionary, community, socialistic programs" rather than "reform programs," the Black Panthers' community services accomplished several goals. They provided much-needed material aid to people; they performed "crucial educational and political work within communities, conveying the insufficiency of the capitalist welfare state to meet even the most basic needs of its citizens, especially black citizens"; and they showed the importance of building independent, Black-led institutions by winning people's support and trust.[86]

Another important aspect of the Panthers' activity was symbolized by the (first) Rainbow Coalition, which coalesced in Chicago in 1968–1969 at the initiative of the Illinois chapter of the Black Panther Party and its young chairman, Fred Hampton. Bringing together groups from different racial, ethnic, and class backgrounds (African American and Puerto Rican gang members, poor whites) in opposition to police brutality, urban renewal, gentrification, and the political corruption of Richard J. Daley's political machine, the Rainbow Coalition was the first of its kind, "not only because it was established and led by teenagers and young people but also because poor ethnic groups led by (indeed, for the first time *including*) African Americans organized as one entity to fight for the political power that was denied to them all and to significantly reduce the rigid racial and ethnic tension between these groups."[87] The coalition was later joined by SDS, the American Indian Movement, and the Chicano Brown Berets.

While the coalition has been remembered as Fred Hampton's brain-child, much of the actual organizing legwork and coalition building across racial lines was performed by Robert E. Lee III.[88] Known as Bob Lee, he had moved from Houston, Texas, to Chicago in 1968 as a VISTA volunteer working in a YMCA facility, where he worked mostly with gang members as a recreation leader during the day and a counselor at night. Again, it shows the porousness of boundaries between social work, religious backgrounds, and radical political commitments and the politicizing opportunities positions in these sectors can yield. The establishment of the Rainbow Coalition translated into coalition members like the Puerto Rican Young Lords and the white Uptown-based Young Patriots aligning their activities more closely with the Panthers'. "To join the [Young Lords Organization], a potential member had to take political education classes and karate instruction, as well as to conduct community service."[89]

Another interesting example of a Black power organization that fused direct services into its self-determination agenda is the Kenwood-Oakland Community Organization (KOCO), in Chicago. Weaving together political groundwork and an electoral perspective, borrowing from Black power rhetoric and political liberalism, this brand of "popular, pragmatic black nationalism" engendered "a hybrid political vision of democratic urban planning that aimed to link economic development to bringing jobs, housing, recreational spaces, and municipal services to working-class communities."[90] KOCO was founded in December 1965 by a group of seven Catholic and Protestant churches that had been engaging in reform action since 1963 within the Kenwood Cooperative Ministry. It operated in Kenwood and Oakland, on Chicago's South Side, north of Hyde Park and the University of Chicago, an area that had undergone rapid demographic changes and aggressive urban renewal projects in the 1950s and 1960s. KOCO was an unusual organization from the start in that it blended IAF procedures and SCLC's philosophy of nonviolent direct action. It was created at the initiative of the SCLC to plan for Martin Luther King Jr.'s 1966 Chicago campaign. "KOCO is built on the standard community organization-Alinsky-premise of organization through tightly knit block clubs (we call them patches of a quilt to keep warm), but is unique in that it is firmly allied with the Freedom Movement, and is a participating member of the Coordinating Council of Community Organizations. KOCO stands for both types of community organization."[91]

KOCO's position at the intersection of nonviolent direct action organizing and IAF militant liberalism manifested itself through the diverse trajectories and organizing experiences of its core leaders and staff. Its first director was Reverend Jesse Jackson, a close advisor to King. He was soon replaced by Reverend Curtis Burrell. An African American Protestant minister who had previously worked as staff for the Woodlawn Organization, where he had been trained in the IAF procedures, Burrell was hired part-time as "executive organizer" in 1966.[92] In a strict Alinsky tradition, KOCO was built upon "patches," block clubs of five people or more—religious institutions, parent-teacher associations, youth groups, and tenant councils—who applied to join the organization and were then voted in by all KOCO delegates. In the fall of 1966, the organization was composed of twenty-four patches, with membership ranging from ten to seven hundred members. It also used a professional rhetoric to describe its staff, as a report from 1966 suggests: "KOCO is a community organization: an architect, a priest, a social worker, a protestant seminarian, a revolutionary, three welfare recipients, and an organizer are the professional servants to KOCO." Earning $390 a month in 1966 ($3,400 in 2021),

Preston Harwell, the community organizer, directed the staff and accomplished mostly outreach and administrative work: "An ex-gang member, former business executive, Press has worked as an organizer and political activist for nine years. His is the responsibility of community organizer. He orients and directs the staff, relates to Commission Heads, acts as advisor to the Executive Committee, and executes the orders of the Chairman. He is also instrumental in the development and coordination of community projects."[93]

Its original strategy of interracial conciliation changed under Burrell, who increasingly tapped into Black power rhetoric, particularly in its cultural-nationalist variant, as the organization's motto made clear: "Black people serious about one another." In the late 1960s and early 1970s, following a national trend among many Black and other non-white-led organizations, and in a local context where the departure of most white households from the neighborhood rendered calls for integration meaningless, KOCO emphasized demands around community control. Against the backdrop of community deterioration, KOCO called for African Americans' political and ideological independence as well as local economic development through a mix of protest actions and community services. In 1971 it pushed the city to open a new high school in the neighborhood. It also developed free direct service programs for community residents, such as a legal aid service and a daycare center. Like TWO and other groups in New York, Los Angeles, and Oakland, KOCO recognized that gangs were an objective part of many people's daily lives and tried to move gangs away from criminal activity and invest their organizational and material resources into defending and promoting the community instead. To implement such a strategy, KOCO sought to welcome gang members into its staff. Several members of the Blackstone Rangers were therefore hired as community organizers to supervise community service programs. KOCO also lent the gang several thousand dollars to open a restaurant, to support Black local businesses. But the partnership soon proved quite rocky and the project petered out.[94] In 1970, partly in order to establish its presence independently from the Blackstone Rangers, Burrell laid off most staff and temporarily closed down the KOCO office.[95]

CONCLUSION

Throughout the long 1960s a new role emerged and took shape within the division of political labor, that of the community organizer as catalyst for individual and collective emancipation, what I've called a spadeworker. As a result, it is inaccurate to claim, as some have done for ERAP or for SNCC's organizing "model," that this particular form of collective action disappeared during the late 1960s. True enough, the projects and organizations that performed and upheld spadework disbanded, chose to focus on issues that were deemed incompatible with the requirements of the work, or lacked the people, the time, and to a lesser extent the money to do the work, as several participants to the 1967 SNCC central committee meeting noted. But the role of the organizer as spadeworker and the skills and expertise attached to the role lived on, albeit in a minor mode.

The role was put into practice and defined through three crucial turning points—SNCC, ERAP, and Black power iterations like the Panthers at the national level and KOCO in Chicago. The role and the expertise differed from the IAF's in terms of its origins, its political horizon, and how its expertise was abstracted. Whereas the IAF-style organizer dug their roots in professional social work and performed an original form of management consulting work, the spadeworker's role originated in radical pedagogy and workers' education movements, with people like Ella Baker and Myles Horton playing key roles as intermediaries and mentors.

Second, contrary to the IAF, the practical, experiential expertise that spadeworkers abstracted from action was not meant to find a professional outlet but to feed into a movement to transform society from the bottom up. By incorporating a paradoxical refusal of institutionalization into the role of the organizer as spadeworker, SNCC field secretaries, ERAPers, CAP working-class nonprofessionals, and Black power organizers at KOCO and in Black Panther Party chapters mounted a deprofessionalizing challenge to the professional claims Alinsky took to a national level around the same time. While IAF organizers worked toward erecting professional boundaries, spadeworkers strove to collapse them. Lastly, the abstraction process was performed haphazardly, with no coherent center (an institution or an individual) who could monopolize the symbolic profits generated from the use of the expertise. Although Ella Baker has been recently hailed as another founding figure in the community organizing tradition, she did not pursue the same strategies to accumulate symbolic capital as Alinsky. She did not write books where she laid out what she meant by "spade work" and why it was so important, for instance.

On other counts, however, the differences between radical spadework and IAF-style community organization were not as clear-cut. In terms of the work itself, there were numerous similarities between the two: the ethnographic immersion into a community, connecting with people to find out what could drive their participation to collective endeavors, the ability to step back to let the people speak and decide, the constant reflexivity on one's own position and practices, and the constant focus on concrete situations and concrete solutions. "Organization" as a specific set of tasks was distinguished from more established domains like leadership and administrative tasks in an attempt to legitimize them. The other resonance between Alinsky's community organization practices and movement spadework has to do with organizers' educational attainment and how higher education institutions were a key site for their politicization. In the case of SNCC and ERAP, the student dimension speaks for itself. But as historian Donna Murch has pointedly emphasized, Black students' activism in places like Berkeley, San Francisco State University, and also Merritt College, where Seale and Newton met, were the backbone to the development of the BPP.[96] This suggests real social distance between organizers and the people they organized, since in the mid-1960s, only 12 percent of people over twenty-five had received some college education or more.[97]

In the early 1970s, shifting political terrains recalibrated the political implications and practical opportunities of spadework. Against the backdrop of heightened political repression, movement exhaustion, strategic and tactical divergences, spadework was further marginalized vis-à-vis other forms of collective action within the ecology of protest politics. On the one hand, several organizations or factions within organizations like the Weather Underground and the Black Liberation Army turned to armed struggle in their fight against white supremacy and US imperialism; on the other hand, others endorsed Marxist-Leninist-inspired party-building efforts and shifted their political focus toward industrial labor and workplaces. In the Black power movements, those who still valued local "community work" increasingly subordinated it to a move "from protest to politics," running candidates for local office.[98] This hardening of political and ideological cleavages was embedded within a more general waning of large-scale radical movements, a lowering of the horizon of radical emancipatory politics, and the conservative backlash led by Richard Nixon, and it moved the spadework expertise diffusely accumulated over the years of struggle into a new direction: building an autonomous, self-reproducing group of professional organizers.

CHAPTER 6

PROFESSIONALIZATION
FROM WITHIN

Building a Skilled Cadre of Practitioners

I n July 1977, radical journalist Studs Terkel sat down with National People's Action (NPA) director Gale Cincotta to talk about the "community movement going on," which the media had shown no interest in. A Chicago native, Cincotta grew up and lived in the white working-class neighborhood of Austin, on the city's West Side.[1] There, she met with former Methodist minister turned IAF organizer Shel Trapp, who worked for the Organization for a Better Austin. The neighborhood struggles they were involved in in the late 1960s led them to creating supralocal institutions to disseminate and support their organizing efforts. In 1972, they convened a national gathering held in Chicago to discuss housing issues; the gathering drew 2,400 delegates from 67 cities and 34 states. It led to the creation of NPA, whose campaigning would be supported by a "national resource center for organizing training, technical assistance, research, and consulting," the National Training and Information Center (NTIC).[2] A spearhead of the urban reinvestment movement, NPA/NTIC was instrumental in pushing Congress to adopt the Home Mortgage Disclosure Act of 1975 and Community Reinvestment Act of 1977.[3]

As the interview with Terkel was ending, Cincotta issued a cry for help: "Community organizations need organizers, they need professional help."[4] It was neither a "regular" nor a "glamorous" job. "But if you want to work with people and make change, this is the place." No college degrees were needed to apply. "You just have to have the will to change something," she concluded. The job might not be glamorous, but in the late 1970s it seemed that it was indeed one of the only places where you could actually effect change. More significantly, it seemed that such essential but unacknowledged work was accomplished by an increasingly autonomous and self-conscious group of full-time, paid organizers.

The editorial history of a forgotten book shows how this fact came to be understood by academics over the course of the decade. When sociologist Joan Ecklein published *Community Organizers* in 1972— the year Alinsky died, ironically—she wanted to focus on "a relatively new occupational grouping of people who intervene, organize, and plan with and on behalf of others. . . . Their activities are not by any means new, but it is only during the past two decades that community organizers have emerged as a distinct grouping of people, many of whom have professional training for their work." At the time, what she meant by "community organizers" also included social planners, a testament to the ill-defined nature of the label. Twelve years later, Ecklein published a second edition, which now excluded social planners, with almost entirely new material. "The fact that this edition is entirely concerned with community organizers . . . is a tribute to the fact that community organizing during the past decade has become an enormously complex and often sophisticated phenomenon."[5] Community organizers were now an autonomous occupational group.

In their own ways, these two anecdotes point to a central characteristic of what people meant by "community organizing" at the end of the 1970s. The work that community organizers accomplished was of a professional nature, it was grounded in abstract knowledge that was put to very practical use, but its object differed from more "regular jobs." The 1970s and 1980s marked a fundamental turning point in the formation of a self-conscious group of professional community organizers. Why did Cincotta and her peers endorse professionalism as a collective project? Why did they come to see themselves as professionals whose "help" was necessary?

In this chapter I want to contend that the occupation came into existence when two hitherto distinct groups, the people who were trained by the IAF and the radical spadeworkers from the sixties, came together some time in the mid- to late 1970s around a shared project of professionalization from within. The possibility of such a project rested on four pillars: an organizational framework; individuals who were ready to work as organizers but who wanted to find a balance between work and their personal lives; a body of knowledge and skills; and the development of institutions binding the group together.

THE CONSOLIDATION OF AN ORGANIZATIONAL FRAMEWORK

The first pillar supporting professional community organizing was the development of a rich, multilayered organizational infrastructure throughout the country. In 1980, political theorist and community organizing enthusiast Harry Boyte claimed that "more than 20 million Americans [had] become active in some form of neighborhood group."[6] Several years later, Gary Delgado, a founding member of ACORN who later created the Center for Third World Organizing (CTWO), estimated that there were eight thousand neighborhood groups.[7] Many of these groups were short lived and never expanded beyond a neighborhood scale. But others were integrated into newly formed supralocal networks and federations that gave neighborhood activism a particular style and orientation.

Beyond Localism: New Federations Vying for Power

The five national federations that were founded between 1970 and 1986 who took up the "community organizing" label all had direct or indirect ties with Alinsky and the IAF. They were founded by people

who had been trained by Alinsky or his staff and wanted to keep building and expanding on his procedures. In a classic case of rivalry between disciples after the death of the charismatic leader, the federations
competed with one another to claim Alinsky's mantle, contributing
to establishing the idea that there was a legacy to be claimed and that
Alinsky was a founding figure of what was now rebranded "community organizing"—a term that Alinsky himself never used to describe
his work.[8]

The first three directly came out of the IAF's networks. In 1972, the
Oakland Training Institute—which became the Pacific Institute for
Community Organization (PICO) in 1976—was founded by former
Jesuit priest John Baumann to organize individuals, families, and then
congregations throughout California. The year 1972 was also when
Cincotta and Trapp founded NTIC/NPA. Baumann, Cincotta, and
Trapp had all been trained by Tom Gaudette, who was himself trained
by Alinsky. Another former Jesuit priest and Gaudette trainee was Greg
Galluzzo, who in 1980 founded a new community organization on the
southeast side of Chicago with his wife, Mary Gonzales, to fight back
against the steel industry laying off thousands of workers. In the next
few years, the United Neighborhood Organization expanded to other
neighborhoods, mostly Black and Latino, and became a prominent
player in city politics.[9] In 1986, Galluzzo was hired to lead the Gamaliel
Foundation, which had been created in 1968 to help a group of Black
homeowners fight discriminatory housing deals.[10] Galluzzo's recruitment shifted Gamaliel's activities toward the repertoires of professional
community organizing: providing training, leadership development,
and consulting advice to local groups that affiliated with the federation.

The ties that the other two federations, Citizen Action and ACORN,
maintained with the IAF were more indirect and articulated with their
origins in the 1960s' large-scale movements. The first, Citizen Action,
was created in 1980 by some of the former sixties radicals (Heather
Booth, Steve Max) who had launched the Chicago-based Midwest
Academy in 1973. It innovated with Alinsky's legacy on two counts:

as a national network, it brought together statewide membership organizations and coalitions of labor unions and citizen groups, whereas until then IAF organizations had been mostly neighborhood or city organizations, and it also sought to influence policy making more directly by pushing for progressive legislation and endorsing Democratic candidates for office.

ACORN was also born out of the cradle of mass movements. It was founded in Arkansas in 1970 by Wade Rathke, a middle-class white man from Louisiana and a former organizer for the Massachusetts branch of the National Welfare Rights Organization (NWRO). Borrowing directly from sociologists Frances Fox Piven's and Richard Cloward's work on poor people's movements and the levers of action they could activate, the NWRO had been created in the mid-1960s to represent the interests of welfare recipients against state bureaucracies. Against the backdrop of the Nixon administration's backlash against welfare benefits, the NWRO tried to expand into the South and picked Rathke as its main on-the-ground organizer. Rathke convinced NWRO's director that Arkansas would be a good place to start. A firm believer in the possibility of interracial coalitions, he also insisted that the new local organization should broaden its base beyond welfare mothers and their children to build a majority constituency organization against the wealthy. The organization was called Arkansas Community Organization for Reform Now, ACORN. Tensions soon arose with the NWRO, in part driven by Rathke's own ambition, and ACORN set out on its own. After initial successes in Arkansas, it rapidly expanded to other states, changing "Arkansas" to "Association" in the process. By the mid-1980s, it had chapters in twenty-six states. It also started to make forays into labor, organizing low-wage service workers in several cities.

ACORN's roots in the welfare rights movement are only part of its story, however. The organization also grew out of Alinsky's community organization practices, with Rathke playing a crucial pivot role. IAF "procedures" got passed on through the NWRO, whose leadership was trained at a Syracuse University program where Alinsky and Fred Ross worked as consultants in the late 1960s. But Rathke also read Alinsky's books and studied Fred Ross's work with the Community Service Organization in California. ACORN's door-to-door approach and use of house meetings actually borrowed from Ross.

These federations' origins and politics depended on their founders' social characteristics and organizing backgrounds as well as the struggles that opposed them over the future of Alinsky's legacy. On the one hand, the entry of former New Leftists like Booth, Max, and Mike Miller into the budding field pushed the meaning of Alinsky's work to the left, challenging long-held assumptions about local, "winnable" campaigns, pushing for mid- to long-term goals while endorsing the "rigor" of his know-how and bringing to the table the question of race as a legitimate question that organizers and organizations should grapple with.[11] On the other hand, others called for a "post-Alinsky agenda" that put an end to conflict and confrontation and emphasized instead self-help and economic development.[12] Social scientist and Gamaliel board member John McKnight became the most famous proponent of this revisionist approach in the 1980s, calling for an anti-welfare, bootstrap embrace of "asset-based community development" that influenced many, including Obama.[13]

Fighting for turf and resources as they grew in size and scope, seeking to move beyond the impasse of neighborhood-level action, all federations formalized their relations with local organizations, which became their exclusive affiliates. Supralocal federations provided individual consulting services and financial resources to their local affiliates. Local affiliates did not always indicate publicly their federative ties, since they had a symbolic and strategic interest in putting forward their "community" roots, a guarantee for independence and autonomy given the "enclave consciousness" that was built into the US notion of community.[14] It was far from obvious, for instance, that the Chicago-based Developing Communities Project where Obama worked in the late 1980s was part of Gamaliel. ACORN was different from other networks since its local chapter presented themselves as part of a broader entity. Institutionalization and organizational growth also increased specialization and hierarchy, which translated into the creation of new, middle-management positions. At the IAF, for instance, regional organizer positions were created.[15]

Finally, supralocal federations started to formalize training curricula, defending their own methods to achieve what they called "real," "effective" change. These methods determined clear steps, goals, and tasks to accomplish. Ed Chambers had already initiated the spelling out of a particular IAF "method" when he took over as executive director in 1972, in the wake of Alinsky's death. But the federation that pushed formalization the farthest is certainly ACORN, where Rathke put in writing a "community organizing model" in 1972 that "clearly delineated a modus operandi for organizers, especially when they entered a new town; it elaborated a replicable organizational structure, which included membership-based local indigenous leadership, and a citywide alliance of ACORN groups; it trained organizers; and it defined a method by which organizers could use almost any neighborhood issue to build an ACORN group."[16] The whole model revolved around a six- to eight-week organizing drive. When they became staff members, each new organizer was given a booklet that introduced and explained the model and its seven stages.[17] Incidentally, ACORN was also the federation with the most explicit ambitions to reach national prominence, as is illustrated by its "20/80" plan spelled out in 1976 to build chapters in twenty states by 1980. Rathke was convinced that "ACORN has an organizational and professional responsibility to demonstrate the potential of community organizing as a mechanism for social change."[18]

Front-Porch Politics in the Background

The competition between supralocal federations, which contributed to solidifying community organizing as a distinct field of practice

by increasing people's stakes in it and developing ties of interdependence, also tapped into two interrelated phenomena unfolding against
the backdrop of the New Deal order unraveling: the proliferation of
neighborhood struggles and the legitimation of community-based organizations as political players. The 1970s witnessed a notable shift in
repertoires of collective action and forms of mobilization. The protest
waves of the long 1960s, at the center of which stood the Black liberation movement and the antiwar movement, were characterized by
large marches and demonstrations that were national in their framing
and scope. In the 1970s, they were gradually supplanted by more local,
diffuse forms of contention, which some saw as a "new populism" or a
"backyard revolution."[19]

These forms of collective engagement, which historian Michael
Foley calls "front-porch politics," were fundamentally heterogeneous,
whether in terms of their repertoires of action, the social origins and
trajectories of their participants, or the issues they fought for—air pollution, toxic waste, bank lending practices, highway construction, and
also property taxes or defending the traditional, heterosexual family
and fighting against women's reproductive rights. But all iterations of
such politics were grounded in people's immediate lived experience
and started from "an immediate sense of threat—from government,
corporations, the law, or other citizens with opposing interests—that
required something more than a vote. It required action."[20] Against
the elite's perceived geographical distance and class contempt, those
struggles led by "regular folks" emphasized their wisdom and common
sense, promoting a "populist sensibility" grounded in "a renewed vision of direct democracy coupled with a mistrust of large institutions,
both public and private."[21] At NPA's founding convention in 1972, it
was clear whom "the people" must close ranks and mobilize against:
the realtors, the banks, the Washington lobbyists, and the Department
of Housing and Urban Development.

Front-porch politics were founded on a deep sense of distrust toward the state, and the federal government in particular, tapping into

the long tradition of antistatist self-help that had been promoted by liberal philanthropy since the mid-nineteenth century and that was now part of a bipartisan political consensus. Indeed, throughout the 1970s Democrats and Republicans alike agreed on the necessity of preventing further government intervention into public matters—hence cuts in federal social spending and the handing over of social service delivery to the private sector, which reinforced the power of the local level of government. A series of federal laws held up the neighborhood as the most effective unit and level to implement policies to tackle deindustrialization, unemployment, and the coming apart of the social fabric in many urban centers.[22]

Such political choices fostered the development of a fully-fledged nonprofit sector, which also benefited from generous tax deductions. Nonprofit organizations, a great deal of which were community-based organizations, became essential components in this new configuration where pacified partnerships between public and private actors became the norm in urban governance. Organizations that registered as 501(c)(3) organizations—after the name of the Internal Revenue Service code section created in 1969 to regulate nonprofits—could receive tax-deductible private donations and were exempted from federal taxes. Not only did such policies redefine the relations between the state and so-called civil society, but they also spurred the number of community organizations throughout the country.[23]

Fault Lines in Work Practices

Organizational growth was in part driven by the invention of new practices or application of existing ones to new constituencies. Although the local groups and supralocal federations involved were committed to "[forming] coalitions among different racial and income groups" and to democratizing power relations through "a greater involvement of ordinary people in decisions affecting their lives,"[24] they did not agree over the "right" way to do so. As other social science studies emphasize, such practical and symbolic debates, far from splitting a group apart, tend to bind it together.[25] As a result, the field and the category of "community organizing" consolidated because of these very disagreements.

Two dividing principles structured competition between organizations and between individual organizers. The first principle opposed different visions of what sectors of "the community" organizers must reach out to, which translated into different work practices. Some favored institution-based organizing—also called "faith-based," "congregation-based," or "broad-based" organizing—where preexisting local institutions were the initial building blocks for future organizing efforts and coalition building. In keeping with the IAF's practices during the Alinsky era, organizers' work consisted in identifying local congregations, meeting one on one with their ministers and lay leaders, and convincing them to pool their efforts and resources together to give birth to an organization representing all voices and interests in the community and organize for a shared, common collective goal that they alone could determine. Member organizations paid dues to fund the new entity (and hire staffers).

Carrying on building "organizations of organizations" did not mean uncritically reproducing Alinsky's legacy. After his death, Ed Chambers and other IAF cadre took issue with the focus on interest-based "power politics" and localism; instead, they pushed for more exclusive alliances with religious groups to build coalitions around "communities of interest" that did not necessarily imply living in the same neighborhood or even city.[26] When congregations or other traditional urban institutions like settlement houses unraveled, organizers turned to creating other institutional units such as block clubs, which had a rich history in cities like Chicago.[27]

Such a definition of what portion of the community should be organized carried a number of blind spots. Such civic engagements are not socially neutral; they tend to express a relative position of social stability—working public-sector jobs or being a homeowner, for instance.

Such a class status pushed these individuals who upheld norms of social respectability to favor moderate issues and consensual rhetoric.

As a result, "individual-based organizing" targeted individuals directly, to reach out to the lower strata of the working classes, those who lacked in the cultural, economic, and social capital often required to develop and maintain civic engagements. The approach was promoted most forcefully by ACORN, which claimed it sought to organize the unorganized through campaigns that could win majority support on the part of residents. To do so, ACORN organizers avoided issues around race and gender (affirmative action, abortion, busing). Individual-based organizing put a heavier emphasis on systematic door knocking as an essential recruitment tool. ACORN's door knocking borrowed directly from organizing practices developed within the welfare rights movement and the NWRO, which themselves grew out of the "house-meeting" practice developed by Fred Ross and the CSO in the 1940s and 1950s.

Just as Alinsky's expertise resonated with certain sectors of business in the postwar era, so did canvassing techniques signal direct links with commercial sales. For decades, door knocking to remind people to vote (and to vote correctly) had been a core component of what precinct captains in Chicago and elsewhere did during election season, but in the early 1970s it intersected with direct marketing techniques and produced a highly rationalized form of door-to-door solicitation called "canvassing." One of its alleged inventors was Marc Anderson, an encyclopedia salesman who had volunteered on the campaign of a reform candidate for city council in Chicago in 1970. Anderson decided to blend his professional training and political experience and founded Citizens for a Better Environment to sell the environmentalist cause while raising funds effectively.[28] Multiple citizen organizations contracted with Anderson for his services. The Illinois Public Action Council, for instance, which maintained close ties with the Midwest Academy and Citizen Action folks, hired Anderson in the 1980s to organize a canvass, which at its peak was operated by around two hundred paid canvassers.[29]

The second dividing line, which partly overlapped the opposition between institution-based and individual-based, was the relation to electoral politics and ideology. Alinsky built the IAF's expertise around a distrust toward elected officials combined with a great deal of political opportunism. It did not really matter who was in office as long as officeholders could be pressured into negotiating with local power groups. "No permanent enemies, no permanent allies, only permanent interests" was one of Alinsky's mottos. While PICO and the IAF under Chambers's leadership honored this tradition, others like ACORN, Citizen Action, and NPA, groups often created or led by people coming out of protest movements and who agreed with the "from protest to politics" orientation, broke with this norm and engaged more directly with the political field at the supralocal level, organizing voter registration drives, lobbying state and federal elected officials on a more systematic basis, opening up offices in DC, and drafting policy to defend the voices and interests of their constituents. In ACORN's case, the organization even sent delegates to the 1980 Democratic National Convention to try to weigh in on internal debates.[30]

Ideology, too, had been written out of the organizer's role by Alinsky—even if such a rejection of ideology was of course the classic expression of a dominant ideology, in this case Cold War liberalism. In Alinsky's eyes, organizers should focus on "the world as it is" and not be bothered with big theories about capitalism, racism, and imperialism. Most of his disciples upheld this dictum, including those who turned to electoral politics, like ACORN and Citizen Action. Yet there existed a number of critical voices who took issue with the focus on nondivisive, "winnable" fights at the expense of more long-term work that would challenge structures of oppression. One of these critics was Gary Delgado, a former welfare rights organizer who contributed to founding ACORN but who left the organization to create the Center for Third World Organizing (CTWO) in Oakland in 1980. In the 1990s Delgado formalized his critiques against what he called "traditional community organizing" and its localist bend into a widely discussed essay titled "Beyond the Politics of Place."[31] CTWO was in- itially meant as a training center for organizers of color, but over the years it expanded its activities to on-the-ground local coalition-building work, organizer coaching, and fundraising training.[32]

The two intertwined, fundamental oppositions in work practices and electoral politics set the parameters for competition between organizers and organizations. Within such a competition was grounded an expanding material base, which spurred the profession's development. Indeed, the growth of this community-oriented organizational apparatus resulted in many staff positions opening. All community-based organizations were nominally run by volunteer citizens and boards, but the work of recruiting new members and fostering their participation was performed by part- or full-time paid organizers. And in the 1970s, there actually existed a pool of people who were willing to take up these positions and intentionally build the career as a whole.

PREDISPOSITIONS, TRANSFORMATIVE EXPERIENCES, AND PROFESSIONAL OPPORTUNITIES

The fact that there were people who were ready to work as organizers, both in the sense of being available at that moment and socially predisposed to perform such work, and the fact that they were intent on defending a professionalization strategy is the second condition of possibility for the advent of professional community organizing.

As I have argued before, staff shortage was one of the IAF's main problems to expand its activity from the 1940s to the 1970s. But the mass movements of the Long Sixties changed that situation by drawing tens of thousands of people into various forms and degrees of engagement. Not all participants became full-time revolutionaries, but through participation in protest action they came to care, or care more, about justice and sought to act on it; they acquired or actualized the predispositions, the practical skills and knowledge that are necessary for what social scientists call "contentious politics."[33] For many, the political radicalization induced by movement participation also recalibrated or even upended their professional expectations and aspirations, as the examples of SNCC field secretaries and ERAP staffers have already shown.

In the mid-1970s, against the backdrop of movement decline, political repression, economic stagnation, aging, exhaustion from years of struggle, and hesitations about their own commitments, organizer positions in the burgeoning community organizing field appeared to many as a place where they could convert their militant resources and critical dispositions into employment opportunities. These positions could allow them to keep the fight going by other means or revive their political faith. Various elements were particularly appealing. One had to do with the relational dimension of the work, the prospect of connecting with people and building social cohesion and community at a time when, in many ways, traditional forms of everyday life in urban neighborhoods were hit hard by deindustrialization and gentrification. Another reason for the appeal was the fact that the highly rationalized practices that the community organizing label encompassed were believed to work, to be more effective than other forms of collective action: contrary to the large-scale demonstrations that were associated with the antiwar movement, they led to victories that improved people's living conditions.

These processes led people from many different backgrounds to take jobs as community organizers, but two pools of candidates in particular left their imprint on how the work and the professional group institutionalized: estranged clerics-to-be and disaffected radical students.

From Priesthood to Organizing

Jim Field offers a good example of the first main channel of entry into the work. He was born in 1948 in a very Catholic family in Lexington, Massachusetts. His father, who "grew up real poor" in Boston, was in the Marines (he became a lieutenant colonel), and the family often moved up and down the East Coast. His mother, who "grew up in the Depression on a farm in Nebraska," started working as a nurse but quit her paid job to become a full-time housewife to raise Jim, his four other siblings, and one of their cousins. At nine, Jim decided to become a priest and entered the seminary at fourteen. "I wanted to help people," he sums up.[34] At nineteen, as he was taking his novitiate in Ohio, he went to Chicago for a three-month internship. Far enough from home to feel the exhilaration of discovering new horizons, he broke with the injunctions to chastity and began dating a young African American woman. But time and again, in various daily social scenes he experienced the racist hostility generated by interracial dating.

When he got back to college, in Indiana, he became involved in the civil rights movement on campus, which cast new light on his dating experience: "I found out that our relationship was still illegal. Not frowned upon, not something people didn't want to happen, but illegal in eleven southern states. So, I went from wanting to help people to wanting to change the world." Despite this, Jim did not find his place within local activist circles. After a year, he entered a phase of demobilization. A negative reevaluation of his urge to "change the world" led him to focus on smaller-scale goals ("At the end of that school year, I just wanted to change *one person*") and was followed by genuine disengagement from activism and putting the sacerdotal way of life on hold.

In 1971, Jim enrolled in a master's program in theology at the Chicago Theological Union. Just as he was about to leave for a ministerial internship in Yellowstone National Park, he bumped into a friend of his who had recently been interviewed by Saul Alinsky. Jim had never heard about the guy, but his friend was so shaken up by the encounter with this "professional slum organizer" that Jim decided to see for himself what Alinsky and the IAF were up to. He interrupted his theological studies and went to work for several months on an IAF project in the suburbs of Cicero, Illinois, to fight against the construction of a highway. "I saw people coming together, Blacks, whites, and

Latinos, around fighting Mayor Daley, who was the most powerful politician, local politician, in the United States. Fighting with him on one of his expressways. He wanted to build a crosstown expressway. And they actually beat him. And I saw them doing that, and I was astounded."[35] Jim reinterpreted his activist experience in light of this discovery and traded his earlier commitments for the pragmatism and effectiveness of Alinsky's practices, whose insistence on the value of the individual and face-to-face interactions dovetailed with Jim's religious background and vocation as a priest. After an IAF internship, he went back to his theological studies and worked in a parish as a deacon for four years, but he left the seminary before being ordained. He did not apply for organizer positions and worked in a bank for three years instead. But the work did not fit him, and when the opportunity arose in 1977 through a friend of his, Jim was hired as an organizer for the Southwest Parish and Neighborhood Federation, a federation of parishes and neighborhood associations that blended the Alinsky tradition and SNCC's practices.

Jim's trajectory is neither an isolated case nor a novel one. Recruitment among the social-justice-oriented fractions of Christian institutions had been a founding pillar of the IAF since it was created. In the late 1960s and 1970s, many others like him who took up community organizer positions and were drawn toward Alinsky's activities had a deeply religious upbringing. They were often destined to become Catholic priests or nuns or Protestant ministers. Because of their own experiences in the civil rights struggles and other movements, however, and against the backdrop of the more structural, long-term crisis of religious vocations, their social destinies bifurcated.[36] They found in the consolidating field of professional community organizing a substitute channel for the realization of their religious dispositions, a "kind of secular sacrament" that was socially less constraining, activated their dispositions toward living a life of poverty, and allowed them to put forward their ambition to help the weak help themselves or even "change the world."[37]

Madeline Talbott

Madeline Talbott's trajectory illustrates the other main channel of entry into paid organizing positions: that of the politicized, college-educated student.[38] Born in 1950, Madeline went to Harvard-Radcliffe in the fall of 1968. The next spring, she participated in demonstrations against the Vietnam War on campus. A few months later, she and other students occupied administrative buildings to protest the war. Her rapid politicization was fueled by her conflicts with her father about Vietnam. A colonel in the Army Corps of Engineers, he had spent a year in Vietnam a few years prior, and he was one of many moderate Kentucky Democrats who supported the war. Her class background and family history could have prepared her for Harvard's elite environment: her mother, one of the few women who had a college degree at the time, had helped intercept and decrypt Japanese communications during World War II. Yet Madeline felt that she did not really belong at Harvard-Radcliffe, being estranged both from campus radical activists and from her old friends.

When she was a sophomore, in the fall of 1969, a friend of hers from college took her to a community action program operating from a church in the majority Puerto Rican neighborhood of Chelsea, Massachusetts, near Boston. Church volunteers had realized after investigating the issue among neighborhood women that they had no access to any form of daycare. They had started knocking on people's doors to talk women into getting together to demand a daycare center. Madeline participated in the campaign, where she met numerous women. In the process, she felt the weight of social and cultural boundaries, but she also shared with them deep, intimate connections, which contrasted with her experience on campus. The Chelsea experience was a turning point in her life. At the end of her sophomore year, she took a gap year, moved into Chelsea for five months, and worked full time on the daycare center campaign. When she finished her junior year, she took another year off, which turned into two, during which she went to Ethiopia to work as a volunteer for the Harvard Africa Volunteer Project.

When she came back, as she was about to graduate, she went to the university's group placement office and found a binder with nonprofit ads. She had already heard about ACORN a few months before during a seminar on community organizing where members of different community groups had presented their activities—the man speaking for ACORN, Steve Kest, was a Harvard alum who presented ACORN's successful campaign against a coal-burning power plant in Arkansas and dwelled on ACORN's five thousand low-income dues-paying members. "So, I found a flyer and it said something like, 'Work for social justice. Make forty-five dollars a week.' And I looked at that. And even in 1975, forty-five dollars a week was way below the minimum wage. I said, 'Oh! They'll take me!'"[39] In 1975, the minimum wage was $2.10 an hour (or $11 in 2021), so people working a forty-hour week earned around $80— twice as much as what ACORN offered. At the time, the organization was still operating in Arkansas only, so Madeline moved to Little Rock. Over the years, she was one of the organization's key staffers who drove its expansion to other states and created new ACORN chapters.

Beyond their irreducible singularities, Jim's and Madeline's trajectories offer precious information on the type of social characteristics, skills, dispositions, and movement experiences that could resonate with community organizer positions. Contrary to what Gale Cincotta argued in her interview with Studs Terkel, people needed more than just "the will to change something" to take up jobs as organizers. The positions recruited among certain pools of candidates. Of central importance was the ability to know how to cross social and racial boundaries, connect with people and listen to them, and find satisfaction, pleasure, and meaning in doing so. In terms of the politics associated with the role, what Andrew Kopkind wrote about "out-of-state" ACORN organizers in 1975 holds more broadly:

> [They] seem to have come with no heavy ideological baggage. They
> are not radical intellectuals who seek their work "among the people"
> as direct steps to a predictable revolution. They clearly express a rad-
> ical sensibility; most are recognizable children of the movements of

the sixties, but not adherents to particular sects. Perhaps they are the kind of people who would have been Peace Corps volunteers in 1963. But the social history of the last decade has given them a different political context for their interest in community development.[40]

Community organizer positions matched with people whose upbringings had taught them dedication to a cause through self-effacement but for whom politics was more about concrete deeds than theoretical debates. When they had had extensive experience in sixties movements, they were more likely to be rank-and-file participants than national leaders. As Kopkind points out, they were also more likely not to have received the dense ideological training that was commonplace in left-wing cadre organizations because the work itself required a degree of political pragmatism that was incompatible with ideological debates and infighting. But they had also acquired enough cultural resources to feel authorized and entitled to cross boundaries of race, class, and geography. Although they recognized the weight and prevalence of racism as a structure of power and oppression, and called for their organizations to hire more organizers of color as a political necessity, they still believed that interracial organizing was possible. And they believed that the relational, the interpersonal aspect of political work was a crucial one.

For all these reasons, not all former sixties radicals turned to community organizer positions. Many of the people who were active in the various Maoist, Trotskyist, and other socialist groups that formed the backbone of the New Communist movement,[41] many of the spade-workers of color who were active in the Black power, Puerto Rican, Chicano, and Native American movements, had incorporated a political education that did not fit into community organizer positions.

A More Diverse Group?

The most obvious element in the establishment of the profession is that, from the 1980s on, it became possible to live *off* community organizing, and not just *for* it, even if "organizers generally work long hours for little pay and almost no recognition."[42] This resulted in an increase in the number of full-time, paid community organizers throughout the nation. But the process also signaled, more surprisingly perhaps, a diversification of the group's demographics and social composition.

Various studies by funders and social scientists sympathetic to the profession yield interesting analyses in that regard. A survey conducted in Chicago in the early 1990s found that working long hours for almost no recognition was indeed the norm, yet community organizers earned wages that were "roughly comparable with similar positions in similarly sized non-profits nationwide" and in Chicago. Even more counterintuitive, they were actually slightly better off than social workers.[43] In 1991, when the median income was around $32,000 in Illinois and around $30,000 nationally ($66,000 and $62,000 in 2021), median income for National Association of Social Workers members was $27,500 ($57,000 in 2021). For Chicago organizers, it was around $33,000 ($68,000 in 2021). While most respondents benefited from some health care, only a quarter of them had an employer-sponsored pension plan, whereas national coverage was around 35 percent at the time.[44] Well over half of the respondents had been working as organizers for ten years or more, which contrasted with the previous generations where, apart from Alinsky and a few others, most organizers never stayed long in their job. This was not specific to Chicago. By the mid-1990s, a local IAF organizer made between $25,000 and $30,000; a lead organizer, between $40,000 and $50,000; and a national staffer, over $70,000.[45] The fact it was now possible to "make a career" out of community organizing was a sign that the profession had established a real grounding in the professional order.

The fact that organizer positions had been stabilized as positions people could enter "for the long haul," as the popular saying went, translated into a broadening of organizers' social backgrounds. As was already the case at the IAF, organizers still had received far more formal schooling than the rest of the population, and even more so

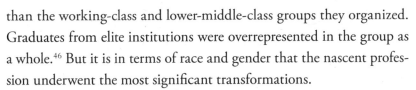

than the working-class and lower-middle-class groups they organized. Graduates from elite institutions were overrepresented in the group as a whole.[46] But it is in terms of race and gender that the nascent profession underwent the most significant transformations.

Until the 1980s, community organizers were mostly white college-educated men, and the dominant culture in these circles was definitely sexist and heteronormative. In his study of ACORN, Gary Delgado indicates that no national federation employed more than 10 percent organizers of color.[47] The picture began to change drastically in the 1980s and 1990s. In the Southwest, sociologist Mark Warren notes that thanks to new funds from large philanthropic foundations and the development of new staff positions, the number of IAF organizers went from twenty-five in 1990 to sixty in 1999. Out of the sixty, there were twenty-seven women, thirty organizers of color, and twenty individuals who started out as community "leaders."[48] Another study on the evolution of ACORN's staff's racial composition shows that the share of organizers of color went from 10 percent in the 1970s and 1980s to 64 percent in 2003.[49] A national survey from 1999 on one hundred faith-based community organizing groups on behalf of Interfaith Funders also found that "the organizing staff operating in the faith-based community organizing field is fairly diverse racially. Half are white, nearly 29% Black and 16% Hispanic. Asians make up 2.7% of the staff with Native Americans at less than 1%."[50] Out of the 325 respondents, about 56 percent were men and 44 percent were women. However, women and people of color were much less likely than men and white people to hold supervisory roles.

These profound transformations coincided with changes in the standards and norms governing the organizer's role. Alinsky and the IAF had built into the organizer's position the rule that organizers should be outsiders in the neighborhoods in which they organized. Exteriority was a necessary condition to effectiveness because it guaranteed rational cool-headedness and distance from interpersonal disputes. But in the Long Sixties, the Black liberation movements challenged this assumption and legitimized the notion that people who intended to act with a racially defined group, whether it be through protest or direct service provision, must share the group's racial identification.[51] As a result of former sixties radicals entering the profession in the 1970s and of new generations following their lead, the IAF norm was challenged by calls for racial representation.

Because many of them had learned from their movement experience that asymmetrical relations of race kept operating within movement spaces and should not be overlooked as secondary issues, newcomers—and in particular African Americans, Hispanics, and women—challenged the prevailing assumptions and pushed for local organizations, national federations, and the occupational group as a whole to reckon with its demographic makeup and act on it. Contrary to what Alinsky's disciples believed to be tried-and-tested truth, the fact that an organizer occupied an insider's position vis-à-vis its intended target constituency was not an obstacle, but a resource. As Madeline Talbott put it, "People of color, organizing in their own communities, have the ability to build a movement. White people organizing in communities of color have the ability to build a damn fine organization, but you're never going to get to movement, because you're a white person."[52]

These evolutions were pushed by several external forces. First, increasing "diversity" in job recruitment began to be inscribed in law, prompting a broader social and cultural consciousness of the issue. The federal affirmative action programs, which translated into policy some of the demands made by the Black liberation movements in the 1960s and 1970s, were redefined by corporate officials and management specialists and redefined in terms of economic performance in the 1970s and 1980s, giving birth to "diversity management."[53] Second, at the organizational level, there were evolutions in recruitment policies, with the creation of new, intermediate supervisory positions with clearer job profiles; intentional attempts to hire community "leaders" into organizer positions; and establishing racial statistics as a first step toward changing hiring practices.[54]

Finally, the demand for organizers sharing similar racial identities with the people they organized came from the people themselves. One of the legacies of the Black power movement was an increased sense of pride on the part of African Americans and other racial minorities who now felt empowered to speak up against white people when the latter did not take their concerns seriously and trampled their basic dignity. For instance, the community organizer position Barack Obama applied for in Chicago in 1985 had been created as an implicit "minority job" after African American women leaders blamed white organizer Mike Kruglik for systematically refusing to take their opinions and ideas into account.[55]

ORGANIZING AS A CRAFT: ABSTRACT KNOWLEDGE AND PRACTICAL SKILLS

Beyond the different recruitment channels that led to the organizer positions that multiplied in the 1970s and 1980s, a third element bound the professional group in the making together: the commonly held belief that organizing was "a highly skilled craft" that was superior to other forms of social action and commitment and that this craft needed to be developed and taught.[56]

The body of knowledge and know-how that was believed to legitimize the superiority of organizing came from two different sources: the IAF's expertise in fostering militant voluntary association and the experiential know-how about politicizing spadework that was passed on from the sixties. Both sources converged as professional community organizing came into existence, blending knowledge about people's behaviors and motivations, group dynamics, and organizational mechanisms that borrowed from sociology, political science, psychosociology, and management theory. The skills necessary to perform the craft were a practical sense of organization, attention to detail, and an ability to plan, sort out, and anticipate; an aptitude to develop a critical mindset to "draw lessons" from past collective action experiences or from one's own practice;

relational skills to "start where people are," recruit them into the organization, and convince them to commit further and identify with the organization; and most important, an ability to step back and let the members and leaders make their own decisions. What gave coherence, purpose, and legitimacy to these elements was the appeal to legitimating cultural values like effectiveness, egalitarianism, and altruism.[57]

Possessing this body of applied knowledge was one of the factors that explained the authority that individual organizers claimed and projected when they entered a given community. In a way, such a social production of militant authority was nothing new; the moral authority that Leninist professional revolutionaries drew from their knowledge of Marxist science was not fundamentally different. The innovation that community organizers introduced over the course of the 1970s and 1980s was the creation of institutions that specialized in the production and circulation of what had grown into "a systematic body of knowledge and experience."[58]

Several training manuals were published at the time that offered synthetic accounts of how various forms of "social change practice" had emerged over the course of the twentieth century and delineated the particular skills associated with the organizer's work.[59] Although they substantiated Alinsky's own claims that there existed "rules" for radicals and a "science of revolution," these books differed from Alinsky's writings in their tone and style and in their intended practical uses.[60] Called "handbook," "guide," or "manual," they were often written by professional social workers or social-work academics, sometimes in collaboration with grassroots organizers. They were not political essays but specialized works conceptualizing and formalizing a set of information, prescriptions, situations, step-by-step guides, warnings, and methods. They analyzed a wealth of individual case studies, and they offered practical exercises on identifying local leaders, increasing commitment and turnout, and building neighborhood organizations. They also differed from the mimeographed pamphlets published by movement participants and organizations in the 1960s not only because of who distributed them and how (small, independent presses rather than institutional publishing houses) but also because they were meant to contribute to academic knowledge and professional know-how rather than building self-organization of the oppressed outside of institutional channels.[61]

The manuals point to an important but overlooked phenomenon: the incorporation of community organizing into academic curricula. Universities are a major resource for the validation of professional dynamics because "academic knowledge legitimizes professional work by clarifying its foundations and tracing them to major cultural values" such as rationality, logic, and science.[62] In the 1980s, social-work programs at the School of Social Administration at the University of Chicago, Hunter College in New York, and the University of Michigan all included courses on the history and theories of community organizing in their curricula. Ecklein's *Community Organizers*, mentioned in the beginning of the chapter, "grew out of a curriculum development project within the field of social work."[63] There were also former professional organizers like Harry Boyte, who worked for Martin Luther King's SCLC in the 1960s, and Marshall Ganz, the lead organizer for the United Farm Workers from 1970 to 1980, who entered academia in the 1980s and 1990s and focused on the mechanics of grassroots organization and leadership.

This incorporation should not be overemphasized. It happened in the margins of academia. Community organizing courses were mobilized as new resources to revitalize older community organization curricula, which historically occupied a dominated position within social-work education as opposed to clinical work, planning, or administration and which were further marginalized in the context of a political backlash against federal programs spurring people's participation in the 1970s and 1980s.[64] Because of an inbuilt distrust toward academic knowledge and analysis, which goes back to Alinsky's own ambiguous relationship with the social sciences, and even if a large part of them had received undergraduate or graduate education, professional organizers did not see universities as a particularly strategic institution to support their professional claims.

The key that gave meaning and coherence to the systematization of organizing knowledge and know-how was the organizer's role. Despite the fragmentation of targeted constituencies and the stark opposition between institution-based and individual-based organizing, the core work tasks and functions claimed by the profession as a whole remained largely unchanged. This is where the IAF-trained community organization consultant and the movement spadeworker came together.

In a 1973 text titled "What Is an Organizer?" by Richard Rothstein, which he wrote at the request of Heather Booth, the founder and director of the Midwest Academy, Rothstein defined the role and the type of work it sought to control. All organizations, he argued, functioned under the assumption that they had "members who decide broad policy; leaders who guide the group in a fashion responsible to members' instructions; and staff who carry out the mechanical work of the organization." Yet, there was a fourth function, organizing, which meant being "most concerned with pushing the organization's growth, [having] the greatest vision about how to get from here to there and patiently [trying] to organize that vision." In certain organizations, the organizing function could be performed by leaders, staffers, or members, and there might not be "formally designated 'organizers,'" but from an analytical perspective it remained a distinct, autonomous function.[65]

The problem, according to Rothstein, was the illusion of bottom-up internal democracy, which held that members participated spontaneously and out of their own free will. As a result, organizing was unacknowledged, conflated with administrative tasks, or intentionally hidden so as not to undermine the democratic illusion. Such dissimulation was a danger for organizations because it transformed "the open functions of teaching, counseling, confidence-building, modeling, guiding," which were "all the functions of organizing," into "the hidden functions of manipulation." Worse still, it distorted the way "real organizations" worked and led people to blame leaders for failing to achieve internal democracy. Instead, people should start by acknowledging that "real organization members come with everyday lives to lead, with limited time, with normal prejudices and personal needs." The division of labor was an inescapable fact of collective organization. For organizations to grow, function more effectively, and achieve real social change, it was therefore necessary to consider organizing as a "publicly defined and approved" function, the performance of which could be improved through accountability and constructive criticism.[66] Collective reflexivity and honesty were the best and only ways to dispel the specter of manipulation.

A Harvard graduate from New York, Rothstein had been one of the pillars of SDS's ERAP in Chicago. As the projects stumbled on, he "emerged as a strong critic of informal and decentralized organization in both SDS and ERAP," targeting in particular what he saw as organizers' self-delusion in believing that they did indeed "let the people decide."[67] His own experience largely shaped the way he defined the role. Rothstein's text echoed other analyses written by sixties radicals on the threats posed by the myth of bottom-up participation, horizontality, and spontaneous protest—what feminist Jo Freeman called "the tyranny of structurelessness."[68] But the distinction between what he called "the conventional description" of organizations and "real organizations" also resonated with Alinsky's pragmatic defense of "the world as it is" against "the world as it should be." Rothstein's analysis reiterated the central tenet of the role: leadership development was "the most important part of an organizer's job."[69] The dialectic relation between organizer and leader was the profession's foundation: there was no organizer without a leader to identify and "develop," and conversely there was no leader without an organizer "developing" them.

In legitimizing organizing as a distinct and necessary organizational function, Rothstein responded to the often-made accusations that organizers manipulated leaders, that they were the ones wielding real power in the organization, not the volunteer community leaders and boards, that organizers were the ones who took the necessary day-to-day decisions about the selection of issues, campaigns, policy agendas, and strategy. Yet in naturalizing the division of labor and looking at organizations as the sum of complementary functions, Rothstein downplayed the real social antagonisms at play in community-based organizations. Being honest about the reality of the organizing function did not dispel the fact that the organizing social relation was predicated on a double form of power imbalance: first, staffers usually came from different social backgrounds than the people they organized; second, the work itself was about power and control—it imbued those who performed it with the sense of cognitive superiority that was built into it. Even if the individuals who worked as organizers sincerely believed that they did not tell people what to do and were committed to building a more just and equal society, the organizer's role was still predicated on a fundamental power imbalance: the organizers knew things that the leaders did not, and that knowledge allowed to have the leaders do things that they wouldn't have done otherwise. For the organizing relation to happen, it was necessary that the organizer felt authorized to ask potentially uncomfortable questions to the people they met and that the potential leaders acknowledged their informal license to do so.

Yet, leaders did not systematically consent to the organizing social relation. Clashes between organizers and leaders are not often mentioned in the literature, but they were very real. Delgado recalled that in 1979, for instance, the volunteer chairman of ACORN's Nevada chapter resigned because he was denied access to copies of the ACORN organizing model and financial information. In Chicago, the Campaign Against Pollution (CAP), a citywide project launched by Alinsky in 1970 to bring together working-class and middle-class residents into a popular majority against a common enemy, Chicago's Commonwealth Edison company, dissolved after a few years because of bitter fights between staff and leadership over the organization's direction and finances.[70]

Because those who endorsed professionalization as a collective strategy to strengthen community organizing practices thought that their craft was indeed "highly skilled," it followed that it "[deserved] respect, recognition, and the benefits afforded other occupations."[71] The profession's fourth pillar, therefore, was a collective effort to bolster its internal structure and secure social recognition.

THE PROFESSION'S SOCIAL ORGANIZATION

Sociologists have identified three main aspects to how professional groups develop their internal structure to gain recognition: (1) worksites; (2) mechanisms like training schools, licenses, and ethics codes, which establish control over the selection of candidates and restricts their range of action; and (3) professional associations. Looking at them for professional community organizing indicates how and why professionalization from within was endorsed as a collective project.[72]

In terms of worksites, faith-based community organizing groups operated with small paid staffs; the vast majority only had one or two organizers, and only 10 percent of the groups hired between five and eight organizers.[73] In individual-based organizing networks such as ACORN, local chapters employed more organizers, and efforts were made to establish connections across chapters. But overall, because of the nature of the work itself, organizers were seldom in contact with their colleagues on a daily basis.

As the profession developed, however, several collective spaces emerged where people could establish interpersonal connections and informal networks beyond organizational boundaries. One of these spaces was a magazine called *Just Economics: The Magazine for Organizers*, the main outlet that transcended organizational boundaries (tellingly, it changed its name to the *Organizer* sometime in the late 1970s). Another nascent collective space were the "retreats" organized by the Midwest Academy every summer between 1975 and 1987. "We would always invite people from other networks," Jackie Kendall, who directed the academy from 1982 to 2010, remembers. "We would regularly get people from the other networks. Not huge numbers, but we would get them to come and be on panels together and have discussions about this stuff." In their heyday, the retreats brought together up to 1,500 people.[74]

The Institutionalization of Training

Formalizing training was a more robust tool to strengthen the profession and its claims for recognition. The IAF had already started to focus on training as a strategic site for further expansion and consolidation of its professional project in the late 1960s; movement spadeworkers also tried to formalize training programs. But it was really in the 1970s and 1980s that training institutionalized as a specialized activity.

Training programs changed the way the work was learned. By creating semiautonomous institutional subspaces and formalizing training curriculum, they made a dent into on-the-job learning. They stimulated a distanced, reflexive relation to the organizer's role. Such critical thinking was already at the core of how IAF organizers learned to do their jobs, but training was now abstracted from informal, interpersonal relations. Developing training programs and centers became one of the main sites of competition between national federations, but the relations between the two entities varied. Certain training centers were part of national federations, as was the case with the IAF and the Gamaliel Foundation. Their priority was to train the staff—and sometimes the leaders—from their local affiliates. Others, like NTIC/NPA and CTWO, had first started out as autonomous training centers, putting forward their consulting skills, and they morphed into supralocal federations and networks after a few years' activity. Others still remained independent organizations providing training services at a local or supralocal level. This is the case of the Midwest Academy.

Founded in Chicago in 1973 by former sixties radicals, the Midwest Academy was meant to pass on the lessons learned from the decade's movements to gain in effectiveness at building grassroots support and improving people's living conditions. According to Steve Max, a former SDS staffer who played a major role in overseeing ERAP in Kentucky but left the organization in 1964 to work for the League for Industrial Democracy, the Midwest Academy represented "a coming together of the politics of the New Left with the science of organizing from Alinsky."[75] The academy was created right where the two main social forces that structured professional community organizing converged.

Looking at the background and trajectory of the academy's founder sheds critical light on its origins. Heather Tobis was born in 1945. Her father was a doctor and her mother a housewife who later became a special education teacher after resuming her studies. She acquired the disposition toward involvement and a commitment to social justice at an early age, first through her Jewish upbringing. When she was in high school in Long Island in 1960, she participated in CORE and joined the sit-ins against Woolworth's in New York City. She then studied sociology at the University of Chicago, and in 1964 she went to Mississippi to join the Freedom Summer. Like many other women who shared a similar experience and who would later shape the women's liberation movement, Tobis realized how essential feminist struggles were through her experiences of daily sexism in movement circles. In 1965, at the first sit-in against the war in Vietnam, she met Paul Booth, then SDS's national secretary. They got married a year later and had two children. Although she took up her husband's last name, she refused to comply with the gendered division of domestic labor. She kept up her activism and became "one of the central figures in the burgeoning women's liberation movement in Chicago," participating in founding the Jane Collective (an underground feminist abortion network), the Chicago Women's Liberation Union, and the Action Committee for Decent Childcare (a militant organization demanding decent and accessible childcare for all).[76]

In 1972, two years after receiving her master's in educational psychology from the University of Chicago, she helped fellow clerical staff at a publishing house stand up against their boss's abusive behavior. She was fired, but she filed a grievance with the National Labor Relations Board and won. She invested the money from the settlement into what became the Midwest Academy. She ran it until 1978, when she founded a new national organization, the Citizen/Labor Energy Coalition, which brought together labor unions and citizen groups to address the energy crisis. She then directed the Citizen Action national network; managed various political campaigns for Democrats at the local, state, and national levels; and became the Democratic Party's training director of the Democratic National Committee in the 1990s. Later she worked as a consultant on a range of issues at the national level, such as women's rights, voter turnout, and health care.

Booth and her husband, who did not agree with the turn taken by the New Left toward armed struggle or Marxist-Leninist party building, both applied their experience to the growing "neighborhood movement" by getting involved in Alinsky's CAP. Paul Booth was CAP's first cochair. Heather Booth participated in IAF trainings. Because of the organization's inbuilt sexist and chest-thumping approach, many IAF organizers believed that women could not be real organizers and felt, like many others in the political and civic arenas, that feminist issues were secondary and potentially "divisive." The institutional innovation formalizing strategy into something everyone could learn grew out of Booth's "relative marginalization" within the existing state of contentious politics writ large: Booth occupied a dominated position as a woman, but she also had a significant amount of cultural capital and years of deep movement experience that gave her enough resources and legitimacy to challenge existing organizational arrangements and create a new one.[77]

> So one of the reasons I think I developed [the Midwest Academy] was that I didn't find that [IAF organizers] explained strategy. I found them brilliant in explaining broad conceptions of power and brilliant on tactics. But being an unconfident woman, I felt, "Well, they know how to do it, someone else knows how to do it." But I didn't know how to *do* it, how to figure out what to do when you don't know what to do.[78]

Booth's solution was to break down "strategy" into a number of objective, debatable elements: a "strategy chart." It had five columns: goals, from short- to long-term; organizational considerations; constituencies and allies; institutional targets; and tactics. It was meant to be used as a collective tool to parse the various components of a given campaign and elaborate a rational, effective strategy—to figure out what to do when you don't know what to do. The strategy chart helped turn strategic planning from an informal, intuitive individual practice that required unspoken skills and qualities and looked like an innate quality into a collective process whose every component could be discussed, learned, and appropriated by anybody, regardless of their prior experience. Expressing a lack of confidence like Booth's and plenty other women activists, Jackie Kendall put it most succinctly when she remembered,

> The [Alinsky folks] had an organizing gene, a strategy gene that I didn't have. I'll go do the craziest tactics, just wind me up! But I just thought I couldn't do the strategy. And then I have to go over to the Midwest Academy, a two-week session. . . . And every day, it was mind-blowing, but especially the session on strategy was like, "Oh, this is not rocket science. You can figure this out, you can teach it to people."[79]

The whole paradox is that the desacralization of the "strategy gene" and the discovery that it is not "rocket science," which transgressed the expert/amateur dichotomy, was powered by professional claims and the promotion of a group of experts in building people power through citizen participation and issue campaigns.

Initially designed as a training institute for women, the Midwest Academy quickly became one of the main training institutions for organizers in the country and a *passage obligé* for men and women, would-be organizers and seasoned ones. As the academy grew, it diversified its services and formalized the curricula. The original training material was compiled into a manual that went through five different editions between 1984 and 2010. According to Kendall, "For a while people called it their Bible, their organizing Bible."[80] In keeping with the academy's central position within the nacsent profession, its training sessions were open to any organization. They were organized throughout the country—participants could be sent from local community organizing organizations, student unions, consumer organizations, and large national or international nonprofits and nongovernmental organizations like Amnesty International and the American Cancer Society. Between 1974 and 2014, five thousand people were trained there. The academy also positioned itself as a hotbed of organizational innovation, building coalitions between labor and citizen groups, developing intermediate organizational tiers at the state level, and making forays into electoral politics.

The development of training institutes also opened new professional opportunities, taking experienced organizers off the hook of on-the-ground organizing and putting them in a position where they could pass on the experience they had acquired in the movement. Trainers occupied a strategic role in identifying and selecting the new talents through whom the profession could produce and reproduce itself. A good example of this is Mike Miller. Growing up in a left-wing household (his father was a labor educator), after several years of student unionism at Berkeley in the late 1950s Miller served as an SNCC field secretary from 1962 to 1966, first in the Mississippi Delta and then in Northern California. In December 1966, after SNCC expelled white organizers and volunteers, Miller met Alinsky and was hired on an IAF project in Kansas City, where he worked until 1968 before moving to San Francisco. In 1972, he founded the ORGANIZE! Training Center.[81]

Binding the Group Together: The National Organizers Alliance

For the profession to gain social recognition and come into social existence, there also needed to be people and institutions who spoke on behalf of the group of community organizers, who defined what their activity was and what it was not, therefore binding the group together around shared beliefs, norms, and self-representations. A core task for in this perspective was to enhance organizational and financial stability and make sure that it was possible to live off of organizer positions.

Dedication to the cause and self-effacement were appealing symbolic rewards, which drew many to the work in the first place, but the sacrificial model of commitment was rejected as antithetical and detrimental to organizing for the long term.

Certain structures were created to improve the group's material conditions. The Chicago Community Organizing Cooperative (CCOC) was one such example. Founded in 1984, it was initially housed by the charity branch of the Catholic Church and brought together a dozen Chicago organizations. It implemented a cooperative health insurance system that, after a few years, covered 160 workers from 46 different organizations.[82] Some of the people who were involved with the CCOC went on to play leading roles in a professional association for organizers called the National Organizers Alliance (NOA).

Created in November 1992 in Oakland, in the premises of Gary Delgado's CTWO, NOA claimed to represent the interests of all organizers at the national level—community organizers but also union or "issues" organizers as well as freelance consultants who identified as organizers. Significantly, many of its founding figures were highly critical of the localist, "winnable issues" focus of many community organizations as well as the reproduction of racist and sexist behaviors in work environment and practices. Instead, they felt that supralocal structures had to be built to support movement-oriented work and nurture the workers themselves.

The invite letter to the first national gathering in August 1994 indicates that NOA tried to create "a vocation with infrastructure that enables us to make both a life—and a living—within its borders, a network of resources and colleagues that teach, carry on tradition, and celebrate organizing as a calling and a profession."[83] The editorial to the first issue of NOA's bulletin, ironically called the *Ark*, drove the point home: "Building a growing, skilled cadre of practitioners—who can make both a life, and a living, as long-term organizers" was the best way to "transform the fractured way the progressive wing is structured and funded to forge us into a more cohesive and powerful movement." Simultaneously,

NOA's goal was to "create a culture of organizing that is supportive, ecumenical, creative, generous and humorous, as well as effective."[84]

Published several times a year, the *Ark* compiled information about the association's life, opinions on topics of interests for professionals (ongoing struggles, political and strategic debates, individual features, historical vignettes), job offers, and grant applications. NOA organized national "gatherings," blending seminars, conferences, and roundtables, with more informal moments like parties and other social events. In the early 2000s, it published a best-practice guide that listed the existing range of union contracts and personnel policies and included "best and worst" situations in areas like staff training, management and evaluations, and hours of work, as well as racism, sexism, and other oppressions on the job.[85]

Like many other professional associations, and in direct reference to prestigious professions such as medicine and law, NOA tried to establish rules and codes of ethics that would regulate people's practices and show further proof of professionalism. In the preliminary discussions that led to NOA's creation, Mike Miller, who was close to various members of the steering committee, suggested the association should write "some short 'Hippocratic . . . Oath' that broadly merges what we do with why we do it, something people can sign on to."[86] But the association never tried to secure legal protections or control entry into the group through an alliance with universities, as other professional associations had done. Its immediate task was to increase the profession's visibility and recognition and show to its intended audiences that it played a necessary but underestimated role in social change.

In a letter announcing the creation of the association, thirty founding members tried to convince their "dear colleagues" that creating NOA was necessary for authentic people's representation and strong, durable social movements to exist. The underlying argumentative logic was metonymic: defending and supporting the part (organizers) meant defending and supporting the whole (progressive movements). As a result, those who sided with progressive movements must in all logic side with organizers. And because the work was challenging, devalued, and made invisible, it was necessary to "change the conditions that thin our ranks, deter newcomers and discourage the recognition and celebration of our part in a larger movement."[87] NOA sought to do exactly that.

If organizers were essential, albeit invisible, it followed that they must not operate on the sacrificial model of commitment, which pervaded social movements. "People who see themselves as the empowerers of others will also take care of themselves, while those who see themselves as sacrificing for others often forget,"[88] NOA founder and director Kim Fellner argued. Self-sacrifice represented a threat to people's individual well-being and ability to balance their work and their personal lives, but it also ran counter to self-reproduction and institutionalization for the long haul. Nurturing the profession's material bases and support systems, NOA spokespeople argued, offered the only effective solution to the twin pitfalls of experienced organizers' burnout and newcomers' high turnover. Consequently, one of the organization's main initiatives was to establish a national pension plan for all organizers, in a context where the vast majority had no retirement safety net whatsoever, to "help experienced organizers remain in the field, and to encourage younger practitioners to view social change as a long-term career."[89] The plan, the first of its kind according to NOA, was officially launched in 1996. It was regularly advertised in the *Ark*'s columns and in newsletters.

NOA's membership went from five hundred in 1992 to one thousand at the end of the 1990s. Five thousand people received NOA's publications.[90] The pension plan was indeed implemented for several years. But overall, the association never quite managed to bind organizers together and gain enduring social recognition. First, even if NOA claimed that all organizers across the nation shared "a vocation: to help build democratic structures, leadership and power to gain social and economic justice," the targeted constituency was too wide, its boundaries too fickle, and the interests of its members too disparate because of the sheer heterogeneity of their organizational and working and unemployment conditions.[91] Part of the difficulty also had to do with the work itself and how people conceived it. Beyond bitter competition for turf, members, and resources between organizers themselves, professional organization potentially clashed with organizers' ethos of self-effacement and dedication to the cause. When Rathke offhandedly told Fellner that NOA was a good idea, but that "I'm a bit too busy these days trying to organize the members, and don't really have the time or energy to try and organize the organizers," he touched on something that resonated with many.[92]

Second, the type of institutions NOA reached out to for validation undermined its project from the start. Universities and public authorities are key sites for professional control to be secured. But the question of securing legal status and protection was never on the table. And the few efforts made by social-work academics to sponsor the nascent organization did not come to fruition.[93] Instead, NOA turned to the philanthropic field. A couple of philanthropic foundations—Wieboldt and Woods in Chicago, the New World Foundation in New York—were instrumental in the project's genesis and initial funding. Throughout the 1990s, lengthy conversations among NOA's leadership focused on improving relations with foundations, both quantitatively (pushing for larger grants to make organizer positions more attractive to potential candidates) and qualitatively (recognizing the profession's expertise and effectiveness). A 1991 letter from Fellner to the president of a philanthropic foundation sums up this strategy: "Organizers are perhaps the most critical—and most underrated—resource for social change. But, like the innovators and inventors much touted by modern scions of capital, these ecclectic [sic] movers and shakers need some nurturing to survive."[94] Over the years, funders lost interest in nurturing the "movers and shakers" through a professional association. In 2010, NOA eventually collapsed, without leaving many institutional tracks behind it.

CONCLUSION

In June 1994, a dozen community organizers from the South Side of Chicago and staff members from the Woods Fund met to discuss "the results of organizing" and talk about the aspects of the work that

Woods should pay more attention to in the future. Woods had funded community organizing groups for ten years by then, and its board of directors was intent on evaluating its own effectiveness. Although they disagreed on what "good organizing" was as well as future prospects, all participants considered that further professionalization was the way forward. "The continuing professionalization of organizing" was "a boon to recruiting new talents," with a particular insistence on recruiting racial minorities.[95]

That meeting encapsulates the four pillars upon which the profession was constructed: the community-oriented organizations people worked for; the people who staffed them; the body of applied knowledge that legitimized their claims to being effective in improving people's lives and rejuvenating democracy; and the group's internal organization. Not all organizers agreed on how race and gender should be taken into account in their work; nor did they all agree on the building blocks they should start from (preexisting organizations or individuals), but they all saw themselves as professional "democratizers" whose role was "to give low- and moderate-income Americans a genuine opportunity to influence the political system without being controlled by organizers."[96] And they believed that the existence of a stable profession was the most effective solution to do so. Professionalism was not a shameful stigma; it was a resource, a source of pride and distinction.

As it coalesced into a self-reproducing entity, the profession was undermined by contradictory forces. First, its structure pulled in two opposite directions: toward self-effacement behind leaders; toward recognition in the professional order. The contradictory dialectic was grounded in the work itself. Organizers' ability to step back was what made their work possible in the first place, but it also created a relation of power that undermined the broader democratic philosophy undergirding community organizing. Adjustments were made to mitigate the power imbalance, such as the call to recruit more organizers of color, but the relation itself could not be challenged—it was the profession's raison d'être.

Furthermore, the proponents of professionalized community organizing feared a looming risk of definitional dilution. Organizing strategies "[branched out] into a remarkably diverse set of groups and activities, ranging from block-level service delivery to national issue coalitions to multimillion-dollar housing development corporations," which could render the category meaningless.[97] In the introduction to the 1984 edition of its training manual, the Midwest Academy suggested that the term "community organizing" should be replaced with something more encompassing, like "direct action" or "citizen organizing," to reflect the fact that territorial implantation was no longer a defining criteria.[98]

The professionalization-from-within collective strategy and the defense of organizers' professionalism and effectiveness could not in themselves lead to exclusive control over the work of producing rationalized community participation and representation. Such professional claims needed to be validated and legitimated by other institutions. And as the next chapter shows, organizers' professional projects yielded mixed results.

CHAPTER 7

"YOU RUN FOR PRESIDENT?"

Fitting into the Division of Political Labor

"**W**hen classmates in college asked me just what it was a community organizer did, I couldn't answer them directly. Instead, I'd pronounce on the need for change. . . . Change won't come from the top, I would say. Change will come from a mobilized grass roots. That's what I'll do, I'll organize black folks. At the grass roots. For change."[1] These words, which Obama wrote tongue in cheek in his first autobiography in the mid-1990s, speak to the fact that the professionalization dynamics that I just described went largely unnoticed in the eyes of the general public. Barack Obama's classmates were far from the only ones who did not know in the early 1980s that "community organizer" was indeed the name of a job. Nor was Obama the only one who could not go past vague pronouncements about the need for "change" coming from "the grassroots" to explain what he thought a community organizer did.

The confusion was not just Obama's, however. In a large part, what made community organizing so appealing to those who turned to it in the 1970s and 1980s as opposed to other available forms of collective action had to do with its inbuilt definitional vagueness and the vast territory it claimed to control through professional work. Producing a mobilized grassroots for change was indeed an ambitious agenda to which different people could give different meanings. As I argued in the introduction, to understand how a profession's claims over a given set of work tasks can hold and be granted long-lasting institutional recognition, it is important to look not only at the work itself and the profession's attempts to bolster its internal organization, as I elaborated in the previous chapter, but also to take into account the struggles with other groups and entities who also seek control of the same tasks, or bits of them. Interprofessional competition and, sometimes, cooperation are central elements in any professionalization story.

The stage over which these struggles happened is the complex division of political labor connecting the ruling classes and the ruled. Even if the electoral arena is an important site in this system, it also includes sectors and social fields like organized labor, social movements, nonprofit organizations, corporate lobbying groups, and government agencies, which all contribute to producing competing collective interests. Complex relationships of competition and collaboration bind together a wide array of political intermediaries, campaign directors, political consultants, pollsters, pundits, outreach workers, policy analysts, labor educators, and more, who haphazardly work toward producing and managing collective interests and representation.

At the time when the professional group of community organizers was coalescing into a self-conscious form, the division of political labor was undergoing structural transformations. The 1970s and 1980s were not just marked by the advent of neoliberalism as the new dominant bipartisan consensus or by the conservative counterrevolution and its attacks on the working class, organized labor, and minorities in general. Those decades also witnessed a multiplication of intermediary positions between citizens and political professionals writ large. Although the division between professionals and laypeople is a fundamental opposition structuring the political field, an antidemocratic feature built into the fabric of representative democracy, the extension of what political scientists call "party networks" to think tanks, policy institutes, media companies, consulting agencies, and private foundations meant a proliferation of intermediate layers that further estranged citizens from elected officials. The process went far beyond electoral politics: it also affected the realm of citizen participation in general.[2]

As sociologist Edward T. Walker has highlighted, for instance, since the 1970s and 1980s the production of "grassroots," citizen political action, "has been adapted as a commercial practice deployed by consultants of behalf of corporations, trade associations, the wealthiest and most professionalized advocacy organizations, and electoral campaigns in their Get-Out-The-Vote efforts."[3] As a result, the logics of professional work extended to new territories, blurring the lines between the private and the public spheres, between volunteer commitment and compensated work. At the same time, it multiplied the chances of competition and conflict between established and nascent professional groups.

How did community organizers fit within these long-term transformations? This last chapter points to an ambiguous story of institutionalization and legitimation. It starts with the professional group coming into existence, in the 1970s and 1980s, and it ends with a former community organizer being elected to the White House in 2008.

Community organizing and organizers' expertise gained legitimacy through their incorporation into other neighboring social fields (philanthropy, organized labor, electoral politics), but the ways in which these forms of incorporation happened nested community organizing into a minority, subaltern position. The incorporation of professional community organizing into the division of political labor represented an ambivalent challenge to the increased professional closure of the US political field. The capacity to present oneself as being close to "the people" and to be recognized as such, to claim the ability to "organize for change at the grassroots," as Obama put it, became a political resource with increased value.[4] But the whole paradox, the fundamental contradiction, is that building such "grassroots," nonprofessional, "community" presence in public affairs has been claimed as a new territory for professional control.

To map how this ambiguous position consolidated between the 1980s and 2008, I want to look at four interdependent developments: a structural subordination to the philanthropic field; frequent skirmishes over the most effective way to bring about social change with social movement and advocacy groups; closer partnerships and alliances with labor unions; and an ambiguous incorporation into the political field of which Obama's career was just a symptom.

THE SUBORDINATION TO THE PHILANTHROPIC FIELD

As I have mentioned earlier, charges against the nonprofit-industrial complex and the stifling, domesticating role played by organized philanthropy are very popular on the left in current opinions on and conceptions of community organizing. This is the reason why I want to address them first.

Part of that story is already well known. As community-focused organizations grew and professional community organizing consolidated over the course of the 1970s and 1980s, there were intentional efforts by volunteer neighborhood leaders and paid organizers within these groups to develop their organizations' financial autonomy and independence through original and creative fundraising initiatives: implementing membership dues systems, engaging in systematic door-to-door canvassing in middle- or upper-middle-class neighborhoods, and holding parties, bake sales, and bingos. Such homegrown efforts often helped establish an organization's presence and credibility as a potential vessel for people's grievances, yet they were insufficient to attain financial stability. In a large part, this was due to the nature of the terrain itself: the poor lacked the stable, mobilizable financial resources that were necessary for organizational survival and for paid staff to keep getting paid and keep the organizations running.[5]

As an autonomous philanthropic field took shape in the 1970s, grants from private foundations appeared as a way out of this vicious circle. They became the primary source for funding community organizing groups, and alternative funding channels were soon marginalized within organizational budgets, if not altogether abandoned.

Philanthropic money fueled the drive toward professionalization: in order to fill a grant application correctly and then manage the money, administrative skills and formal schooling were de facto required. Philanthropic money was a mixed blessing, as organizations became more and more dependent on foundation grants for organizational survival.

The relation of subordination to the philanthropic field went actually deeper and was more complex than this standard story suggests.

A Philanthropic Field Takes Shape

The autonomous philanthropic field that emerged in the 1970s broke with previous charitable traditions by claiming its effectiveness to bring about ill-defined "social change" and ability to address the root causes of social problems. Between 1977 and 2017, thanks in part to the public policies that established all nonprofit organizations, including foundations, as tax-exempt entities, and that defined contributions to nonprofits as tax-deductible, the total amount of philanthropic donations tripled, from around $140 billion to $410 billion (in 2018 dollars).[6] Institutions like the Ford Foundation bolstered their claims that they were better equipped than public authorities to define and shape the common good.[7] Because of the large financial and organizational resources they muster, they became the prime source of funding for the overwhelming majority of nonprofit organizations, exercising immense discretionary power without being accountable to anyone.[8] As a result, although they hide behind the mask of pluralism, they actually "define much of our political culture, while channeling social change to protect corporate wealth and power."[9] Even critics who are committed to milquetoast redistributive policies see private foundations as "an exercise of power and plutocratic voice that warrants democratic scrutiny."[10]

The formation of the philanthropic field went hand in hand with a concerted effort on the part of private foundations to jockey for position as the prime representative of philanthropy in general. Although they only account for a small part of all donations, which are mostly made by individuals, private foundations' organizational resources allowed them to position themselves as spokespeople and impose their own norms, work practices, and worldview. In so doing, "organized philanthropy" tried to legitimize its activities by using a rhetoric of skill, professionalism, and responsibility to belie the commonly held view that philanthropic actors were elitist, unaccountable institutions wielding arbitrary power and operating in the shadows. By stressing the moral obligations associated with the act of giving, private foundations redefined their relationships with grantees in a collaborative light. "Philanthropy" was no longer just onetime charitable donations; it now encompassed long-term logistical support, technical assistance, and strategic consulting.[11]

Within the field, a sector specializing in funding "social change," sometimes radical in language and scope, became one of the ways in which philanthropic actors could substantiate this renewed definition of philanthropy.[12] In the early 1950s, only three foundations funded social movement organizations; in 1990, there were 186. This process was undergirded and accompanied by intentional efforts on the part of certain philanthropic actors to strengthen and mobilize the small number of social-justice-inclined donors and organizations to create spaces where grantees could meet one another, to give them more informational and organizational resources, but also to try and encourage other foundations to include "progressive" considerations in their grant-making programs.

In 1978, for instance, the National Network of Grantmakers (NNG) was launched to offer "a progressive complement to associations of more traditional foundations."[13] Over the course of the 1980s and 1990s, NNG tried to push other actors to start funding or increase their grants for progressive organizations. Of particular interest to NNG was the claim made by professional community organizers that they knew how to effectively improve people's living conditions and create new representation channels for marginalized groups. As a result, NNG teamed up with NOA and established a "partnership to fund organizing" and "strengthen the community organizing field" to "educate funders to the importance of community organizing and seek increased foundation support for community organizing." To do so, half a dozen meetings were set up across the country with funders and professional organizers in the mid-1990s.[14]

The number of "social-change foundations" remained small in comparison with large corporate foundations, whose prime goal was to "look good and do good" in the public's eyes and avoid subversive causes—or fund initiatives and organizations that actively fought against them.[15] The overall share of funds attributed to "social-change organizations" was a drop in the bucket compared to domains like health, education, and direct social services. But the power relation that subordinated social-change grantees to funders was very real. It turned private foundations into an indirect employer, one that was seldom brought into the picture but that wielded real power over working and employment conditions. Hence NOA's pointed argument, in its endeavor to stabilize and improve paid organizers' material conditions at work and beyond, that any pension plan for organizers should include contributions by private funders, and that the latter should also participate in the design:

> To a very real extent, foundations are a third corner of a tri-partite employment structure. We will be asking foundations to (a) include a pension contribution incentive over and above the grant amount for grantee organizations that agree to join, and (b) establish a fund to make up the difference between 3 and 5 % for organizations that want to participate but cannot meet the entire minimum commitment in the first year.[16]

Over the years, several philanthropic foundations did participate in funding NOA's pension plan, but it did not translate into a binding, long-term partnership; rather, the funding was part of their usual grant-making activities and depended on funding trends and fads.

Social-Change Philanthropy Funds and Moulds Community Organizing

Unsurprisingly, philanthropic funding came with all sorts of restrictive strings attached. The channeling effect of foundation money on the Black liberation and women's movements is well studied—how funders selected and groomed candidates and organizations, promoted pacified repertoires of action and moderate campaign goals that led to electoral politics and policy making, and pushed for hiring more staff and rationalizing internal structuring.[17] In the process, they defended their own vision of what the public sphere, civic engagement, and democracy should look like, placing a strong emphasis on notions like leadership, compromise, and pluralism.[18] What is less often emphasized is that private foundations also affect social movement organizations at a macro level, by embedding them into networks and sets of standards that they themselves shape and that fall outside of the organizations' control.[19]

In the case of professional community organizing, philanthropic foundations gave the "vocation" increased visibility and legitimacy. They helped operationalize the community organizing label into their own systems of classifications and concrete grant selection criteria. In the 1980s, "community organizing" became a label that funders used to differentiate between different sectors of activity they wished to fund and label their grant programs. By deciding what application corresponded to what fundable community organizing should be, they gave a particular twist to the category. Furthermore, they funded research efforts to understand professional community organizing better through a number of national, regional, and local surveys.[20] In the early 1990s, for instance, the Ford Foundation commissioned a report from Gary Delgado about the challenges and limits of local community organizing and how large funders might play a more active role, which caused quite a stir in the professional organizing milieu.[21] Although initiatives like NOA and NNG's "partnership to fund organizing" were meant to facilitate conversations between professional

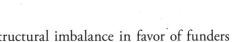

organizers and funders, the structural imbalance in favor of funders implied that in the end they were the ones who defined the criteria for "good" organizing.

Chicago offers a good example of these interwoven processes and their practical effects on professional community organizing efforts. In 1984, the Woods Charitable Fund, which, like the Schwarzhaupt Foundation, had funded citizen participation for decades, decided that it would launch a new grant program called "Participation and Leadership in Communities." The next year, the program was renamed Community Organizing Program after Ken Rolling was hired to implement it.[22] A former Catholic priest, Rolling had worked for several years at the Catholic Campaign for Human Development (CCHD), created in 1970 by community organizing partisans like John Egan to promote the Church's social mission. CCHD soon became one of the major funders for the IAF, ACORN, and other national networks.[23] Woods's program was "based on a belief that Chicago needs strong, sustained citizen participation and a continuing emergence of new leaders. We particularly see a need to strengthen the effectiveness of organizing and to involve more people, especially minorities, in leadership positions."[24]

In spite of being a small local philanthropic actor, Woods became one of the major funders for community organizing in the city.[25] In 1994, as it overhauled its entire organization and changed its name to the Woods Fund of Chicago, an evaluation of the Community Organizing Program estimated that $4.2 million had been attributed to community organizing groups over a decade (or $8 million in 2021). Driven by concerns that were typical of organized philanthropy, the board of trustees concluded that it was necessary for the foundation to improve the program's impact and effectiveness. It commissioned a report from a group of academics and consultants who conducted meetings with organizers throughout Chicago like the meeting with South Side organizers of June 1994 mentioned in the previous chapter. The report concluded that there was a deficit of grants to the city's poorest neighborhoods, located primarily on the predominantly Black South and West Sides.[26]

In 2003, staff members again assessed the foundation's impact in funding organizing groups.[27] The foundation commissioned another evaluation report, which concluded after a year that "there is a lack of organizations on the South Side of Chicago that are doing any work that broadly falls within the parameters of community organizing. There are even fewer that have demonstrated the capacity to sustain this work at a high level of efficacy, and still fewer that are run and staffed by African⊠Americans."[28] In order to solve these three problems, Woods issued a call for projects for new or existing groups: the South Side Initiative.

The initiative combined small capacity-building grants (from $5,000 to $20,000, or from $7,600 to $30,000 in 2021) with various training workshops. Eight organizations were selected. The arrangement came "with strings attached," as the foundation put it since the grants were conditioned on mandatory attendance of the workshops.[29] The foundation also mobilized the expertise of experienced organizers who monitored and evaluated the grantee's progress. At the same time, Woods invited other funders in the city to cooperate and share advice and feedback while showcasing the work of its protégés. Over two years, the eight organizations receive a total of $220,000 ($337,000 in 2021) "in support of capacity building activities such as developing leadership training curricula, advancing organizing campaigns, strategic planning, grants development and fundraising, and increasing membership."[30] In addition, four organizations received regular grants totaling $160,000 ($245,000 in 2021 dollars). The project lasted until 2009, when Woods decided that it had met its original goals.

The South Side Initiative epitomizes the intricacies of what the subordination to the philanthropic field meant in practice and how external pressure was articulated alongside of community organizing's professionalization from within. First, the program was meant as a tool to measure the fund's social impact, to optimize the allocation of funds to organizing groups, and to promote the development of "real" organizing. Whereas groups like the Black Panthers had integrated the provision of direct services into what they meant by organizing and politicized these tasks in the 1960s and 1970s, the foundation now pitted service provision and direct-action organizing against one another by using a self-help, anti-welfare rhetoric that still structures similar grant-making activities across the country: "The social services emphasis has become so entrenched in extremely low income communities that it will take multiple efforts to find and build organizations that are truly committed to principles of empowerment and civic engagement."[31]

The type of organizing that Woods favored, on the other hand, was defined as "the ability of a community to mobilize its members and leverage resources to influence social justice or economic equity."[32] Impact was assessed in terms of quantifiable outcomes in bullet-point lists: the number of leaders an organization trained, people who attended meetings, volunteers who got involved in various campaigns, the amount of money the groups received from other funders, and so on. The injunction to produce measurable outcomes was not new; it represented an instrumental rationality that had been woven into the very fabric of organizers' claims to control the making of popular participation for decades, but the norm was now also defined and imposed from outside.

Doubling down from the outside on an internal professional dynamic manifested itself in another way: the emphasis placed by the South Side Initiative, and funders in general, on organizing trainings. In the words of Travis, the program officer who oversaw the program, "We thought most of these groups didn't have a grounding in the basic organizing principles. And if you want to build that organizing capacity, sending people to training is one way to do that. And because we didn't want them to have to take that out of the regular grants that we were giving them, they had a few thousand dollars extra just for that, that they could take." Travis had firsthand

knowledge of what "organizing capacity" could mean: prior to joining Woods he had worked as a community organizer for a local
Chicago group after graduating from the University of Illinois with a
bachelor's degree in anthropology. The other way to "build capacity"
was the intentional development of local, interorganizational networks of organizers that would bolster the organizations' strengths
and ties and support a sense of shared purpose and interests. Travis
explained that "most of these groups were small, they didn't know
each other, so we felt that bringing them together in a room, building those kinds of relationships was ultimately going to be critical to
their growth and success."[33]

Nurturing collaboration and exchange between fledgling groups
was not necessarily a bad thing in itself. It could lead to more collaborative efforts, help the circulation of information and the building
of shared commitments, and translate into more success for newly
formed coalitions. But it is worth keeping in mind that encouraging
coalitions grew out of concerns about Woods's "impact," which is another word for maximizing resource allocation, and that the groups
that Woods funded had little if any say over how such allocation
happened, what standards were used to assess it, and how long it
would last.

How Organizers Respond to Philanthropy

As with any relation of power, formal subordination to the philanthropic field did not entail full consent or subjugation. In the words
of political scientist and anthropologist James Scott, even when power
seems to crush resistance, subaltern groups have weapons to mitigate,
bypass, circumvent, and resist domination.[34] There is plenty of evidence suggesting not only that community organizers were well aware
of the power imbalance and the structural dependence that came with
philanthropic funding but also that under certain conditions critical
voices emerged.

The dominant mode of criticism was not radical but reform-oriented: it did not take issue with the very principle of philanthropy's involvement but called for funders to take professional organizing more seriously and fund it accordingly. Throughout the decades, the voices within the professionalizing sector of community organizing who pushed for private funders to secure organizational stability and recognize their expertise regularly brought this up. At the end of the national report on faith-based community organizing for Interfaith Funders (a group of religious and secular donors that came out of the NNG in 1997), a section on "strategic self-assessment" synthesized organizers' opinions of what funders could do to "help advance the field." Three main roles stood out. First, funders should provide more funding and "educate other foundations and agencies about the field, in order to meet the need for greater resources." Second, they should collaborate more closely with professional organizers to "steer the field in constructive directions." Finally, they should foster research on and for the field (best-practices memos, surveys on the profession's demographics and recruitment patterns and gaps) to nurture organizers' collective reflexivity.[35]

Another interesting example of reform-oriented criticisms is the attempt by NOA to formalize accountability mechanisms. In 1998, the professional association created a "report card on progressive funders" where organizers were instructed to evaluate ten program officers from progressive foundations—"preferably the 5 best you've actually tried to work with, and the 5 worst."[36] NOA identified eight criteria to assess whether the officer aligned with organizers' needs, constraints, and ideas or with funders. The initiative grew out of a discussion spurred by the publication in the *Nation* a few months earlier of an article titled "Why do Progressive Foundations Give Too Little to Too Many?" Written by the former director of a policy institute, it argued that the main problem with progressive funders was not that they had fewer resources than conservative ones but that they did not invest it effectively. The small, single-issue, single-year grants that progressive foundations designed forced organizers to spend more time fundraising than performing actual organizing work.

The opportunity for organizers to voice their complaints about funding patterns was made possible by philanthropists' concerns about being effective in their grant-making activities and improving their impact.[37] This is what transpired from the various meetings organized by Woods in 1994 to assess its Community Organizing Program. But the wording of the question (what role should Interfaith Funders play to help advance the field, and by implication other funders in general?) and its underlying assumptions (funders do have a role to play, advancing the field is a given, consensual goal) and the institutional origins of the survey, which was launched by the funders themselves, framed the interaction in such a way that more critical challenges were less likely to be voiced.

By the late 1990s, criticizing the power dynamics "inherent in the organizer/funder relationship" had become somewhat of a trope, which organizers and funders alike regularly talked about.[38] A more marginal—but nonetheless present—line of criticism, which in many ways prefigured the criticisms against the nonprofit-industrial complex, called into question philanthropy's very existence. In 1998, for instance, against the backdrop of lively debates about the role and scope of philanthropy in public affairs, and the tepid response by "progressive" and mainstream funders to Republicans taking over Congress in 1994, NOA's *Ark* bulletin organized a roundtable conversation with five people: three professional organizers, a program officer from the Unitarian Universalist Veatch Program, and a staffer for the National Committee for Responsive Philanthropy who was a foundation watchdog.[39] All participants agreed that there were very few really progressive, left-wing foundations, and lamented that "appallingly little money has gone to support grassroots work that has as its goal to empower low and moderate income constituencies" while right-wing foundations had been pouring money into think tanks and political action committees since the 1970s.[40] When the discussion moved to how funders can support "the progressive movement," which some also called "the Left," one roadblock the participants highlighted was the structural lack of accountability. Aside from the legal requirement that private foundations must distribute at least 5 percent of their assets every year, they were not bound by much.

Ironically, it was the program officer from Veatch, Jane McAlevey, who went even further in her criticism: "I think that foundations are largely illegitimate structures to begin with. The whole idea that little pockets of privately held capital get to pass judgment on anyone is a problem."[41] McAlevey was no stranger to the world of politics and professional organizing.[42] She was born in the 1960s, and her father was a local politician in New York. As the president of the Student Association of the State University of New York in Albany in the early 1980s, she helped set up a partnership between the US Student Association and the Midwest Academy to organize student-led week-end trainings about power, strategy, and tactics.[43] After working for several years with environmental justice groups organizing international campaigns, she worked for three years as the associate director of the Highlander Research and Education Center. She was then approached by Veatch, who wanted to hire her. After dispelling her initial doubts, she accepted the job, in part because Veatch had "funded every organization I'd worked for, so they knew me well."[44]

McAlevey's political and professional experiences led her to look at foundations with a mix of critical skepticism and pragmatic opportunism. In the *Ark* roundtable, indeed, she explained that there were several small-scale bypass tactics that program officers like her could use to advance the interests of the people they stood for. "One method I use, five of us progressive funders regularly get together with the leaders of the environmental justice movement. We tell them what's the foundation lingo of the month. We help them repackage their proposals to sell to the mainstream funders. There's a lot of structured stuff we can do behind the scenes." McAlevey recognized that she could strategically use the assumptions large donors would make about her to gain better access: "I'm a white, female, blond, middle-class funder, and I'm a lot less scary than someone from the grassroots, so I can get into Ford and Rockefeller." She acknowledged the fundamental contradiction at play in no uncertain terms: there was a real danger that she and others like her would become new gatekeepers between "the grassroots" and donors, thus reproducing the structural lack of accountability they challenged in the first place.[45]

The structural subordination to the philanthropic field introduced professionalizing dynamics from above over which organizers as a group had little control. But it does not mean that foundations imposed their power onto unwilling organizers. Rather, social-change philanthropy's rhetoric of rationalized social change, the need for leadership, political pluralism, and a commitment to individualized racial and gender equality resonated with some of the core tenets in the professional excellence that organizers stood for. Subordination was not the only type of relation that pinned down community organizing's place within the division of political labor. Another crucial dimension was competition with other intermediaries who also claimed that they knew how to bring about social change.

ORGANIZING, ACTIVISM, AND ADVOCACY: COMPETING AND COLLABORATING WITH SOCIAL MOVEMENTS

Establishing community organizing as a recognizable social entity within the chain of political labor implied actively erecting symbolic boundaries separating the group and the professional territory it claimed as its own from other nearby competitors. To carve out their place and give meaning to their role, organizers sought to delegitimize several competing figures who also sought to be recognized as the legitimate producers of people's interests outside of electoral channels. I want to focus more particularly on two key competitors: the ineffective activist and the groundless advocate.

"We're Not Activists, We're Organizers"

Although most people assume that "organizer" and "activist" are just two synonyms to refer to people who engage in collective protest, for people who identify as organizers and claim that label with pride, being called an activist is an insult. The two must be distinguished, as the following anecdote illustrates. In April 2016, at the biannual Labor Notes Conference, which took place in a hotel near Chicago's O'Hare airport, several thousand trade unionists, union officials, and political activists were having dinner in the hotel's main conference room and watched a series of awards and prizes be given to various individuals, organizations, and campaigns whose defense of workers' rights was particularly praiseworthy. One of these awards, the "Troublemaker Award," was given to the Dyett coalition, which led a thirty-four-day hunger strike the previous summer to prevent the closure of the Dyett public high school on the South Side of Chicago. The Kenwood-Oakland Community Organization (KOCO) was the coalition's main driving force. When Jitu Brown and Jeanette Taylor-Ramann, two of the coalition's spokespeople, went onstage to receive the prize, they started their acceptance speech with the statement that "we're not activists, we're organizers."[46]

To understand why Brown and Taylor-Ramann dismissed the activist figure, it is important to remember that contrary to a dominant narrative, radical social movements did not disappear in the second half of the 1970s and 1980s. Movements' mass appeal and scope certainly decreased, but it did not mean that protest activity and contention stopped altogether. Not only was there the myriad of "front-porch" struggles I alluded to in the previous chapter, but there was also "a proliferation of movements, causes, and political identities" around a variety of issues[47]—LGBTQ rights, women's rights, environmental causes, workers' rights, and international solidarity—performed by small affinity groups with dense social ties, whose creativity led to profound cultural and social changes. Many of them resorted to various forms of direct action and civil disobedience that were meant to disrupt the ordinary course of things and trigger some form of moral outrage that would shock people out of apathy and into action.[48]

Although they did not necessarily share the same politics, these forms of collective action were often dismissed as "activism" in the press, on TV, and in political speeches. As I explained in the introduction, the "activism" label has a fairly recent history. As the group of community organizers grew increasingly conscious of itself and actively pursued professionalization as a pathway to legitimacy, being equated with "activists" became an object of collective concern. Not so much because of fundamental political divergences but rather because activists acted in an amateur fashion, they lacked the know-how to lead victorious struggles. Professional community organizing emerged as a response to the decline of the 1960s' mass movements; professionalism became the favored collective solution to sustain citizen participation and engagement outside of movement waves. The "activist" became somewhat of a bogeyman that organizers could invoke to bolster their claims to being uniquely able of bringing about effective social change. The distinction between organizing and activism as two different and distinct forms of collective action became a touchstone for the group's professional project and the claims that it was more effective than, and superior to, nonprofessionally powered collective action efforts. As a result, ironically, professional community organizing consolidated its position and built its legitimacy around distrust for movement activity.

The way community organizers responded to the nascent antiglobalization movement in the late 1990s offers a good example of these processes. The "battle of Seattle," which took place in Seattle in November 1999 against the World Trade Organization (WTO), the subsequent demonstrations in Washington in April 2000 against the International Monetary Fund and the World Bank, and the counterdemonstrations outside of the Democratic and Republican conventions in the summer of that year, were welcomed as founding moments in the building of a transnational movement against neoliberal globalization. According to Kim Fellner, who reported on the events in Seattle in the *Ark*, it brought together "a dynamic hodge-podge of interests and organization," from anarchist groups to large labor unions, religious organizations, and environmental justice NGOs. Fellner argued that organizers should support the movement's goals and challenges to profit-driven globalization. The diversity of organizations and styles offered stimulating opportunities for participants to broaden their horizons and learn from one another. She hailed the large turnout and unexpected shutdown of the WTO as positive developments. But beyond these victories, she went on, the overall picture was less rosy. The movement was "too white to win": "Given that the three entities most responsible for coordination were predominantly white, with almost exclusively white spokespersons, it is not very surprising that organizations of color did not feel themselves in partnership." Against the short-term goals to create a working, operational coalition, Fellner opposed "the imperative to build racially diverse and equitable relationships and organization for the long haul—to forge a new way of being with each other." In her eyes, what was at stake had less to do with what protest tactics to use or the issues themselves than with the movement's lack of social and racial representativeness.[49]

In developing such a line of argument, which did point out some real fault lines within the antiglobalization movement, Fellner voiced two core beliefs that collectively justified and gave meaning to organizers' commitments: the belief that organizing was primarily and fundamentally about interpersonal relationships, and building and nurturing these relationships was a collective, political goal in itself; the belief that it was possible to cross organizational, racial, and social divides and change a movement's demographics provided that the right methods and techniques were used.

The organizer/activist distinction was regularly rekindled throughout the 2000s, during the antiwar movement and the immigrant rights protests of 2006, but it was reactivated with a vengeance in the wake of the Occupy Wall Street movement in 2011. In a more global context where established political organizations like political parties, labor unions, and civic associations were undergoing what's often described as a crisis of legitimacy, characterized by dwindling membership figures, consensus decision-making, anti-organizational sentiment, and the valorization of moral indignation and spontaneous outrage gained traction within social movement circles.[50] Such organizational trends combined with the advent of what Zeynep Tufekci calls "networked protests," with the "assimilation of digital technologies into their fabric" and subsequent gains in how fast (and cheaply) information could circulate beyond social and spatial borders, a new parameter of contemporary protests that the Arab Spring in 2011 and the Gezi Park protests in Turkey in 2013 made abundantly clear.[51] These growing trends directly challenged organizers' expertise and negated their long-standing claim that organizing, while arduous, should be acknowledged as a legitimate and necessary component of any political endeavor.

The distrust toward "spontaneous" protest movements has been structured by two fundamental arguments that feed on one another. First, there is a stark opposition between idealistic, ineffective amateurs and pragmatic, strategic professionals. While the former appeal to the broader public's moral sense through a rhetoric of urgency, the latter consider that lasting change can be achieved only through a careful plan unfolding over the long term. Derided as being mostly idealistic college kids, volunteer activists might act out of goodwill, and sometimes good ideas, but they do not have a clear sense of "what to do when you don't know what to do," to use Heather Booth's telling expression. Organizers, by contrast, tap into practical, tried-and-tested knowledge; they master a set of stages, principles, and prescriptions about how to identify leaders and push an organization toward strategic campaigns.[52] Their calculating mentality leads them to be obsessed with numbers and constantly count how many doors they must knock on, how many phone calls they must make, how many people they must bring to an event, how many interviews they must do, and so on.

The second argument builds upon the interested/disinterested dichotomy, which is so central to the entire narrative around commitment and the distrust toward its salarization, but it does so in an original way. Activists do not include building a real, lasting, growing base of support into the set of tasks that develop through their practice. They work for themselves, not for others. As a result, their protests are socially and racially very homogeneous. Their claims to represent people's interests do not match their deeds. Organizers, however, have the necessary relational skills to reach out to people who are affected by a given problem and convince them that taking action collectively is the best way they could solve it. They have the emotional intelligence to relate and empathize with people whose politics they might not necessarily agree with. The leaders that they identify and groom are volunteers, like activists, but it is the organizing relation that turns them into leaders. Organizing is best seen as a dialectic relation: there's no leader without an organizer; and there's no organizer without leaders. Activists, by contrast, are volunteers who fall outside the scope of the organizing relation.

Groundless Advocates

The other specter professional organizers raise and dispel is the professional advocate, who claim they speak in the name of a given constituency who has little access to public voice and representation (the elderly, people with disabilities, children, people of color, women, and so forth).[53] Although advocacy practices emerged in the late 1950s, their massive growth and proliferation were the result of transformations in political and civic life inaugurated in the 1960s and 1970s. Broadly speaking, advocacy organizations specialize in defending an ever-growing number of public interest causes. To do so, they attempt to "bring greater attention, raise awareness, and create urgency around claims," favoring discreet institutional repertoires (initiating education and media campaigns, lobbying public officials, testifying at hearings, writing policy proposals, issuing reports and surveys) over more boisterous public displays of discontent.[54] For sociologist Theda Skocpol, such a process went hand in hand with a shift from membership-based organizations to memberless groups run by college-educated, legalese-speaking professional staffers, which did not foster a civic culture of debate or actively engage their membership.[55]

Because of advocates' professional and academic credentials, organizers cannot pull the same professionalism card they use with activists to support their claims. Besides, advocacy organizations do not exactly play on the same field as organizers and activists. Organizers and activists can literally bump into one another during a march or a demonstration; they directly compete for turf and physical occupation of space. Advocates, on the other hand, navigate the halls of city, state, and federal power. As a result, organizers insist on the gap between advocates and the constituents whose voices and interests they claim they defend but with whom they enjoy little demonstrable connection. The lack of representativeness and democratic accountability combines with a policy-driven, socially disconnected vision of social change. By contrast, community organizers bring to the fore their own abilities to bridge the distance between the ruling and the ruled, maintain authentic relationships with the so-called community, and organize actions that show that there is indeed power in numbers.[56]

There are real differences in what social scientists call "styles of political commitment" between collective action powered by community-based organizations, by social-movement-type groups, and by advocacy and public interest organizations; in practice, however, the boundaries between these three figures can be quite porous.[57] There are several examples of activists and organizers, or advocates and organizers, working together on common campaigns. There are also plenty of examples of community-based organizations using both organizing and advocacy in their campaigns or advocacy organizations developing "grassroots lobbying" strategies to demonstrate to elected officials the salience of the issues they defend. Large national community organizing networks started establishing "some presence" in Washington, DC, in the early 1980s to follow legislative debates and monitor federal politics more closely.[58] And in terms of people's careers, organizer positions can function as training grounds for later involvement in social movements, as Black Lives Matter demonstrated but also as recruitment pools for careers in advocacy groups and policy-oriented staff positions.[59]

These symbolic distinctions have real, practical implications in terms of material constraints. Because advocacy presupposes respect for the established rules of the game and trust in the political system's ability to deliver, actors like philanthropic foundations have an inbuilt interest in recognizing its value. As a matter of fact, when philanthropic actors fund organizing, what they like the most are applications and projects that combine both supralocal advocacy and localized organizing. Between 2004 and 2014, for instance, the program that the Woods Fund funded the most in Chicago was not community organizing per se but a mix of organizing and advocacy called "intersection."[60]

While social movement activists and advocates appear as direct competitors from whom professional organizers distinguished themselves to carve out and defend their place in the political division of labor, from the 1980s on they also increasingly cooperated with another major player: organized labor.

LABOR AND COMMUNITY, A NEW COMPLEMENTARITY?

Two intertwined processes signaled community organizing's growing legitimacy in the eyes of organized labor. Certain sectors of organized labor embraced the organizing practices that had developed in the cradle of workers' mass movements in the 1930s but that were abandoned during the Cold War. And people who had worked as community organizers took up positions as union staffers, which spurred the circulation of organizing expertise within labor circles.

The initial impetus behind the rapprochement came from community organizing and other civic-engagement groups. For most of the IAF's history, ties with labor had been tenuous, to say the least. The

United Farm Workers union, launched in the late 1950s by IAF-trained organizer Cesar Chavez to organize agricultural workers in California, was an outlier in the projects sponsored by the IAF, one that Alinsky was initially highly skeptical of. But in the 1970s, the attitude toward organized labor and workplace organizing began to change. This was in part due to the arrival of people whose political training in the Black liberation, antiwar, and women's movements led them to push for the integration of economic justice issues into community organizing's focus. Folks at the Midwest Academy, for instance, were instrumental in building the Citizen/Labor Energy Coalition in 1978 and developed a close relationship with organizations for white-collar women workers like Women Employed and 9to5.[61]

Other efforts focused more directly on organizing workers at the point of production, particularly poor workers in nonunionized sectors. In the late 1970s, ACORN launched its own autonomous labor organizing projects, the United Labor Unions (ULU), as part of the organization's ambition to reach out to the unorganized. ULU organizers targeted poor workers in the rapidly growing service industry, which established unions showed little interest in representing. "By the mid-'80s, ULU locals had used direct action methods to obtain the first fast food industry union contract in US history, to unionize thousands of 'invisible' poverty-wage home care workers, and to make inroads into New Orleans's gigantic and nonunion tourist industry."[62] ULU locals spearheaded union representation campaigns, negotiated union contracts with employers, and created enduring institutions.

ULU locals were formally independent of ACORN, but they shared the same broad goal of "economic justice for low- and moderate-income people in the neighborhoods and in the workplace."[63] At first, the power imbalance that linked organizers and leaders in ACORN was reproduced in these new institutional arrangements. After a couple of years, the social composition of staffers differed significantly from ACORN's. In violation of the professional norm that clearly distinguished organizers and leaders, rank-and-file members were commonly hired as staff. In the mid-1980s, ULU organizers were approximately 60 percent African American and about half female, which pushed ACORN to be more intentional in its recruitment strategy and to hire organizers of color and women out of its own membership.

The growing openness to workplace and economic justice issues on the part of community organizing professionals in the 1980s mirrored the newly found interest of several labor leaders in community organizers' expertise and skill set and a broader turn (back) to organizing. By then, organized labor was in shambles. The 1947 Taft-Hartley Act, the advent of Cold War labor politics, and the failure of Operation Dixie in the South all marginalized labor shop-floor militancy and organizing practices in favor of "business unionism," which meant both close partnerships with management and the depoliticized provision of services like pension and health-care benefits. The Black liberation movement and women's struggles actually infused into the workplace, and so women, people of color, and other radicals drove a wave of union organizing into the 1970s, but it was met with an offensive led by employers and professional union busters like Alinsky enthusiast John Sheridan to thwart union organizing drives.[64] After Ronald Reagan fired eleven thousand striking air traffic controllers in 1981, union busting became a normalized practice in both the public and private sectors.

At the same time, the mostly nonunionized service sector grew at a steady pace, which deeply affected the balance of forces within organized labor and opened a window of opportunity for unions like the Service Employees International Union (SEIU). In the face of rapidly dwindling membership bases and intensifying interunion rivalries, certain unions turned to corporate campaigning strategies, focusing on exposing corporations' weak spots and discrediting them in the public arena.[65] Others, like SEIU, recruited massively, hiring full-time staffers who did not come out of the labor milieu. SEIU's national office went from employing a dozen staffers to more than two hundred over a few years. Working in the organizing and research departments, a significant portion of them had gained their political socialization in the struggles of the 1960s and '70s. As journalist and labor special-ist Vanessa Tait points out, "By the late '80s, organizers with social justice or community organizing experience had made headway in-side local, regional, and national trade unions. Experience with UFW and ACORN was common; others came with backgrounds in inter-national solidarity movements and anti-apartheid struggles."[66] They brought with them a blend of experiential know-how as well as an interest in management theory. But they were also recruited on their academic titles and background rather than from the rank and file, as had been the case for decades.[67]

The election of the "New Labor" slate of candidates at the head of the AFL-CIO in 1995 signaled a major shift in official rhetoric and practice. To move away from a servicing model of unionism, which provided union members with wages and benefits while maintaining good relationships with management and suppressing militancy on the shop floor, the new leadership emphasized the need to resort more sys-tematically to "union corporate campaigns," a form of union action pi-oneered in the late 1970s used to exert broad pressure on an employer, usually by targeting its public image and brand, but it also pushed for a strategic plan to engage union members more actively and, more significantly, to recruit new members en masse.[68] "Organizing the un-organized" was one of New Labor's campaign slogans. The new lead-ership unveiled its organizing plan in the spring of 1996: a "Union Summer" training program modeled after Freedom Summer for a thousand college students. The plan hinged on multiple things: the allocation of more funds to organizing campaigns, the creation of an Organizing Department (the AFL-CIO did not have one until then), and the increased use of the Organizing Institute, created in 1989 to recruit and train union organizers.[69]

Organized labor's newfound interest in organizing expertise and the circulation of people with experience in professionalized com-munity organizing resulted in the advent of "labor-community coali-tions"[70] to reach workers who had hitherto been excluded from union representation: precarious workers (fast-food restaurants, retail, and logistics), part-time or interim workers, service employees, and immigrant workers. Several famous examples actually predated the 1995 AFL-CIO election and New Labor's acknowledgment that "union politics must start in the neighborhoods where our members live and vote."[71] They include SEIU's national Justice for Janitors campaign, kicked off in the late 1980s, to organize custodial staff, as well as Jobs with Justice, an independent nationwide coalition of labor unions and community organizing groups founded in 1987 in Miami that, ten years later, was composed of thirty local chapters and was backed by a dozen national unions and community organizing networks like ACORN and Citizen Action.[72] What these campaigns had in common was an aggressive organizing outlook that relied on community-based, social movement-style tactics. Like the work of most of the independent unions, this organizing tended to be based in communities of color and among the growing immigrant workforce."[73]

Certain labor-community coalitions were more concerned with symbolic posturing and did not survive the campaigns they were supposed to support, but others outlived their short-term goals. A good example of this is the Chicago-based Grassroots Collaborative. It was founded in the early 2000s as a result of a campaign for a minimum wage increase that brought together a wide range of labor and community organizations in the city. The coalition originated in a close partnership between the local ACORN chapter and SEIU's health-care local. Organizational and individual trajectories were deeply interwoven: the SEIU affiliate was at first a United Labor Unions local, created in 1983 by Madeline Talbott's husband, Keith Kelleher, after she was sent to Chicago by Wade Rathke to start a new ACORN chapter. The local, which first organized homecare workers, affiliated with SEIU in 1987. For a long time, the newly formed SEIU Local 880 and ACORN shared the same office spaces. During the 2000s, the coalition led campaigns on many fronts, like the status of undocumented immigrant workers and a fight against the construction of a Walmart store, creating a site of counterpower that threatened and challenged Mayor Richard M. Daley's pro-growth agenda. Tellingly, in 2006 Daley used his first veto—and the only one he ever used during his twenty-two-year reign—to block a proposed municipal ordinance that would have created a minimum wage in the retail sector.[74]

Such partnerships paved the way for a more integrated, comprehensive approach to workers' actual living conditions and experiences.[75] But coalitions were also often unbalanced in terms of internal division of labor. Community organizations did most of the unacknowledged groundwork, knocking on people's doors, making phone calls, and distributing leaflets and literature, while labor leaders negotiated with the bosses.[76] Furthermore, there were considerable disagreements on the left over what labor-community coalitions meant and where they were headed. While some praised new organizational forms that provided a stepping stone to address people's "daily struggles as working people trying to get around the city, as consumers paying for services, as rights-conscious citizens,"[77] other critics emphasized the overreliance on professional staff and rationalizing marketing strategies, which would certainly introduce new institutional obstacles preventing rank-and-file workers' active participation and liberation.[78] Indeed, these efforts relied heavily on paid staff, who left little room for members to commit on their own terms. In 1995, for instance, Justice for Janitors employed 110 professional organizers.

Recently there have been lively debates about New Labor's legacy and outcome, particularly since union ranks have continued to plummet despite the commitment to "revitalize" unionism though intentional organizing and corporate campaigns. In a much-discussed piece from 2015, which she later expanded into the book *No Shortcuts*, Jane McAlevey traces New Labor's failure back to Alinsky's sway over the New Labor leadership.[79] Regardless of how one assesses New Labor's impact and contribution, McAlevey does point out a significant phenomenon: the practices put forward by professional community organizers were seen as potential solutions for labor's woes, which

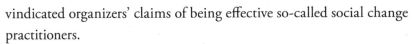

vindicated organizers' claims of being effective so-called social change practitioners.

The increasing interplay between the community organizing field and labor, philanthropy, and social movements, both in terms of partnerships between organizations and people's individual professional trajectories, contributed to the circulation of community organizing practices and norms. This, in turn, strengthened their legitimacy and anchored more firmly community organizing's position within the division of political labor, even though such a position was a subaltern one. The final social site that pinned down and legitimized community organizing within that ecosystem, electoral politics, gave that minor, ambiguous incorporation a particular twist.

AN AMBIGUOUS INCORPORATION
INTO THE POLITICAL FIELD

From the 1970s on, thanks to new campaign finance rules allowing corporate and wealthy individual donors to make barely regulated political contributions, the US political field became increasingly permeable not just to corporate power and money but also to the valorization of economic and management skills in determining political legitimacy. As the neoliberal prioritization of market interests over constituents was steadily upheld by political professionals, strategic experts grew in prominence to continue obtaining popular support at the polls.[80] Political consultants emerged as a professional group whose skills and expertise allowed them to take control of political campaigns, which became increasingly candidate-centered, shaping a "modern business of politics" where "the pursuit of popular support came to rely almost exclusively on products and services that consultants alone could provide."[81]

Just as the arrival of new intermediaries lengthened the chain of political labor even further, the overarching beliefs legitimating political rule shifted. In postwar America, promises of economic growth and material well-being were the basis of the authority of urban elites. But with the collapse of belief in the prospects for growth beginning in the 1970s and 1980s, urban elites had to base their authority on other legitimizing beliefs, such as the promise of neighborhood self-determination through participation. Therefore, a paradoxical public-engagement industry took shape whose main purpose was to elicit such popular participation.[82] It is against this backdrop that professional community organizing was incorporated into the margins of the political field. Incorporation happened on two interrelated levels: synchronically, with community-based organizations being embedded into the political process, and diachronically, with organizer positions functioning as a springboard for elected office.

The Active Margins of the Political Field

Exerting "community" pressure on elected officials to extract concessions had been at the core of the IAF's political vision when Alinsky was in charge. As emerging networks competed to claim the Alinsky legacy, some of them broke with the Tocquevillian civil-society mindset and tried to shape more directly the outcome and direction of electoral struggles in the 1980s and 1990s to build a progressive populism that could counter right-wing populism.[83] Local ACORN chapters supported candidates for office or even ran their own in various local elections, for instance.

Conversely, developing ties with certain community organizing institutions propped up elected representatives' democratic credentials and claims that they indeed took their constituents' interests to heart, at the time when the Democratic Party accentuated its shift away from mild redistributive politics and toward its white-collar and elite constituencies, becoming "a professionalized, well-funded, and elite-run multitiered conglomerate with a permanent bureaucracy at its core."[84] By the end of the 1980s, the Midwest Academy annual retreat had become a go-to for Democratic Party socialites, from congressional candidates to entertainment celebrities like Jane Fonda. At the 1987 retreat, Kendall points out, "every Democratic candidate for Congress came."[85] Citizen Action's growing presence in many states meant that it was a political player to be reckoned with. "The organization's growing political savvy has not been lost on the Democrats," one reporter noted in 1988. "Jesse Jackson, Paul Simon, Joseph Biden, Michael Dukakis, Bruce Babbitt, Patricia Schroeder, Edward Kennedy, and Alan Cranston all spoke at last summer's retreat."[86] Not all community organizing federations went as far as Citizen Action in its association with Democratic electoral politics, but the field as a whole was still attracted by the Democratic Party's gravitational pull.

The election of Harold Washington as the first African American mayor of Chicago in 1983 offers a good example of the multifaceted, complex incorporation of people, organizations, and the rhetoric embodying professional community organizing into the electoral arena and the political field more broadly. Opening the formulation and implementation of public policy to community input and scrutiny was central to Washington's commitment to break from decades of political corruption and clientelism under the Democratic Party machine. During his campaign, Washington heavily relied on input and advice from neighborhood groups and people from the world of professional organizing (Heather Booth was one of his campaign advisers, for instance). After he was elected, he put together a team of 250 people from two hundred private and public organizations to write a transitional report that would provide the initial push for a new political program. Emphasizing "balanced growth, neighborhood development, job creation, affirmative action, and public participation," it aimed at cementing the role of neighborhood groups as recognized agents for local planning and development activities.[87] Washington also created a short-lived Department of Neighborhoods to organize neighborhood forums throughout the city. It was directed by top political adviser Joe Gardner, a former organizer for the Woodlawn Organization and Jesse Jackson's Operation PUSH.[88]

Not all community organizing groups sided with Washington, however. The 1983 campaign and Washington's first term unfolded in a context of intense political polarization, which overlapped a clear-cut racial divide.[89] After Washington was elected, two of the main institution-based organizing federations in the city, the Southwest Parish and Neighborhood Federation and the Northwest Neighborhood Federation, came together in a coalition ominously called Save Our Neighborhoods, Save Our City (SON-SOC). Both organizations were started by IAF-trained organizers in the 1970s in neighborhoods where white ethnics responded to the arrival of African American and Hispanic families with reactionary language and methods. In these neighborhoods, the dog-whistle rhetoric used by people like Republican mayoral candidate Bernard Epton and alderman Ed Vrdolyak, the leader of the anti-Washington faction during the infamous "Council Wars," resonated widely. During SON-SOC's first convention in 1984, the 750 delegates issued a "Declaration of Neighborhood Independence," soon nicknamed the "white ethnic agenda," centered on neighborhood preservation and opposition to racial integration.[90]

Its racist overtones notwithstanding, the parochialism and "us versus them" mentality saturating SON-SOC's rhetoric and worldview was actually an inbuilt feature of neighborhood politics in the 1970s and 1980s across the country, with "many urban dwellers [seeing] their neighborhoods as imperiled entities precariously existing in openly hostile territory."[91] When professional organizers made the conscious decision to steer the prospection phase toward locally framed issues that bypassed broader questions of exploitation and oppression or aligned with dominant norms—when, for instance, they avoided bringing race to the table or chose to organize around the existence of a pornographic bookstore rather than corporate tax evasion—they reinforced parochialism. In such occasions, many organizers were placed into a real predicament: they were torn between the "let the people decide" outlook at the heart of their own professional ethos and standards, and their own politics and commitments. As a result, many of them were fired or resigned from such organizations—sometimes they quit the work altogether. Arguably, the development of citywide and statewide coalitions from the 1990s, bringing together several local community groups as well as unions and advocacy groups, made a dent in localist tendencies, but they did not disappear altogether.

Because most community organizing groups were tax-exempt, 501(c)(3) nonprofit organizations, their participation in the electoral process could happen only on a minor scale, from the margins. They could not endorse candidates running for office, whether in the form of direct financial support or setting up canvassing operations. They could engage only in overtly nonpartisan activities, such as civic education campaigns and voter registration efforts. However, one cannot deduce community groups' actual practices from these legal restrictions. Sociologist Nicole Marwell's analyses on community-based organizations (CBOs) in Brooklyn show that these organizations are part of a larger three-way, indirect patronage exchange system between voters and elected officials, where CBOs are the prime organizational vessel to mobilize and organize voters on the one hand and influence the allocation of public resources such as service contracts on the other.[92] The position they really occupy in the local political field is that of a power broker, "connecting [poor neighborhoods] into larger organizational systems of economic and political decision making."[93] Their intermediary position is grounded in three interdependent activities: educating members about electoral issues and building reliable voting constituencies; displaying the constituency during large public events and community forums where candidates for office are invited to participate; and converting these performances into an electoral force capable of influencing the outcome of elections.

Although Marwell provides a welcome analytical alternative to approaches that reduce poverty and inequality to interpersonal relationships and a dearth in social capital by bringing formal organizations into the picture, she does not delve into interorganizational competition and the symbolic struggles that give meaning to these relationships.

And yet, such struggles matter because they shape positions that are interrelated. This is particularly true of the struggles over the definition of who the community's legitimate representatives should be.

Based on an investigation of nine Boston community development organizations conducted in the early 2010s, sociologist Jeremy Levine proposes another reading of these organizations' political role. They occupy a structurally ambivalent position because they are both essential to state functions largely based on public-private partnerships and are relatively autonomous from bureaucratic or electoral control. They are "nonelected neighborhood representatives" who have "actually superseded elected officials as the legitimate representatives of poor neighborhoods."[94] It is not so much that elected officials have become irrelevant but that community-based organizations appear to be more legitimate representatives in the eyes of both residents and private funders: only they can really capture and redistribute financial resources intended for urban development more effectively, while elected officials are confined to roles of political figuration (inaugurations, social events, and so on). What is central in the "privatization" of representation is that the claims made by community-based organizations are not validated through electoral channels but certified by agents of the philanthropic field, whose subordinating contributions give them "significant influence in urban affairs."[95]

Community-based organizations are not monolithic, however. They are a wide umbrella that hides real differences between organizations.[96] Although they all share a common attachment to the notion of community, there are also differences between the way they operate, which fuel fierce battles for the definition of the right way to push for residents' interests. Community organizers often see community development with deep skepticism, for instance. In the words of one Chicago organizer who worked for ACORN in the 2000s and went on to head one of the city's largest community organizing groups, "Community development often is outsiders coming in telling the community 'This is what's best for you, we have a plan for you.' I think it's good to develop a community through economic influx and things like that, but oftentimes community development is done in a vacuum, and is not, doesn't have the actual people who are indigenous to that community."[97] In a political context where, since the 1970s, the ability to encourage such indigenous participation from ordinary citizens has become a legitimating resource for the ruling classes, people who claim that this is precisely their area of expertise produce a symbolic good that can yield substantial profits when converted into the electoral arena.

A Community Organizer in the White House

The other mechanism that pushed for the incorporation of community organizing into Democratic Party networks can be located not at the organizational level but at the level of job positions themselves. As a long-standing research tradition in political sociology has shown, not all occupations predispose equally to running for office. Nor do they leave the same imprint on political professionals' electoral fortunes.[98]

Of course, the most famous example of a former community organizer getting elected to office is Barack Obama. His 2008 election brought about a fundamental change: the label gained significant symbolic currency and was now seen as a springboard for political careers. The year 2008 therefore represents a moment of supreme legitimation for professional community organizing, as the first Black president was also the first ex–community organizer president.[99] The profession received the recognition it had struggled for for decades. It signaled the incorporation of community organizing into the political field. But this recognition came at a price. The title was inextricably woven into the fabric of Obama's mythicized trajectory at the expense of the profession as a whole. Through a classic dazzling effect, Obama's election completely obscured a much older, more structural phenomenon: around the same time as community organizing consolidated into a self-conscious professional group, organizer positions predisposed some of the people who held them to run for political office. In other words, that a community organizer became an elected official was nothing new.

Incorporation happened mostly at the local and state levels, where the costs to run a campaign are relatively lower and can therefore be met by candidates with fewer financial and political resources. A good example of this, again, is Chicago. In the 1980s, several people who had occupied previous positions as full-time paid organizers were elected to the city's fifty-member city council. Illinois Black Panther Party chapter cofounder Bobby Rush, who operated its Free Breakfast for Children Program and became the chapter's chairman after Fred Hampton's assassination in 1969, was elected in 1983. He served until 1993, when he moved up to the US House of Representatives.

Another example is Helen Shiller, whose political and professional trajectory, straddling volunteer and paid organizing work, illustrates the now-familiar processes that led to the consolidation of community organizing as a professional group. A former SDS member who got into Panther-inspired community work in the Uptown neighborhood when she came to Chicago from Wisconsin in 1972, Shiller was involved throughout the 1970s in forms of local organizing that built bridges between movement-oriented spadework and IAF-style community organization. In 1979, for instance, she worked as the executive director of the Employment Action Coalition, which fought against plant closures and pushed city government to support workers and their families. The organization was hosted by the Community Renewal Society, a century-old faith-based organization that defended a social justice understanding of religion and that took up IAF community organization techniques in the 1960s.[100] Shiller's position and politics also pulled her closer and closer toward electoral politics. In the context of Harold Washington's 1983 campaign and first term, she was one of the thousands of radicals who flocked to the (second) Rainbow Coalition that brought together white, Black, and Latinx people and who targeted local political office as an institutional opportunity to push for progressive reform. After a first unsuccessful bid, she was elected to Chicago City Council in 1987, where she stayed until 2011.[101]

In the 1990s and 2000s, other former community organizers throughout the country were also elected to political office, like Miles Rapoport in Connecticut and Karen Bass in California.[102] Such careers bore witness to community organizing's institutionalization as a recruitment channel to elected office, but they remained a minority channel. Out of the 190 people who have served as alderpersons on the Chicago City Council since 1983, only a dozen or so had worked as community organizers in a professional capacity before getting elected. Similarly, it does not mean that these positions mechanically shaped and educated future leftists. In 1996, for example, Chicago mayor Richard M. Daley appointed Danny Solis to head one of the city's fifty wards to replace the incumbent Democratic alderman, who had been convicted of corruption, as reward for Solis's political loyalty to the party. The former executive director of United Neighborhood Organizations from the predominantly Hispanic neighborhood of Pilsen, trained in the Alinsky tradition, Solis was one of a group of Latinx political professionals who had openly supported Daley in the 1989 election amid the growing demographic and political weight of the Latinx population.[103]

CONCLUSION

The relationships of interdependence that community organizing developed with philanthropy, the social movement arena, organized labor, and the political field all played into securing community organizing's place within the division of political labor and legitimating the organizer's role as a necessary cog in the wheel. This process of institutionalization went hand in hand with the circulation of practices and norms associated with the organizer's role and the claims made by the professional group that it knew how to solve a crucial contemporary political problem: how to produce citizen participation.

These structural relationships did not all carry the same weight, however. The mix of competition and collaboration with certain social-movement organizations, advocacy groups, and labor unions was the main terrain where community organizers formulated and defended their claims to being effective at bringing about social change and fostering ordinary people's participation and empowerment. These direct interactions were instrumental in spreading a professionally powered model of rationalized collective action beyond the confines of the community organizing world. But the most decisive legitimizing push came from other sources, philanthropy and the political field—two social arenas that absorbed community organizing into their margins while subordinating it.

The boundaries that shaped these intertwined yet unequal relationships were far from impenetrable, as the trajectories of Travis, Jane McAlevey, and Barack Obama demonstrate. After working for the Woods Fund, Travis went back to community organizing, working for several years for various groups, national and local, before doing a short stint at the Midwest Academy. When McAlevey left philanthropy in the mid-1990s, she entered organized labor, first as a coordinator of the AFL-CIO Stamford Organizing Project in Connecticut and later at SEIU in various capacities (senior national staffer, executive director, and chief negotiator for a union local in Nevada). And until Obama's political career went national in 2004, he kept a foot in the social-change philanthropy milieu through the Woods Fund. But a common characteristic to these trajectories and many others is that community organizing appeared early in people's careers, as a springboard that led to other endeavors, not the other way round.

Such trajectories also allowed the circulation of an ambiguous professional ethos and project, one where pullback and control, conflict and compromise, spadework and management consulting were so interwoven that it was impossible to disentangle them. Community organizing found a particular place within the division of political labor, at the unstable point where existing claim-making institutional actors encounter new actors, who do not (yet) master the rules and routines of the game, where "contained" and "transgressive" contentious politics meet, where nonprofessional protest movements challenge professionals' monopoly.[104] To secure such a position, community organizers offer a paradoxical antidote to political professionalization: a professionally powered deprofessionalization of politics.

What do community organizers look like today? Elements from my research in Chicago provide some answers. A database I compiled over the course of my PhD in the late 2010s suggests that a large majority of Chicago community organizers are women (66 percent). In terms of race, people of color seem to be an overwhelming majority (76 percent), with Hispanics and African Americans making up respectively 39 percent and 27 percent of the total. Chicago organizers are young too: 57 percent of them were born in the 1980s and 1990s. As a result, they belong to a "millennial generation" that, according to political scientist Ruth Milkman, can be seen as a distinct political generation "whose lived experiences and worldviews sharply distinguish them from previous generations of youthful activists." One of this generation's main characteristics is the fact that

> Millennials' aspirations have been frustrated by the growth of precarious employment and by an increasingly polarized labor market. Although these trends have affected all generations, they have influenced the worldviews of youthful labor market entrants most profoundly. The emergence of precarious and polarized employment preceded the Great Recession but was exacerbated by it, and this helped galvanize Millennial activism, especially among the college-educated.[105]

Although the socio-occupational origins of the individuals in the sample were difficult to identify, works on the imbrication of race and class and the overrepresentation of racial minorities in the urban working classes suggest that the community organizer professional group recruits beyond the middle and upper-middle classes and taps individuals with working-class origins who attained upward mobility through education.

In terms of education, indeed, there is a wide gap between community organizers and the constituents they work with. Sixty-seven percent of them have a bachelor's degree or higher, whereas between 2013 and 2017 it was the case for only 37.5 percent of the adults twenty-five and older in Chicago—the figure being lower for minorities and the residents of the poor neighborhoods whom organizers try to organize. Their salaries are lower than what people with a similar level of qualification make on average ($56,000 dollars for a bachelor's degree holder in Chicago in 2017): a lower-level community organizer, often called a field organizer, earns between $38,000 and $48,000. In this regard, in a city that is highly polarized along race and class lines, community organizers are not so different from the members of the intellectual fractions of the dominant classes who, as Pierre Bourdieu put it in the 1970s, "may find in the structural homology between the relationship of the dominated classes to the dominant class and the relationship of the dominated fractions [of the dominant class] to the dominant fractions the basis of felt and sometimes real solidarity with the dominated classes."[106] My ethnographic survey also suggests that, in the case of organizers who grew up in working-class families and neighborhoods, this sense of solidarity feeds on upwardly mobile trajectories where working-class origin further legitimates their position.

The surveys from the late 1990s and early 2000s that I mentioned in chapter 5 that pinned down some of the core sociological and demographic characteristics of the group throughout the country pointed to similar trends: a democratization of the group's class and race characteristics as well as a marked and consistent feminization. As a result, it is fair to say that the typical community organizer in Chicago today is a young, college-educated woman of color.

CONCLUSION

"**H**ere's the interesting thing that happens when you're president, or when you go through the experience of being president." Several of the 650 or so young people from Chicago and all over the world in the audience laugh. These attendees were hand selected to be part of the Obama Foundation's second summit in Chicago, and they listened to the community-organizer-turned-president converse with best-selling author and philanthropist Dave Eggers. Obama mused on his political trajectory and experience, his vision of power and human relations. Sitting comfortably in one of the two armchairs on the stage, dressed in an elegant dark suit and a gray shirt, he went on:

> So you start off, you're a community organizer and you're struggling to try to get people to recognize each other's common interests, and you're trying to get some project done in a small community, and you start thinking, "OK, you know what? This alderman is a knucklehead, they're resistant to doing the right thing, and so I need to get more knowledge, more power, more influence, so that I can really have an impact." And so you go to the state legislature, and you look around and you say, "Well, these jamokes . . ." (*laughter*) Not all of them, but I'm just saying, you start getting that sense of, "This is just like dealing with the alderman. I gotta do something different." Then you go to the US Senate and you're looking around, and you're like, "Oh, man!" (*laughter and applause*) And then when you're president, you're sitting in these international meetings, and it's the G20, and you got all these world leaders—and it's the same people! (*laughter*)

For Obama, this was a lesson about power and the exercise of power, about how "at every level, at the United Nations or in your neighborhood," power depended on "[having] a community that stands behind what you stand for. And if you do, you'll have more power, and if you don't, you won't."[1]

At the time, however, it was doubtful whether Obama still had such a community standing behind what he stood for—at least in Chicago. In 2015, three years before Obama gave his speech at the Obama Foundation's second summit, the University of Chicago was selected to host the future Barack Obama Presidential Center, a real estate project housing his presidential library and a museum. City hall, the university, and the Obama Foundation decided to build the library in Jackson Park, just south of the Hyde Park neighborhood, on the city's South Side. Hyde Park, where the University of Chicago and Obama's house are located, where almost half of the population is white, stands in stark contrast with the predominantly Black and low-income neighborhoods in its vicinity. Various community organizing groups, including the Kenwood-Oakland Community Organization (KOCO), warned that the anticipated increase in rent and real estate prices produced by this prestigious development would negatively affect poor residents in the surrounding neighborhoods. The community groups banded together to demand the signature of a binding agreement, a "community benefits agreement" to make sure that the Obama library would not accelerate a gentrification process already underway.

The demands did not sit well with Obama. During a conference in 2017, he conjured up his own past to remind everyone that he knew better: "I was a community organizer. I know the neighborhood. I know that the minute you start saying, 'Well, we're thinking about signing something that will determine who's getting jobs and contracts and this and that,' [and] next thing I know, I've got twenty organizations coming out of the woodwork." But the charismatic authority that Obama once held had eroded. During the 2019 municipal elections in Chicago, where six socialists with strong ties to the local organizing scene were elected to city council, a nonbinding referendum was held in polling stations near Jackson Park over the community benefits agreement proposal that KOCO and other groups argued was the best way to avoid the Obama library accelerating gentrification in the area. The proposal won 90 percent of the vote. Even Lori Lightfoot, Chicago's new mayor, supported the proposal. Alderwoman Jeanette Taylor, a former KOCO organizer who participated in a victorious thirty-four-day hunger strike in 2015 to prevent a public high school from closing, and who helped form a new socialist caucus in Chicago City Council, teamed up with another alderwoman and introduced a community benefits agreement ordinance in the city council. Taylor took issue with Obama for betraying his past, noting, "He's got a lot of nerve saying that. He's forgotten who he is. He forgot the community got him where he is."[2]

The gap between Obama's words and his acts bear witness to the ambiguous processes of legitimation and professionalization of community organizing, both as an ill-defined label and a particular form of collective action, that I have charted in this book. They also offer a clear summation of what community organizing looks like post-Obama.

On the one hand, Obama's words clearly point to the material and symbolic incorporation of the "community organizer" label and the practices it encompasses into the mainstream of US institutional life and the political order, to the point where it has almost lost its political, critical edge. Community organizing's institutional legitimacy is illustrated by the following example from Chicago: in the search for civilian commissioners to form the Community Commission for Public Safety and Accountability, a body that oversees the city's notoriously violent and racist police department, the posting explicitly listed community organizing as one of the "areas of expertise" being sought out, alongside law, public policy, social work, and psychology.[3]

As I have argued in the book, Obama's 2008 election was a turning point in that story. Yet the meanings of the "community organizer" and "community organizing" labels remain extremely murky. Aside from implying firsthand knowledge of ordinary people's living conditions and the ability to relate with the positively connoted "grassroots," they can refer to a lot of different things. Some use them as trendier terms to rebrand traditional party politics; others use them to signify prior experience in the civic-engagement sector of the nonprofit world; others still use them to refer to radical local politics that unfold outside of or against the electoral arena. A case in point is the way Ella Baker has been rediscovered and reinterpreted over the past twenty years, and in particular how her notion of spadework has been taken up by political actors as diverse as Black feminists, democratic socialists, and young progressive Democrats.[4]

On the other hand, both the campaign for a community benefits agreement and Jeanette Taylor's own trajectory, from community organizer to socialist alderwoman, speak to the position that the community organizing field occupies within the production of protest and left-wing politics that resist being co-opted into the status quo. In the various movements that have erupted in the wake of the Great Recession of 2007–2008, many core participants and leaders had prior experience as full-time, paid community organizers. The most famous example is probably that of Patrisse Cullors and Alicia Garza, two of the three Black women who initiated the Black Lives Matter hashtag in 2013, but there are plenty other examples in the movements against evictions, in the DREAMers' fight for immigrant rights, in the environmental justice movement, in international solidarity with Palestine, and in the waves of teachers' strikes that first started in Chicago in September 2012.

For professional community organizing, the resurgence of the left and the burgeoning of protest activity in the 2010s has translated into the multiplication of platforms and networks such as LeftRoots, the Forge, and *Organizing Upgrade* (now *Convergence* magazine) that seek to build more bridges with "activist" circles, certain sectors of organized labor, and progressive political groups. While a pragmatic bent eschewing ideology had dominated professional community organizing for decades—a lasting legacy left by Alinsky's IAF—the organizers who developed these collective spaces were intent on spelling out left-wing positions within the community organizing world and articulating a more structural critique of capitalism, racism, patriarchy, and imperialism.

I have argued throughout this book that these contradictory developments were best understood not so much in terms of nonprofitization but through the combined lenses of professionalization, professionalism, and professional work. Community organizing, as a professional practice encouraging the representation of members of the urban working classes and lower-middle classes through active participation in mostly local issue-based campaigns, was not born in the 1930s with Saul Alinsky, as is often believed. It emerged at the end of the 1970s after two hitherto independent expertise-shaped practices converged: the IAF's rationalizing militant liberalism, which I've called its political crème brûlée; and the radical spadework associated with Ella Baker and SNCC. While the former emerged from an original blend of reform-oriented urban sociology, social work, labor militancy, and management consulting, the latter that grew out of education and pedagogy and disseminated within certain sectors of the sixties movements. The formation of the group of professional organizers resulted from several factors converging toward one another—the development of an organizational apparatus, the symbolic legitimacy of neighborhood-based protests, the availability of private funds, and the existence and readiness of people who had been socially predisposed to take up organizer positions.

As a result of this process of group formation, the very definition of what an organizer was and should do changed. The IAF's norm of exteriority was challenged on political and practical grounds by newcomers with a background in sixties-style protest politics and replaced with demands that organizers should share similar experiences and social characteristics with the groups they sought to work with—in terms of race, in particular. One of the effects of this competing norm is that today in a city like Chicago, the majority of people working as community organizers are people of color. While redefining the contours of the organizer's role did have a lasting impact on the group's demographics and social composition, it did not fundamentally alter the nature of organizing as a professionally grounded relation of power. The organizer/leader distinction was upheld and reinforced by the organizer/activist dichotomy, which was itself justified and legitimized by a rhetoric of effectiveness (the claim that organizing "works").

Of course, things could have turned out differently. Had the IAF not managed to secure something of a monopoly over contentious citizen participation in the 1960s and 1970s and disseminated it throughout the country; had there been other institutional sites where former sixties radicals could have kept their political commitments going without pursuing a professionalization-from-within strategy (had more robust left-wing institutions existed, in other words); and had certain philanthropists and private funders not turned to social justice philanthropy, maybe professional community organizing would not have come into social existence. Had Obama not been elected president in 2008, the label would definitely not have gained such currency; the tension between a decades-long drive toward professionalism and professional control on the one hand and, on the other, the difficulties—if not impossibilities—to assert such professional control, would not have consolidated in such a way.

There is one true constant throughout the history of community organizing: paid community organizer positions have been overwhelmingly held by college graduates since Alinsky first started to carve them out in the early 1940s.[5] Being a college graduate in Alinsky's time and today mean very different things. While only 5 percent of adults over twenty-five had a four-year college degree or higher in 1940, in 2007 the proportion had reached 29 percent. Along similar lines, only 32 percent of employed workers held white-collar jobs in 1940; by 2006, the proportion had almost doubled to 60 percent.[6] The share of college graduates is relatively higher among so-called millennials, and that share has steadily increased over the years: in 2007, 31 percent of people between twenty-five and thirty-four had completed at least four years of college; in 2021, that percentage rose to 41 percent.[7] Whereas the share of people with college degrees has increased, it does not mean that cultural-capital-induced social distance has decreased. This qualifies organizers' recurring claim that they have more intimate connections with the communities they organize (in) than their competitors, activists and advocates. It might be true in terms of race or social and geographical origins, but definitely less so in terms of cultural capital.

The inbuilt tension between spadework and management consulting does not manifest itself at all times and evenly across people, organizations, and local community organizing fields. The balance between the two components is a dynamic one; it varies depending on imbricated factors: who occupies the job position—their prior backgrounds and social characteristics, their experiences, political education, and socially acquired predispositions toward dedication and care work—what position they have within the organization, what position the organization occupies within the local ecosystem of community-based organizations, and what position the community organizing field occupies within even broader ecologies of political power and representation.

For instance, a left-leaning white college graduate who works as a youth organizer in Black and brown impoverished neighborhoods in Philadelphia for an organization that maintains close ties with other social movement groups will probably emphasize more the spadework aspect, as opposed to a Black middle-aged former social worker working for an institution-based organization that mixes organizing, direct services, and legal counseling, who might stress the post-Alinskyite management component more and look at movements like Occupy Wall Street or Black Lives Matter with a mix of gusto and condescension. But the crucial thing here is that in both cases, the two people do not really *choose* a particular balance the way they would choose between two brands of cookies at the store. Rather, the balance very much imposes itself on them with the cumulative weight of layered social constraints and determinants. And in both cases, the minor component does not disappear either: regardless of what the individuals doing the work think (or hope) that they're doing, there is always an element of management consulting within spadework, and vice versa.

Saying that community organizer positions have become a major recruitment channel on the left does not mean that working as a community organizer mechanically produces politicization, as a cursory look at post-organizer career trajectories shows. Well-trodden paths include moving on to work for labor unions and policy institutes as well as think tanks, universities, and philanthropic foundations, but there are also lesser-known channels like yoga studios, management consulting firms, and business operations. A good example of how an organizing experience can lead to corporate consulting and business is Donnel Baird, a former community organizer in Brooklyn who later worked as a consultant under Obama and ended up creating a climate tech startup. An even more intriguing trajectory is that of Kathy Wylde, a former SDS member who worked as a community organizer around housing and development issues in New York City in the 1970s and crossed to the other side of the barricade in the early 1980s as she started working for banks, large corporations, and billionaires.[8]

Regardless of the career paths former community organizers later pursue, the experience of working and getting trained as a community organizer does have an impact on people's later professional experiences and worldviews, even if they stop working in that particular line of work. Remember Patrick's pronouncement, made "as an organizer," that Alinsky could have written the management books he stacked in front of me. Another telling example is Jane McAlevey, herself a former community organizer. In her books and trainings on the labor movement, she develops a professionally powered claim to being able to effectively identify the "real," "organic" leaders in a group of workers and, by doing so, win victories, which is not that different from the expertise Alinsky made a career out of. The provocative argument that there are correct and wrong ways to build worker power is not that far from Alinsky's assertion that he had discovered universal laws of change and organization. McAlevey calls for a return to the organizing tactics and strategies developed during the 1930s by the CIO, which saw workers as "[people] embedded in a range of social relationships in the workplace and in the community," and where "full-time organizers were *co-leaders* with rank-and-file organizers, the organic leaders among the workers,"[9] but her "whole worker organizing model" understates the dimension of professional expertise, which is obvious in her taking up the organizer/activist distinction, and the qualitative difference in formalization between the 1930s and today. In the 1930s, many CIO organizers were paid staffers, but contrary to today there was no relatively autonomous social group and layer that existed beyond organizational structures that they could identify with and that shaped their practices and worldviews.

What does it matter that community organizing, or even all forms of organizing in general, is shaped and driven by logics of professionalization? Why should anyone care that Alinsky and Garza and McAlevey and other organizers claim that they are skilled experts in the mechanics of organization building if the work that these professional organizers perform is effective and wins victories that improve people's lives in very concrete terms? And if professional logics hold such a grip over the work, shouldn't the spontaneity of radical upheavals falling outside of staff-heavy organizations be seen as a better hope for emancipatory politics?

To start addressing these difficult questions, I want to touch on two substantial qualifications to the professionalization thesis. First, community organizers are far from being a homogeneous, clearly defined professional group. The distinction between amateurs and professionals is fundamental to understand how the group has carved out its own territory, but as several studies on the history of sports have shown, the boundary between professional and amateur sports can sometimes be difficult to draw distinctly.[10] Whether you are the only staffer in a small neighborhood organization or whether you are one among dozens of staffers in a large citywide coalition that is affiliated with a national organizing network, your working conditions, wages, benefits, and physical workspace can vary greatly. Because working conditions remain particularly straining, especially for organizers occupying subordinate positions within their organization's hierarchy, and because the pay is still relatively low, turnover is quite high and burnout quite frequent. The advent of professional community organizing means that it has become possible to pursue a career as an organizer, but as one female organizer told me in Chicago, "there aren't that many lifers. So when people get frustrated they just leave the field. . . . I'm ancient. I'm an ancient organizer. I became ancient at twenty-eight."[11]

Second, professional community organizing does not exist in a social vacuum as a stand-alone entity; it belongs to a broader political ecosystem, but in a subaltern position. Contrary to how political consultants took over campaign and electoral work, for instance, community organizers have not managed to take full control over their work.[12] When they team up with labor unions, community organizations are very often relegated to performing organizational and political "dirty work," like phone banking or door knocking. More generally, organizer positions in all sorts of political organizations—labor unions, nonprofits, social movement groups, and advocacy groups—might have become more difficult to get for noncollege graduates, but they still occupy a subordinate position vis-à-vis more dominant positions within social justice organizations like policy staffers, full-time advocates, and top leadership positions, and even more so vis-à-vis other larger institutional players in the political ecosystem. To put it bluntly, if there is a management consulting component at the heart of community organizing work, it does not produce the same effects as corporate management consulting. The professional organizer's very existence is also regularly called into question by people who do not agree that the organization of political work should be monopolized by one particular group and should be professionalized, which means that their professionalism does not enjoy society-wide acceptance and legitimacy.

So if professionalization dynamics are actually heterogeneous, and if (community) organizers play a subordinate role in the division of political labor, why bother looking at organizing in terms of professional work? Besides, doesn't the focus on professionalization shift the attention away from the real bad guys, so to speak, the really dominant ones, who definitely stand on the other side of the barricade?

Fundamentally, issues of professionalization matter because the professional group, however much it lacks social recognition, however much it is plagued by structural underfunding and high turnover, has become one of the social constraints that people have to deal with when they get involved in political work writ large, alongside philanthropy, nonprofit status, celebrity contests, and social-media-driven entrepreneurialism. Professional organizer positions have become an unavoidable feature of US politics in general and movement politics in particular. They exist as an objective opportunity for anyone who wants to combine the imperatives of work in a capitalist society and a practical commitment to social justice. Conversely, those who are particularly predisposed toward organizer positions because of their background and politics but who choose not to become full-time paid organizers very often have other employment options or material resources that allow them to have the choice in the first place.

Highlighting professionalization dynamics, therefore, serves as a prism through which to look at how political work is actually performed. Submitting professionalization dynamics to critical scrutiny should not lead to a romantic valorization of unpaid, volunteer political work as being more authentic and more "real" than salaried work. First, the volunteer dimension obviously does not protect from burnout, internal rivalries, infighting, power relations, physical and symbolic violence, and domination.[13] Second, volunteer commitments presuppose that people have spare time that they can allocate to nonwork activities, which of course cannot be dissociated from class status. As Max Weber noted a hundred years ago, granting a financial compensation to elected officials was the only way to make sure that people who did not come from wealth could remain in office. In the case of community organizing, it is worth keeping in mind that changes in the group's class composition and racial and gender makeup happened *after* the professional group emerged. In other words, the consolidation of the professional group made this bottom-up democratization possible.

How can the pitfalls of professional control and power be avoided? What are the alternative practices and options to look to? I'm not really interested in (or capable of) providing a road map or a ten-step plan, but I want to conclude by pointing to possible roads to think on and move forward. To begin with, I don't think that a mass revolutionary uprising that would upend and redefine all social relations, while desirable, is a credible option in the current configuration of advanced capitalist societies. Despite the crumbling legitimacy of prominent political and social institutions and development of powerful practices, movements, and narratives calling into question neoliberal capitalism in recent years, the ruling class and their allies are still protected by thick trenches of all sorts, to borrow Antonio Gramsci's metaphor, which make the prospect of a fast war of maneuver against the state and capital highly unlikely.

A more realistic road, therefore, is to wage a war of position at the community organizing level; the first main possibility is to tinker with the organizer side of the organizing relation. In an analysis of the state and prospects of the US left after the 2020 presidential election, historian and activist Mike Davis noted that one of the key questions for the left was the building counterinstitutions that could sustain the radical activism that proliferated after the murder of George Floyd and produce "a new mass politics" that could "[bridge] social democratic reform and extreme economic conditions." According to Davis, the combination of Bernie Sanders's defeat in the 2020 primaries, distrust toward the possibility that the Democratic Party can ever move to the left, and the gridlocked nature of party politics in Congress means that the electoral road is not the best fit to channel these activist energies. Rather, "the goal must be the creation of more 'organizations of organizers' offering niches that allow poor young people, not just ex–graduate students, to lead lives of struggle."[14]

Davis does not get into the details of what such lives of struggle can look like or how exactly such a course of action might be implemented, but one of the main takeaways from the history of community organizing's professionalization is that the diversification of organizers' demographics was in part the product of a professionalization strategy. One way forward would therefore be to keep designing organizer positions as paid positions, but to find ways to dissociate the paid dimension from the sense of professional pride and cognitive superiority that fuel competition and contempt, fostering instead collaboration and cooperation. Because they break down traditional boundaries and barriers, mass movements and protests are particularly conducive to a challenge of existing practices and norms, as the complex interactions between Black Lives Matter groups and community organizing groups show.[15] But in contexts of movement lulls, it is much more difficult to push for deprofessionalization as a winning strategy since defending the group's dwindling resources can appear as a more reachable and desirable goal. Given how much the subordination to philanthropy constrains organizing work, developing independent sources of funding in order not to replicate the dependence on foundation money will probably be key—even if the recent controversy over the $6 million mansion in California that several prominent BLM leaders bought in 2020 has shown that issues of accountability and transparency in how the money is spent by movement actors are just as important as how much money was available in the first place.[16]

Because so much of the organizer's power of control comes from the monopoly they have (or try to have) over keeping an organization running and growing and developing its strategy, a second site for reflection might be located in actual organizational dynamics, whether you look at their internal structures, their governance, how people commit both to the organization and to one another, chains of accountability among all organizational members, and role specialization.[17] As legal scholar Dean Spade very pointedly puts it, one of the concrete ways in which mutual aid groups can "prevent and address overwork and burnout" is to "make internal problems a top priority" rather than pushing them under the rug or turning them into staff-only issues.[18] Speaking from my own experience and conversations with organizers in the US and France, and in light of research I've done for this book, turning organizer positions into temporary roles that several people, including nonstaffers, could take on over time, rather than entrenching them into fixed identities and job titles, for instance, might lead to a more long-term circulation of information, skills, and sense of authorization at endorsing the organizer's role. Not only would it lower the costs of entry into the role and make it more accessible to a wider variety of backgrounds and social characteristics, but it would also develop more solidly what Ella Baker called "group-centered leadership."[19]

There definitely is a managerial ring to a focus on intentional recruitment strategies or changes in organizational cultures, but I guess it goes with the terrain. The third possibility, which does exist outside of the organizer's contradictory professional hold, is to modify the other side of the equation, the community leader's side. Because as it stands, the organizing relation is largely predicated on the wide gap in terms of cultural capital between organizer and leader, a rising tide on the community leaders' side would probably level off the relation in more profound ways than intentional changes in recruitment patterns. Of course, concrete relationships between individual organizers and individual community leaders cannot be reduced to the one dimension of domination. Not only can these relationships produce genuine emotional bonds, mutual trust, and friendship that mitigate the power imbalance, but leaders can also influence organizers' work through their concerns and previous life experiences. They can, and they do: since the 1980s on, scores of Latin American leftists migrating to the US have brought their politics with them in their community commitments and confronted organizers' biases and attempts to control the entire organization process.

At a more macrosocial level, however, there still are tremendous obstacles to the development of working-class self-organization. Structural factors like educational attainment and class background still play a formative role in shaping electoral and nonelectoral political participation writ large.[20] A fundamental overhaul (and decommodification) of the education system, the implementation of tuition-free and debt-free public colleges and universities, and massive investments in building a strong and durable safety net would probably have a more long-term impact on changes in internal organizational cultures and on the likelihood of working-class self-activity and mass politics than the multiplication of the "niches" that Davis calls for.

In the wake of the worldwide COVID-19 pandemic, and against the backdrop of an accelerating climate crisis and soaring inflation, such prospects are not on the table in the foreseeable future, however. So in the meantime, all initiatives that keep pushing for a democratization of organizers' ranks *while simultaneously* challenging professional closure and autonomization seem like a sound course of action and reflection. To do so, it is probably best to look up to the spadework that Ella Baker and others have developed, and its radical-pedagogy perspective, rather than ogling the latest political crème brûlées.

ACKNOWLEDGMENTS

I am deeply indebted to numerous people for their help at all the stages that led to the publication of this book. I want to start by thanking all the people I met and interviewed for my PhD in Chicago and elsewhere, with particular thanks to Matt Ginsberg-Jaeckle, Alex Goldenberg, Alex Han, Rachel Johnson, Jawanza Malone, Mary Pattillo, Isaac Silver, Deborah Taylor, Micah Uetricht, and Kelly Viselman, who all helped me navigate the city and make sense of its organizing scene. The PhD dissertation that this book is based on was supervised by Laurent Willemez, and I want to take the opportunity to thank him once again for his care and support in critical times. I also want to express my gratitude to Risa, Ed and Kathy, and Joe, Jon, Mike, and Rob for welcoming me in their homes, and Mary Pattillo and Bill Sites for introducing me to my first contacts. Several chapters benefited from the comments and insights of Grégory Bekhtari, Alexia Blin, Heather Booth, Ambre Ivol, Jackie Kendall, Marie Plassart, and Alice and Staughton Lynd. I also want to thank my research center, the Centre de Recherche de l'Institut de Démographie de l'Université Panthéon Sorbonne, for its contribution to funding the book. People at Haymarket Books have played a decisive role in turning what started out as a casual conversation with Jon Kurinsky into a reality. As a former editor myself, I know how crucial yet invisible editorial work is. So earnest, wholehearted thanks to John McDonald, Katy O'Donnell, Michael Trudeau, and Aaron Petcoff for their trust and the quality and accuracy of their feedback. The book would look quite different without them. Finally, I want to thank Marie for her advice, support, and presence—and so much more that language can't adequately express.

NOTES

Introduction

1. Kelly Viselman, interview with author, April 4, 2016.
2. See, for instance, Mark R. Warren, *Dry Bones Rattling: Community Building to Revitalize American Democracy* (Princeton: Princeton University Press, 2001); Kristina Smock, *Democracy in Action: Community Organizing and Urban Change* (New York: Columbia University Press, 2004); John Atlas, *Seeds of Change: The Story of ACORN, America's Most Controversial Antipoverty Community Organizing Group* (Nashville: Vanderbilt University Press, 2010); Jeffrey Stout, *Blessed Are the Organized: Grassroots Democracy in America* (Princeton: Princeton University Press, 2010); Heidi J. Swarts, *Organizing Urban America: Secular and Faith-Based Progressive Movements* (Minneapolis: University of Minnesota Press, 2008); Loretta Pyles, *Progressive Community Organizing: Reflective Practice in a Globalizing World* (New York: Routledge, 2013).
3. Aaron Schutz and Mike Miller, eds., *People Power: The Community Organizing Tradition of Saul Alinsky* (Nashville: Vanderbilt University Press, 2015), 11.
4. Alicia Garza, *The Purpose of Power: How to Build Movements for the 21st Century* (New York: One World, 2020), 57.
5. Mie Inouye, "Starting with People Where They Are: Ella Baker's Theory of Political Organizing," *American Political Science Review* 116, no. 2 (2022): 533–546. See also Barbara Ransby, *Ella Baker and The Black Freedom Movement: A Radical Democratic Vision* (Chapel Hill: University of North Carolina Press, 2005); J. Todd Moye, *Ella Baker: Community Organizer of the Civil Rights Movement* (Lanham, MD: Rowman & Littlefield, 2013).
6. Garza, *The Purpose of Power*, 57–58.
7. The few existing surveys were carried out in the late 1990s and early 2000s by social work researchers or were published in mostly confidential collective works gathering individual portraits of professional community organizers. See, for instance, Sandra M. O'Donnell, "Is Community Organizing 'The Greatest Job' One Could Have? Findings from a Survey of Chicago Organizers," *Journal of Community Practice* 2, no. 1 (1995): 1–19; Terry Mizrahi and Beth Rosenthal, "'A Whole Lot of Organizing Going On': The Status and Needs of Organizers in Community-Based Organizations," *Journal of Community Practice* 5, no. 4 (1998): 1–24; Rose Starr, Terry Mizrahi, and Ellen Gurzinsky, "Where Have All the Organizers Gone? The Career Paths of Community Organizing Social Work Alumni," *Journal of Community Practice* 6, no. 3 (1999): 23–48. For a collection of testimonies by community organizers, see Kristin Layng Szakos and Joe Szakos, *We Make Change: Community Organizers Talk about What They Do—and Why* (Nashville: Vanderbilt University Press, 2007).

8   In the 2019 municipal elections in Chicago, for instance, six socialists were elected
     to City council—the highest number of socialist alderpeople the city has had
     since it was incorporated in 1837. Only one of them is a white male, all others are
     men and women of color and women, and most of them come from a working-
     class background. Four come out of the community organizing milieu.
9   Sanford Horwitt's authoritative biography on the man, published in 1989, is
     entitled *Let Them Call Me Rebel.* In 2010, Nicholas von Hoffman, Alinsky's
     former lieutenant at the Industrial Areas Foundation (IAF) turned *Washington
     Post* journalist, wrote his own memoir about his former mentor and called the
     book *Radical: A Portrait of Saul Alinsky.*
10   Frank Bardacke, *Trampling Out the Vintage: Cesar Chavez and the Two Souls of the
     United Farm Workers* (London: Verso, 2012), 68.
11   Mike Miller, for instance, who worked for Alinsky's Industrial Areas Foundation
     (IAF) as a community organizer in the late 1960s after years spent in the student
     and civil rights movement, portrays him as a "radical democrat" who "saw
     his work as creating the opportunity for self-government. At their core, the
     organizations he built were vehicles for the expression of democratic citizenship."
     Schutz and Miller, *People Power*, 27.
12   I am indebted to Aaron Petcoff for the expression, which is the most accurate
     depiction of Alinsky's politics that I know of.
13   A good overview of these criticisms can be found in Rinku Sen, *Stir It Up: Lessons
     in Community Organizing and Advocacy* (San Francisco: Wiley & Sons, 2003).
14   An influential variation on this theme is Marshall Ganz's *Why David Sometimes
     Wins: Leadership, Organization, and Strategy in the California Farm Worker
     Movement* (Oxford: Oxford University Press, 2009).

Chapter 1

1   Garrow, *Rising Star: The Making of Barack Obama* (New York: William Morrow,
     2017), 471–82.
2   Quoted in Robert Fisher, ed., *The People Shall Rule: ACORN, Community
     Organizing, and the Struggle for Economic Justice* (Nashville: Vanderbilt University
     Press, 2009), 3.
3   Hank De Zutter, "What Makes Obama Run?," *Chicago Reader*, December
     7, 1995, https://www.chicagoreader.com/chicago/what-makes-obama-run/
     Content?oid=889221.
4   Elizabeth McKenna and Hahrie Han, *Groundbreakers: How Obama's 2.2 Million
     Volunteers Transformed Campaigning in America* (New York: Oxford University
     Press, 2014).
5   Sheingate, *Building a Business of Politics: The Rise of Political Consulting and the
     Transformation of American Democracy* (Oxford, New York: Oxford University
     Press, 2016), 184–85. The organization, Organizing for America, was renamed
     Obama for America for Obama's reelection campaign in 2012.
6   Schutz and Miller, *People Power*, 12.
7   Peter Dreier, "Organizer in Chief?," *Huffington Post*, September 12, 2014, https://
     www.huffpost.com/entry/organizer-in-chief_b_6293598.
8   Fisher, *The People Shall Rule*, 3.

9   Quoted in John Atlas, *Seeds of Change: The Story of ACORN, America's Most Controversial Antipoverty Community Organizing Group* (Nashville: Vanderbilt University Press, 2010), 2.

10 Atlas, *Seeds of Change*, 3. John Atlas notes that given the scope of ACORN's voter registration operation—thirteen thousand workers in twenty-one states—problems would inevitably occur. Several canvassers did duplicate or fake voter registration forms, but they amounted to a tiny drop in a large bucket.

11 Atlas, *Seeds of Change*, 227.

12 Atlas, *Seeds of Change*, 240–244.

13 Attacks from the outside were actually worsened by ACORN's own internal predicament. In May 2008 the national leadership found out that Dale Rathke, the brother of ACORN founder Wade Rathke, had embezzled almost $1 million from the group and its affiliates. Not only that, but Wade knew the whole time and covered it up for years. Wade Rathke had been firmly in charge of the organization for almost forty years, but he had been delegating some of his administrative work to his brother for several years. Many outraged staff and board members forced Rathke to resign and to fire his brother. Two months later, the *New York Times* broke the story, which right-wing and far-right bloggers and pundits were happy to circulate and amplify.

14 Glenn Beck, *Saul Alinsky: The Four-Part Series*, August 21, 2016, https://www.glennbeck.com/2016/08/20/saul-alinsky-the-four-part-series.

15 I explain later in the book why it is historically more accurate to use the label "community organization practices" to refer to Alinsky's work.

16 Dreier, "Organizer in Chief?"

17 Saul Alinsky, "Interview with Saul Alinsky," *Playboy*, 1972; Saul Alinsky, *Rules for Radicals* (1971 repr., New York: Vintage, 1989), 152.

18 See, for instance, Peter Dauvergne and Genevieve LeBaron, *Protest Inc.: The Corporatization of Activism* (Cambridge: Polity, 2014); Dana R. Fisher, *Activism, Inc.: How the Outsourcing of Grassroots Campaigns Is Strangling Progressive Politics in America* (Palo Alto: Stanford University Press, 2006); Nancy A. Naples, ed., *Community Activism and Feminist Politics: Organizing Across Race, Class, and Gender* (New York: Routledge, 1998).

19 Eric Blanc, *Red State Revolt: The Teachers' Strike Wave and Working-Class Politics* (London and New York: Verso, 2019), 103–5.

20 See, for instance, Jeffrey Helgeson, *Crucibles of Black Empowerment: Chicago's Neighborhood Politics from the New Deal to Harold Washington* (Chicago and London: University of Chicago Press, 2014).

21 Schutz and Miller, *People Power*; Charles M. Payne, *I've Got the Light of Freedom: The Organizing Tradition and the Mississippi Freedom Struggle* (Berkeley: University of California Press, 2007), 243.

22 Sociologist Aldon Morris was probably one of the first to elaborate on the distinction in his groundbreaking study on the origins of the civil rights movement. Aldon D. Morris, *The Origins of the Civil Rights Movement: Black Communities Organizing for Change* (New York: Free Press, 1984).

23 Ransby, *Ella Baker*; Jennifer Frost, *An Interracial Movement of the Poor: Community Organizing and the New Left in the 1960s* (New York: NYU Press, 2001); Payne, *I've Got the Light of Freedom*.

24 I have found a positive use of "mobilizer" to talk about Malcolm X, Martin Luther King Jr. and other Black radicals in the sixties in the work of historian Peniel Joseph, but it seems to be a highly idiosyncratic use. See Peniel E. Joseph, *Dark Days, Bright Nights: From Black Power to Barack Obama* (New York: Basic Civitas Books, 2010); Peniel E. Joseph, *The Sword and the Shield: The Revolutionary Lives of Malcolm X and Martin Luther King Jr* (New York: Basic Books, 2020).

25 *Merriam-Webster's Collegiate Dictionary*, sixth edition (Springfield, MA: G. & C. Merriam Co., 1949).

26 Joseph Lee, "War Camp Community Service," *The Annals of the American Academy of Political and Social Science* 79 (1918): 189–94.

27 Stanley Wenocur and Michael Reisch, *From Charity to Enterprise: The Development of American Social Work in a Market Economy* (Urbana: University of Illinois Press, 2001), chap. 17. A social work manual from 1922 characterized the community organizer as a type of professional social worker who shared with other prestigious professions or leadership positions (the economist, the management engineer, the labor leader, the public official) an interest in social reform. American Association of Social Workers, *Social Work: An Outline of Its Professional Aspects* (American Association of Social Workers, 1922), 21.

28 Frost, *An Interracial Movement of the Poor.*

29 The name is a pseudonym. Some of the names of the organizers I interviewed have been changed for anonymity purposes.

30 Patrick, interview with author, February 10, 2017.

31 Bardacke, *Trampling Out the Vintage*, 68.

32 Bardacke, 79.

33 Jane McAlevey, *No Shortcuts: Organizing for Power in the New Gilded Age* (New York: Oxford University Press, 2016), 27–70.

34 David Moberg, "Union Buster," *Chicago Reader*, July 23, 1992, https://www. chicagoreader.com/chicago/union-buster/Content?oid=880122.

35 Art Kleiner, *The Age of Heretics: A History of the Radical Thinkers Who Reinvented Corporate Management* (San Francisco: Jossey-Bass, 2008).

36 Charles Tilly, *Social Movements, 1768–2004* (Boulder: Paradigm Publishers, 2004), 156.

37 Theda Skocpol, *Diminished Democracy: From Membership to Management in American Civic Life* (Norman: University of Oklahoma Press, 2004).

38 Amaney Jamal, *Barriers to Democracy: The Other Side of Social Capital in Palestine and the Arab World* (Princeton: Princeton University Press, 2007); Nicolas Jaoul, "Politics Against the Grain: The Dalit Movement of Uttar Pradesh in the Throes of NGOization," *Critical Sociology* 44, no. 4–5 (2018): 611–27; John Arena, *Driven from New Orleans: How Nonprofits Betray Public Housing and Promote Privatization* (Minneapolis: University of Minnesota Press, 2012); Myrl Beam, *Gay, Inc. The Nonprofitization of Queer Politics* (Minneapolis: University of Minnesota Press, 2018).

39 INCITE!, *The Revolution Will Not Be Funded: Beyond the Non-Profit Industrial Complex* (Cambridge: South End Press, 2007), 3.

40 Rosemary Ndubuizu, "Non-Profit over People: Have Organizers Stalled the Advancement of Social Justice?," *Comm-Org* (blog), 2010, https://comm-org.wisc. edu/papers2010/Ndubuizu.htm.

41 Magali Sarfatti Larson, *The Rise of Professionalism. A Sociological Analysis* (Berkeley: University of California Press, 1977), 209.

42 I want to thank Maud Simonet for bringing these distinctions to my attention.

43 Sarfatti Larson, *The Rise of Professionalism*, 45.

44 Julia Evetts, "The Sociological Analysis of Professionalism: Occupational Change in the Modern World," *International Sociology* 18, no. 2 (2003): 395–415.

45 Pierre Bourdieu, *Language and Symbolic Power* (Cambridge, MA: Harvard University Press, 1993).

46 Staughton Lynd and Alice Lynd, eds., *Rank and File: Personal Histories by Working-Class Organizers* (Chicago: Haymarket Books, 2011), 320–21.

47 Max Weber, "Politics as a Vocation," 1918, http://www.columbia.edu/itc/journalism/stille/Politics%20Fall%202007/Readings%20--%20Weeks%201-5/Weber%20-%20Politics%20as%20a%20Vocation.htm.

48 Sarfatti Larson, *The Rise of Professionalism*; Andrew Abbott, *The System of Professions: An Essay on the Division of Expert Labor* (Chicago: University of Chicago Press, 1988); Andrew Abbott, "Things Of Boundaries," *Social Research* 62, no. 4 (1995): 857–82; Andrew Abbott, "Linked Ecologies: States and Universities as Environments for Professions," *Sociological Theory* 23, no. 3 (2005): 245–74.

49 Abbott, *The System of Professions: An Essay on the Division of Expert Labor*, 40.

50 Abbott, 52.

51 Everett C. Hughes, "Professions," *Daedalus* 92, no. 4 (1963): 660.

52 Abbott, *System of Professions*, 280–314.

53 C. Wright Mills, *White Collar: The American Middle Classes* (1951; repr., New York: Oxford University Press, 2002); see also Dustin Guastella, "White-Collar Populism," *Jacobin*, November 25, 2019, https://jacobinmag.com/2019/11/white-collar-populism/.

54 In that sense, my perspective borrows from Adam Sheingate's work on how political consultants as a group managed, throughout the twentieth century, to assert exclusive control over the electoral aspect of political work. Significantly, Sheingate also used Andrew Abbott's concepts and framework.

55 Eliot Freidson, *Professionalism: The Third Logic* (Chicago: University of Chicago Press, 2001).

Chapter 2

1 Alinsky, "Interview with Saul Alinsky," *Playboy*.

2 Irving Cutler, *The Jews of Chicago: From Shtetl to Suburb* (Urbana: University of Illinois Press, 2009).

3 Sanford D. Horwitt, *Let Them Call Me Rebel: Saul Alinsky: His Life and Legacy* (New York: Vintage, 1992), 3–9.

4 Alinsky, "Interview with Saul Alinsky."

5 Martin Bulmer, *The Chicago School of Sociology: Institutionalization, Diversity, and the Rise of Sociological Research* (Chicago: University of Chicago Press, 1984).

6 Andrew Feffer, *The Chicago Pragmatists and American Progressivism* (Ithaca: Cornell University Press, 1993). On the influence of pragmatism on Chicago-style urban sociology, see also Mustafa Emirbayer and Matthew Desmond, *The Racial Order* (Chicago and London: University of Chicago Press, 2015), 1–16.

7 Bulmer, *The Chicago School of Sociology*, 12.

8   Robert E. Park and Ernest W. Burgess, *Introduction to the Science of Sociology*, 3rd ed. (1921; repr., Chicago: University of Chicago Press, 1972), 163.

9   Robert E. Park and Ernest W. Burgess, *The City: Suggestions for Investigation of Human Behavior in the Urban Environment* (Chicago: University of Chicago Press, 1984), 104.

10 Ernest W. Burgess, "The Social Survey: A Field for Constructive Service by Departments of Sociology," *American Journal of Sociology* 21 (1916): 492–500.

11 Lawrence J. Engel, "Saul D. Alinsky and the Chicago School," *Journal of Speculative Philosophy* 16, no. 1 (2002): 50–66.

12 Horwitt, *Let Them Call Me Rebel*, 14.

13 Eric C. Schneider, *In the Web of Class: Delinquents and Reformers in Boston, 1810s-1930s* (New York: NYU Press, 1993).

14 Solomon Kobrin, "The Chicago Area Project—A 25-Year Assessment," *The Annals of the American Academy of Political and Social Science* 322, no. 1 (1959): 19–29; Steven Schlossman and Michael Sedlak, "The Chicago Area Project Revisited," *Crime & Delinquency* 29, no. 3 (1983): 398–462.

15 "Meeting of the Advisory Committee of the Area Project," May 18, 1936, box 14, folder 4, Chicago Area Project records, Chicago History Museum, Chicago, (hereafter, CAP archives).

16 Schlossman and Sedlak, "The Chicago Area Project Revisited," 402.

17 Eric C. Schneider, *Vampires, Dragons, and Egyptian Kings: Youth Gangs in Postwar New York* (Princeton: Princeton University Press, 2001), 190.

18 Park and Burgess, *The City: Suggestions for Investigation of Human Behavior in the Urban Environment*, 106.

19 Clifford Shaw, "Methods, accomplishments, and problems of the Chicago Area Project. A report to the board of directors of the Chicago Area Project," September 20, 1944, 1, box 4, folder 8, Anthony Sorrentino Papers, Part. I, Chicago History Museum, Chicago (hereafter AS archives).

20 John H. Ehrenreich, *The Altruistic Imagination: A History of Social Work and Social Policy in the United States* (Ithaca: Cornell University Press, 1985); Stanley Wenocur and Michael Reisch, *From Charity to Enterprise: The Development of American Social Work in a Market Economy* (Urbana: University of Illinois Press, 2001).

21 Alyosha Goldstein, *Poverty in Common: The Politics of Community Action during the American Century* (Durham: Duke University Press, 2012), 37.

22 Mary Follett, *The New State: Group Organization and the Solution of Popular Government* (New York, London: Longmans, Green & Co., 1918), 3–4.

23 Joyce M. Bell, *The Black Power Movement and American Social Work* (New York: Columbia University Press, 2014), 72.

24 Ehrenreich, *The Altruistic Imagination*; P. Nelson Reid and Gary R. Lowe, *The Professionalization of Poverty: Social Work and the Poor in the Twentieth Century* (New York: Aldine Transaction, 1999).

25 Wenocur and Reisch, *From Charity to Enterprise*, 112.

26 Settlement houses were created in the late nineteenth century in the poor urban areas of large cities in Britain and the United States by upper-class volunteers in order to improve the lives of the poor through direct services (daycare, literacy courses, health care) and, in the case of the US, to help newly arrived immigrants integrate into the mainstream of society and "Americanize" them.

27 Lizabeth Cohen, *Making a New Deal: Industrial Workers in Chicago 1919–1939* (Cambridge: Cambridge University Press, 1990).

28 James R. Barrett, *Work and Community in the Jungle: Chicago's Packinghouse Workers, 1894–1922* (Urbana: University of Illinois Press, 1990), 65, 77.

29 John T. McGreevy, *Parish Boundaries: The Catholic Encounter with Race in the Twentieth-Century Urban North* (Chicago: University of Chicago Press, 1996), 5.

30 Robert A. Slayton, *Back of the Yards: The Making of a Local Democracy* (Chicago: University of Chicago Press, 1988), 195.

31 Slayton, *Back of the Yards,* 198.

32 Timothy B. Neary, *Crossing Parish Boundaries: Race, Sports, and Catholic Youth in Chicago, 1914–1954* (Chicago: University of Chicago Press, 2016); Richard Gribble, "Urban Apostle: Edward Hanna and the City of San Francisco, 1912–1925," *Southern California Quarterly* 86, no. 4 (2004): 369–90.

33 Barrett, *Work and Community in the Jungle*, 240–63; Shelton Stromquist and Marvin Bergman, eds., *Unionizing the Jungles: Labor and Community in the Twentieth-Century Meatpacking Industry* (Iowa City: University of Iowa Press, 1997).

34 Harry Targ and Jay Schaffner, "The Jewish Progressive Tradition: Examples from Chicago's Labor and Socialist Movements," *Tikkun Daily Blog* (blog), February 24, 2016, https://www.tikkun.org/tikkundaily/2016/02/24/the-jewish-progressive-tradition-examples-from-chicagos-labor-and-socialist-movements.

35 Slayton, *Back of the Yards*, 199.

36 Quoted in Slayton, *Back of the Yards*, 202–3.

37 John M. Allswang, *House for All Peoples: Ethnic Politics in Chicago 1890–1936* (Lexington: University Press of Kentucky, 1971).

38 When Edward Kelly became mayor in 1933, after Cermak's assassination, he followed Cermak's insight and rapidly built a powerful political machine with the help of Cook County Democratic Party chairman Patrick Nash. Black voters, on the other hand, remained loyal to what they perceived as the party of Lincoln and were marginalized within the consolidating Democratic machine until the post–World War II era. William J. Grimshaw, *Bitter Fruit: Black Politics and the Chicago Machine, 1931–1991* (Chicago: University of Chicago Press, 1995).

39 Quoted in Eve L. Ewing, *1919* (Chicago: Haymarket Books, 2019), 68.

40 Ewing, 51.

41 Michael C. Dawson, *Blacks in and out of the Left* (Cambridge, MA: Harvard University Press, 2013); James J. Lorence, *Organizing the Unemployed: Community and Union Activists in the Industrial Heartland* (Albany: SUNY Press, 1996); Art Preis, *Labor's Giant Step: Twenty Years of the CIO* (New York: Pathfinder Press, 1974).

42 Alexander Keyssar, *The Right to Vote: The Contested History of Democracy in the United States* (New York: Basic Books, 2000).

43 Lawrence Goodwyn, *Democratic Promise: The Populist Moment in America* (New York: Oxford University Press, 1976); Shelton Stromquist, *Reinventing "The People": The Progressive Movement, the Class Problem, and the Origins of Modern Liberalism* (Urbana: University of Illinois Press, 2006).

44 In resorting to the concept of "claim" to analyze the dynamic, collective making of representation, I am using the conceptual framework developed by Australian political theorist Michael Saward in *The Representative Claim* (Oxford: Oxford University Press, 2010).

45 Kathryn Close, "Back of the Yards. Packingtown's Latest Drama: Civic Unity," *Survey Graphic*, December 1940, box 74, folder 1, CAP archives.

46 Cohen, *Making a New Deal*, 53–99.

47 Two days after the July 14 meeting, national CIO leader John L. Lewis spoke at a mass meeting organized by the PWOC in Chicago. Bishop Sheil spoke in front of the thousands-strong audience, defending workers' rights and shaking hands with Lewis. The photograph of this moment made headlines throughout the country and, the next day, Armour officially recognized the PWOC and conceded a modest increase in wages.

48 Nelson Lichtenstein, *State of the Union: A Century of American Labor* (Princeton: Princeton University Press, 2003).

49 Alan M. Wald, *The New York Intellectuals: The Rise and Decline of the Anti-Stalinist Left from the 1930s to the 1980s* (Chapel Hill: University of North Carolina Press, 1987).

50 Marion K. Sanders, *The Professional Radical: Conversations with Saul Alinsky* (Harper & Row: New York, 1970), 31.

51 Luke Bretherton, *Resurrecting Democracy: Faith, Citizenship, and the Politics of a Common Life* (New York: Cambridge University Press, 2014); Harry C. Boyte, *Commonwealth: A Return to Citizen Politics* (New York: Free Press, 1989); Nicholas von Hoffman, *Radical: A Portrait of Saul Alinsky* (New York: Nation Books, 2010).

52 Horwitt, *Let Them Call Me Rebel*, 34–46.

53 There is no evidence in Sanford Horwitt's biography or Robert Slayton's detailed monograph on Back of the Yards.

54 Hoffman, *Radical*, 94.

55 Ironically, a couple of days after the BYNC held its founding meeting, he recommended Alinsky for a job opening in St. Louis to the director of the Young Men's and Young Women's Hebrew Association: "[Alinsky] is a good public speaker, has published a number of articles in scientific journals and is working with me in the completion of a study of a neighborhood gang which will be published sometime in 1940. Mr. Alinsky has had excellent training in sociology, and he has taken all the courses necessary for his Ph.D." Clifford Shaw to Gilbert Harris, July 17, 1939, box 14, folder 6, CAP archives.

56 *Chicago Daily Times* article, undated, quoted in Horwitt, *Let Them Call Me Rebel*, 105.

57 Quoted in Horwitt, 102.

58 Close, "Back of the Yards."

59 Horwitt, *Let Them Call Me Rebel*, 178–79.

60 Quoted in Goldstein, *Poverty in Common*, 37.

Chapter 3

1 UIC, box 9, folder 128, John O'Grady to Domenico Cardinal Tardini, August 21, 1959, 1–2, box 9, folder 128, Industrial Areas Foundation records, University of Illinois at Chicago, Special Collections and University Archives, Chicago (hereafter UIC).

2 Saul Alinsky to John O'Grady, August 27, 1959, 1, box 9, folder 128, UIC.

3 Saul Alinsky, "Private Memorandum to Msgr. John O'Grady," August 27, 1959, 1, box 9, folder 128, UIC.

4 Alinsky, "Private Memorandum to Msgr. John O'Grady," 3–4.

5   Giuliana Chamedes, *A Twentieth-Century Crusade: The Vatican's Battle to Remake Christian Europe* (Cambridge and London: Harvard University Press, 2019).

6   David Caute, *The Great Fear: The Anti-Communist Purge under Truman and Eisenhower* (New York: Simon & Schuster, 1978); Ellen W. Schrecker, *Many Are the Crimes: McCarthyism in America* (Princeton: Princeton University Press, 1998); Landon R. Y. Storrs, *The Second Red Scare and the Unmaking of the New Deal Left* (Princeton: Princeton University Press, 2013); Marla Stone and Giuliana Chamedes, "Naming the Enemy: Anti-Communism in Transnational Perspective," *Journal of Contemporary History* 53, no. 1 (2018): 4–11.

7   Mary L. Dudziak, *Cold War Civil Rights: Race and the Image of American Democracy* (Princeton: Princeton University Press, 2000); Thomas J. Sugrue, *Sweet Land of Liberty: The Forgotten Struggle for Civil Rights in the North* (New York: Random House, 2009).

8   Eric Foner, *The Story of American Freedom* (New York: W. W. Norton, 1998); Aziz Rana, *The Two Faces of American Freedom* (Cambridge, MA: Harvard University Press, 2010).

9   Harry S. Truman, "Special Message to the Congress on Civil Rights," February 2, 1948.

10   Sanford D. Horwitt, *Let Them Call Me Rebel: Saul Alinsky; His Life and Legacy* (New York: Vintage, 1992), 245.

11   Schutz and Miller, *People*; Bardacke, *Trampling Out the Vintage*.

12   Saul Alinsky, *Reveille for Radicals* (1946; repr., New York: Vintage, 1989), 64.

13   Robert E. Park and Ernest W. Burgess, *Introduction to the Science of Sociology*, 3rd ed. (1921; repr., Chicago: University of Chicago Press, 1972), chap. 9; Robert E. Park, *Race and Culture* (Glencoe: Free Press, 1950).

14   I use a gendered pronoun here because Alinsky's professional and political worldview made next to no room for women.

15   Alinsky, *Reveille for Radicals*, 55, 15, xvii.

16   Knights of Labor, "Declaration of Principles," 1886.

17   Mike Davis, *Prisoners of the American Dream: Politics and Economy in the History of the US Working Class* (London and New York: Verso, 2018), 55–104.

18   Alinsky, *Reveille for Radicals*, 27.

19   Steve Fraser and Gary Gerstle, eds., *The Rise and Fall of the New Deal Order, 1930–1980* (Princeton: Princeton University Press, 1989); Jean-Christian Vinel, *The Employee: A Political History* (Philadelphia: University of Pennsylvania Press, 2013).

20   Bardacke, *Trampling Out the Vintage*, 79.

21   In the late 1950s, he lamented the IAF's lack of editorial production: "It is mandatory that the Industrial Areas Foundation begin to concentrate on a series of publications which would be a synthesis of the ideas, concepts and experiences of the past eighteen years. It is also important that the Industrial Areas Foundation begin to organize and synthesize these materials for the benefit of the Foundation's thinking, as well as for others." The lessons compiled in *Reveille* were now "rudimentary concepts" that practice had since refined and sophisticated. But Alinsky did not manage to publish another book synthesizing his experience and thinking until a decade later. When he complained about the lack of publications synthesizing the "ideas, concepts and experiences" of the IAF, he did so from the perspective of a professional lamenting the lack of up-to-date marketable products, noting that such materials were "acutely needed in the consultation service

programs, in our own training of staff, and in the training of representatives of other organizations." "IAF Annual Report," 1958, 37, box 45, folder 644, UIC.

22 IAF grant application ("The Industrial Areas Foundation was organized in 1940 …"), ca. 1953, 2, box 29, folder 4, Emil Schwarzhaupt Foundation records, University of Chicago Library, Special Collections Research Center, Chicago (hereafter ESF archives).

23 Christopher D. McKenna, *The World's Newest Profession: Management Consulting in the Twentieth Century* (Cambridge, UK: Cambridge University Press, 2006).

24 For a contemporary analysis on these processes written by a former Trotskyist cadre turned anti-Stalinist CIA expert, see, for instance, James Burnham, *The Managerial Revolution: What Is Happening in the World* (New York: Van Rees Press, 1941).

25 Jennifer Karns Alexander, *The Mantra of Efficiency: From Waterwheel to Social Control* (Baltimore: Johns Hopkins University Press, 2008); John M. Jordan, *Machine-Age Ideology: Social Engineering and American Liberalism, 1911–1939* (Chapel Hill: University of North Carolina Press, 2010).

26 Horwitt, *Let Them Call Me Rebel*, 121.

27 Schutz and Miller, *People Power*, 4.

28 "Biographical Sketch—Taken from WHO'S WHO IN AMERICA," ca. 1953–1954, box 4Zd522, folder "Personal, misc, 1965–1972, 2/2," Industrial Areas Foundation records, Dolph Briscoe Center for American History, University of Texas at Austin (hereafter Briscoe).

29 Horwitt, *Let Them Call Me Rebel*, 215.

30 "Annual Budget, Industrial Areas Budget," undated [1952], 1, box 29, folder 4, ESF archives.

31 Lester Hunt, report, September 7, 1957, 1, box 37, folder 599, UIC.

32 [Saul Alinsky, Nicholas von Hoffman, Lester Hunt, in conversation with several Catholic and Protestant clergy members], "What specifically do you propose to do …," ca. 1959, 14, box 36, folder 594, UIC.

33 Nicholas von Hoffman, "Finding and Making Leaders," undated [1963], 1, box 50, folder 697, UIC.

34 [Alinsky, von Hoffman, and Hunt], "What specifically …," 15.

35 Bardacke, *Trampling Out the Vintage*, 12; Gabriel Thompson, *America's Social Arsonist* (Oakland: University of California Press, 2016).

36 "IAF Annual Report," 1955, 34, box 45, folder 641, UIC.

37 "IAF annual report," 1955, 4–7.

38 "IAF annual report," 1957, 14, box 45, folder 643, UIC.

39 Saul Alinsky to Marshall Field III, May 23, 1956, box 4Zd562, folder "Marshall Field, 1956–1962," Briscoe.

40 Saul Alinsky to Robert Hutchins, December 10, 1952, 2, box 4Zd563, folder "Ford Foundation, 1951–1961 (2/2)," Briscoe.

41 Horwitt, *Let Them Call Me Rebel*, 235.

42 "IAF annual report," 1957, 3.

43 "IAF annual report," 1958, 35.

44 McKenna, *The World's Newest Profession*.

45 Nicholas von Hoffman, "Finding and Making Leaders," undated [1963], 4, 9, box 50, folder 697, UIC.

46 [Nicholas von Hoffman], "Analysis of Events at the 61st and University Willis Wagons on June 18th, 1962," undated, 1, box 36, folder 593, UIC.

47 Von Hoffman, "Finding and Making Leaders," 7.

48 [Alinsky, von Hoffman, and Hunt], "What specifically . . . ," 10.

49 Sarfatti Larson, *The Rise of Professionalism.*

50 Nicholas Von Hoffman to the staff, April 5, 1962, 2, box 36, folder 593, UIC.

51 Nicholas Von Hoffman to Bob Squires, December 26, 1962, 2, box 35, folder 583, UIC.

52 [Von Hoffman], "Analysis of Events," 1.

53 [Von Hoffman], "Analysis of Events," 1.

54 Jack Rothman, "Three Models of Community Organization Practice," in *Strategies of Community Organization: A Book of Readings,* ed. Fred M. Cox et al., 2nd ed. (Itasca: F. E. Peacock, 1974), 22–39; Stanley Wenocur and Michael Reisch, *From Charity to Enterprise: The Development of American Social Work in a Market Economy* (Urbana: University of Illinois Press, 2001).

55 Jessamine Cobb, "Report on the Citizen Participation Project," October 24, 1961, 1, box 50, folder 12, ESF archives.

56 Minutes of meeting of Citizen Participation Project staff with Robert MacRae, February 10, 1958, 2, box 52, folder 3, Welfare Council of Metropolitan Chicago records, Chicago History Museum, Chicago (hereafter WC archives).

57 "Survey of the Field of Local Community Organization," 1959, 170, box 202, folder 4, WC archives.

58 "Standards for Evaluation of Community Councils," July 1, 1957, 5, box 51, folder 1, ESF archives.

59 Judith Ann Trolander, "Social Change: Settlement Houses and Saul Alinsky, 1939–1965," *Social Service Review* 56, no. 3 (1982): 346–65.

60 IAF secretary Dorothy Levin to the South East National Bank of Chicago, July 10, 1961, box 36, folder 590, UIC.

61 McKenna, *World's Newest Profession,* 26–50.

62 "IAF Annual Report," 1959, 10–11, box 30, folder 4, ESF archives.

63 Horwitt, *Let Them Call Me Rebel,* 289.

64 Horwitt, *Let Them Call Me Rebel,* 291.

65 "Position Description Data," March 18, 1947, box 35, folder 13, Committee on Education, Training, and Research in Race Relations, University of Chicago Library, Special Collections Research Center, Chicago (hereafter CETRRR archives).

66 Robert Bauman, "'Kind of a Secular Sacrament': Father Geno Baroni, Monsignor John J. Egan, and the Catholic War on Poverty," *Catholic Historical Review* 99, no. 2 (2013): 298–317.

67 Beryl Satter, "'Our Greatest Moments of Glory Have Been Fighting the Institutions We Love the Most': The Rise and Fall of Chicago's Interreligious Council on Urban Affairs, 1958–1969," *U.S. Catholic Historian* 22, no. 2 (2004): 33–44.

68 Quoted in Beryl Satter, *Family Properties: How the Struggle over Race and Real Estate Transformed Chicago and Urban America* (New York: Metropolitan Books, 2009), 171.

69 Daniel T. Rodgers, "In Search of Progressivism," *Reviews in American History* 10, no. 4 (December 1982): 113.

70 [Alinsky, von Hoffman, and Hunt], "What specifically . . . ," 7–8.

71 The first master's program in business was created in 1902 at Dartmouth College. In the 1940s, other elite universities like Harvard and the University of Chicago developed graduate programs for active senior managers. Steven Conn, *Nothing Succeeds Like Failure: The Sad History of American Business Schools* (Ithaca, NY: Cornell University Press, 2019).

72 Ransby, *Ella Baker*, 177.

73 Report, October 21, 1940, file no. 100-3731, "Saul Alinsky," FBI file for Saul Alinsky, https://vault.fbi.gov/saul-alinsky/saul-alinsky-part-01-of-01/view (hereafter FBI).

74 Report, January 22, 1941, file no. 100-522, FBI.

75 Arnold R. Hirsch, "Massive Resistance in the Urban North: Trumbull Park, Chicago, 1953–1966," *Journal of American History* 82, no. 2 (1995): 522–50; John T. McGreevy, *Parish Boundaries: The Catholic Encounter with Race in the Twentieth-Century Urban North* (Chicago: University of Chicago Press, 1996).

76 Saul Alinsky to Carl Tjerandsen, May 22, 1959, 1, box 29, folder 12, ESF archives.

77 Horwitt, *Let Them Call Me Rebel*, 315–62.

78 Bardacke, *Trampling Out the Vintage*, 67.

79 See, for instance, Ryan S. Pettengill, *Communists and Community: Activism in Detroit's Labor Movement, 1941–1956* (Philadelphia: Temple University Press, 2020).

80 Fred Ross to Alinsky, April 2, 1951, box 4Zd525, folder "Catholic Archdiocese, Budget, Letters, etc., 1951–1966," Briscoe.

81 Edgar Jamison, report, March 27, 1961, 3–4, box 36, folder 590, UIC.

82 Schrecker, *Many Are the Crimes*.

83 Businesspeople were the largest group; they accounted for a third of all thirty-seven board members between 1940 and 1972. Conversely, only two union leaders ever joined the IAF board: president of the Kansas Federation of Labor George Harrison, and Ralph Helstein, president of the Packinghouse Workers Union. In the 1940s John Lewis's daughter and secretary, Kathryn, also sat on the board, but she did not stay long.

84 Edwin R. Embree, "The American Council on Race Relations," *Journal of Negro Education* 13, no. 4 (1944): 562–64. *Report* 5, no. 8, August 1950, 1, box 36, folder 8, CETRRR archives.

85 "Memorandum concerning the Industrial Areas Foundation's Application for a Grant from the Fund for the Republic," undated, 1, 3, box 4Zd525, folder "Ford Foundation, 1951–1961 (2/2)," Briscoe.

86 Thomas C. Reeves, "The Foundation and Freedoms: An Inquiry into the Origins of the Fund for the Republic," *Pacific Historical Review* 34, no. 2 (1965): 197–218.

87 Adolph Hirsch to Saul Alinsky, January 10, 1966, box 29, folder 18, ESF archives.

88 Bardacke, *Trampling Out the Vintage*, 69.

89 McGreevy, *Parish Boundaries*; Timothy B. Neary, *Crossing Parish Boundaries: Race, Sports, and Catholic Youth in Chicago, 1914–1954* (Chicago: University of Chicago Press, 2016).

90 Other major Catholic supporters included French philosopher Jacques Maritain. An influential thinker enjoying international recognition, Maritain tried to find a third—Catholic—way between laissez-faire liberalism and communism. The lead theoretician of Catholic social action at the time, his case for a democracy

spiritually regenerated by real, rational, organized citizen participation had an audience in Europe but also Latin America. Maritain became a close ally of Alinsky's, an intellectual confidant, and a steadfast advocate for Alinsky's call to activate democratic participation to fight against the twin evils of apathy and communism. In *Réflexions sur l'Amérique*, for instance, published in French in 1958, Maritain expressed his fascination for the multiplicity of intermediary bodies in the United States and extolled the IAF founder's call for a moral and democratic renewal. To return the favor, Alinsky had a copy of Maritain's book distributed to all IAF board members. See Jacques Maritain and Saul Alinsky, *The Philosopher and the Provocateur: The Correspondence of Jacques Maritain and Saul Alinsky*, ed. Bernard Doering (Notre Dame, IN: University of Notre Dame Press, 1994).

91   John O'Grady to Saul Alinsky, August 14, 1952, box 16, folder 240, UIC.
92   Bardacke, *Trampling Out the Vintage*, 77.
93   Romain Huret, *The Experts' War on Poverty: Social Research and the Welfare Agenda in Postwar America*, trans. John Angell (Ithaca: Cornell University Press, 2018).
94   Goldstein, *Poverty in Common*, 31–76.

Chapter 4

1   "The Alinsky-Carmichael Poverty Team," *Newsweek*, March 6, 1967, box 4Zd525, folder "Stokely Carmichael, 1967," Briscoe.
2   Andrew B. Lewis, *The Shadows of Youth: The Remarkable Journey of the Civil Rights Generation* (Hill and Wang, 2010), 212.
3   See, for instance, "Chicago Doesn't Need Alinsky," editorial, *Chicago Sun-Times*, January 25, 1968, box 46, folder 657, UIC.
4   Peniel E. Joseph, *Stokely: A Life* (New York: Basic Civitas, 2014), 173–97.
5   Max Elbaum, *Revolution in the Air: Sixties Radicals Turn to Lenin, Mao and Che* (London and New York: Verso, 2006); Doug McAdam, *Political Process and the Development of Black Insurgency, 1930–1970* (Chicago: University of Chicago Press, 1982); Michael Stewart Foley, *Confronting the War Machine: Draft Resistance during the Vietnam War* (Chapel Hill: University of North Carolina Press, 2003); Annelise Orleck and Lisa Gayle Hazirjian, eds., *The War on Poverty: A New Grassroots History, 1964–1980* (Athens: University of Georgia Press, 2011); Michael C. Dawson, *Blacks In and Out of the Left* (Cambridge, MA: Harvard University Press, 2013); Laura Pulido, *Black, Brown, Yellow, and Left: Radical Activism in Los Angeles* (Berkeley: University of California Press, 2006).
6   Huret, *The Experts' War on Poverty.*
7   Nancy A. Naples, *Grassroots Warriors: Activist Mothering, Community Work, and the War on Poverty* (New York: Routledge, 1998).
8   Saul Alinsky, "Seminar on Mass Organization," August–September 1965, box 29, folder 17, ESF archives.
9   Arnold R. Hirsch, "Massive Resistance in the Urban North: Trumbull Park, Chicago, 1953–1966," *Journal of American History* 82, no. 2 (1995): 522–50; Satter, *Family Properties*, 46–47.
10   Quoted in Ransby, *Ella Baker*, 140.
11   Great Lakes Institute, *Social Work and Social Tensions*, August 1946, 5, box 52, folder 2, WC archives.
12   Horwitt, *Let Them Call Me Rebel*, 366.

13 Grimshaw, *Bitter Fruit*; Satter, *Family Properties*.
14 Mary Lou Finley et al., eds., *The Chicago Freedom Movement: Martin Luther King Jr. and Civil Rights Activism in the North* (Lexington: University Press of Kentucky, 2016).
15 Quoted in Horwitt, *Let Them Call Me Rebel*, 419.
16 Quoted in Horwitt, 394.
17 Charles E. Silberman, *Crisis in Black and White* (New York: Random House, 1964), 11.
18 Silberman, 207, 318.
19 Silberman, 317.
20 Silberman, 319–20.
21 Gerald Horne, *Fire This Time: The Watts Uprising and the 1960s* (Charlottesville: University Press of Virginia, 1995), 53.
22 Governor's Commission on the Los Angeles Riots, "Violence in the City—an End or a Beginning?" December 2, 1965, 85–86.
23 Dave Niederhauser to Saul Alinsky, September 14, 1964, 2, box 4Zd526, folder "Detroit, 1964–1967 (1/2)," Briscoe.
24 Horwitt, *Let Them Call Me Rebel*, 484.
25 Satter, *Family Properties*, 169–73.
26 See, for instance, "Open or Closed Cities," editorial, Christian Century, May 31, 1961, box 29, folder 14, ESF archives.
27 Joseph, *The Sword and the Shield*, 16.
28 Satter, *Family Properties*, 198.
29 Lois Willie, "Alinsky Here to 'Blow Town Apart,'" *Chicago Daily News*, January 23, 1968, file no. 100-3731-42, FBI.
30 Goldstein, *Poverty in Common*; James Q. Wilson, "Planning and Politics: Citizen Participation in Urban Renewal," *Journal of the American Institute of Planners* 29, no. 4 (1963): 242–49.
31 In *Delinquency and Opportunity* (Free Press, 1960), Richard Cloward and Lloyd Ohlin explain that delinquency resulted from young people's frustration, the absence of social norms that were not "middle class" to which they could identify, and the closure of opportunities. Since juvenile delinquency was not the result of individual pathologies but of a broader socioeconomic environment, delinquency prevention must therefore involve ambitious, broad-based programs channeling their energy toward less destructive modes of expression. Unsurprisingly, Ohlin and Cloward came out of the same intellectual tradition as Alinsky. Soon, their approach was applied into the Mobilization for Youth organization, on New York's Lower East Side, which strongly influenced the design of CAP's organizational vessels, the Community Action Agencies. Noel A. Cazenave, *Impossible Democracy: The Unlikely Success of the War on Poverty Community Action Programs* (Albany: SUNY Press, 2007), chaps. 1 and 2.
32 Saul D. Alinsky, "The War on Poverty-Political Pornography," *Journal of Social Issues* 21, no. 1 (1965): 47.
33 Silberman, *Crisis in Black and White*, 321.
34 Peter Bart, "'Radical' Teaches Revolt to Clerics," *New York Times*, August 2, 1965, file no. 100-3731, FBI.
35 Patrick Anderson, "Making Trouble Is Alinsky's Business," *New York Times Magazine*, October 6, 1966, box 4Zd570, Briscoe.

36   "Chicago Doesn't Need Alinsky."

37   William F. Buckley, "The Fashionable Saul Alinsky—Trouble Maker," *Chicago Daily News*, October 19, 1966, quoted in file no. 100-3731, FBI.

38   Horwitt, *Let Them Call Me Rebel*, 493.

39   Horwitt, 469.

40   Matt Giles, "The Genius of the Playboy Interview," *Longreads* (blog), September 29, 2017, https://longreads.com/2017/09/29/the-genius-of-the-playboy-interview.

41   Sanders, *The Professional Radical*, 34–35.

42   Horwitt, 467–68.

43   Anderson, "Making Trouble Is Alinsky's Business."

44   "Plato on the Barricades," *Economist*, May 1967, box 52, folder 708, UIC.

45   Lewis, *Shadows of Youth*, 204; see also Todd Gitlin, *The Whole World Is Watching: Mass Media in the Making and Unmaking of the New Left* (Berkeley: University of California Press, 2003).

46   Edward S. Herman and Noam Chomsky, *Manufacturing Consent: The Political Economy of the Mass Media* (New York: Pantheon Books, 2002).

47   Hillary Rodham to Saul Alinsky, July 8, 1971, box 4Zd559, folder "Hillary Rodham," Briscoe.

48   Alinsky, *Rules for Radicals,* xix.

49   "The basic tactic in warfare against the Haves is a mass political jujitsu: the Have-Nots do not rigidly oppose the Haves, but yield in such planned and skilled ways that the superior strength of the Haves becomes their own undoing." Alinsky, *Rules for Radicals*, 152.

50   Alinsky, 26, xviii, 7, 21.

51   Alinsky, 9–10, 194.

52   Kirkpatrick Sale, *SDS: The Rise and Development of the Students for a Democratic Society* (New York: Random House, 1973), 338.

53   Alinsky, *Rules*, 195.

54   Minutes of the Annual IAF Board Meeting," December 8, 1966, appendix A, 1, box 4Zd571, folder "IAF board, 1966–1972," Briscoe.

55   Mary Pattillo, *Black on the Block: The Politics of Race and Class in the City* (Chicago: University of Chicago Press, 2007), 118.

56   Saul Alinsky to board member George B. Shuster, January 28, 1969, 1, box 2.325/E457, folder "George N. Shuster," Briscoe.

57   US Census Bureau, *Current Population Reports*, ser. P-60, no. 51, "Income in 1965 of Families and Persons in the United States," US Government Printing Office, Washington, DC, 1967, https://www2.census.gov/prod2/popscan/p60-051.pdf.

58   Saul Alinsky to Edward Burke, January 11, 1960, box 36, folder 597, UIC.

59   *Fortune* journalist Charles Silberman, Arkansas Democratic Senator J. William Fulbright; philosopher Jacques Maritain; philanthropist Charles E. Merrill Jr., the son of one of the founders of the Merrill Lynch investment banking firm; and Democratic federal official turned Nixon adviser Daniel P. Moynihan are some of the names that come up in the archives.

60   "Saul Alinsky—The Organizer," *International Herald Tribune*, January 8, 1971, box 46, folder 657, UIC.

61   "Lectures and seminars given by Saul D. Alinsky during 1968," box 52, folder 708, UIC.

62 Saul Alinsky to Mr. and Mrs. Valentine E. Macy, October 3, 1967, box 4Zd532, folder "Valentine E. Macy," Briscoe.

63 Archie B. Carroll et al., *Corporate Responsibility: The American Experience* (Cambridge, UK: Cambridge University Press, 2012).

64 Thomas Frank, *The Conquest of Cool: Business Culture, Counterculture, and the Rise of Hip Consumerism* (Chicago: University of Chicago Press, 1998); Luc Boltanski and Eve Chiapello, *The New Spirit of Capitalism* (London and New York: Verso, 2018); Morgen Witzel, *A History of Management Thought* (London and New York: Routledge, 2017).

65 CNN Money, "A Database of 50 Years of *Fortune*'s List of America's Largest Corporations," https://money.cnn.com/magazines/fortune/fortune500_archive/full/1966/index.html.

66 Walter Cannon to Saul Alinsky, November 14, 1967, box 4Zd552, folder "A. T. & T., 1967–1969," Briscoe.

67 Walter Cannon to Saul Alinsky, December 18, 1969, box 4Zd552, folder "A. T. & T., 1967–1969," Briscoe.

68 John Sheridan Associates Inc. treasurer Gloria Morgan to Saul Alinsky, January 13, 1972, 1, box 2.325/E457, folder "John Sheridan Associates," Briscoe.

69 John Sheridan to Saul Alinsky, April 18, 1972, box 2.325/E457, folder "John Sheridan Associates," Briscoe.

70 David Moberg, "Union Buster," *Chicago Reader*, July 23, 1992, https://chicagoreader.com/news-politics/union-buster; Mike Davis, *Prisoners of the American Dream: Politics and Economy in the History of the US Working Class* (London and New York: Verso, 2018), 105–58; John Logan, "Consultants, Lawyers, and the 'Union Free' Movement in the USA since the 1970s," *Industrial Relations Journal* 33, no. 3 (2002): 197–214.

71 Box 4Zd563, folder "Auditors' certificate, 1958" and following, Briscoe; box 4Zd564, all folders, Briscoe.

72 Richard Anstett et al. to the Holy Family Rectory, August 15, 1970, 1, box 4Zd527, folder "Tom Gaudette," Briscoe.

73 Schutz and Miller, *People Power*, 124.

74 Charles Sheldon Jr. to Saul Alinsky, May 16, 1966, box 51, folder 701, UIC.

75 Samuel Austell to Saul Alinsky, March 5, 1967, box 51, folder 701, UIC.

76 Howard S. Becker et al., *Boys in White: Student Culture in Medical School* (1961; repr., New Brunswick and London: Transaction, 1992); Doug McAdam, *Freedom Summer* (New York and Oxford: Oxford University Press, 1988); Ziad W. Munson, *The Making of Pro-Life Activists: How Social Movement Mobilization Works* (Chicago: University of Chicago Press, 2009).

77 Donald Janson, "Alinsky to Train White Militants," *New York Times*, August 7, 1968, box 4Zd529, folder "I.A.F. national training institute (preliminary info), 1968," Briscoe.

78 Gordon Sherman to Saul Alinsky, December 19, 1968, box 4Zd532, folder "Marquis, 1968–1971," Briscoe.

79 "Application," grant application to the Rockefeller Foundation, ca. 1968, 13, 15, box 54, folder 730, UIC.

80 [Alinsky, von Hoffman, and Hunt], "What specifically . . . ," 7–8.

81 Karen Ferguson, *Top Down: The Ford Foundation, Black Power, and the Reinvention of Racial Liberalism* (Philadelphia: University of Pennsylvania Press, 2013).

82 J. Craig Jenkins and Craig M. Eckert, "Channeling Black Insurgency: Elite Patronage and Professional Social Movement Organizations in the Development of the Black Movement," *American Sociological Review* 51, no. 6 (1986): 812–29.

83 Schutz and Miller, *People Power*, 196.

84 Quoted in Schutz and Miller, 196.

85 Janson, "Alinsky to Train White Militants."

86 Staughton and Alice Lynd, interview with author, July 15, 2021.

87 Staughton and Alice Lynd, interview with author.

88 Staughton Lynd to Ed Chambers, April 2, 1971, box 4Zd532, folder "Staughton Lynd, 1968–1971," Briscoe.

89 Max Weber, *The Theory of Social and Economic Organizations*, trans. A. M. Henderson and Talcott Parsons (1920; repr., New York: The Free Press, 1947), 358–92.

90 Ed Chambers, untitled document, December 1, 1972, 10, box 70, folder 854, UIC.

91 "The Alinsky-Carmichael Poverty Team."

Chapter 5

1 "Excerpt From SNCC Central Committee Meeting regarding Forging a Relation with Saul Alinsky," January 20, 1967, Civil Rights Movement Archive, https://www.crmvet.org/docs/alinsky.htm. On the Lowndes County Freedom Organization, see Hasan Kwame Jeffries, *Bloody Lowndes: Civil Rights and Black Power in Alabama's Black Belt* (New York: New York University Press, 2009).

2 Ransby, *Ella Baker*; Goldstein, *Poverty in Common*; Payne, *I've Got the Light of Freedom;* Frost, *An Interracial Movement of the Poor.*

3 Frost, *An Interracial Movement of the Poor*, 1.

4 Quoted in Ransby, *Ella Baker*, 118.

5 Payne, *I've Got the Light of Freedom*, 364.

6 Joseph, *The Sword and the Shield*, 106.

7 People like Diane Nash and John Lewis, for the most part devout Christians brought up in the Black church, saw nonviolence as a moral crusade and philosophy that expressed itself through confrontational direct action (sit-ins, Freedom Rides); the other, more secular-minded group, which included Charles Jones and, later, Stokely Carmichael, endorsed nonviolence as a tactic that should not hamper other options, such as engaging in voter registration efforts. Joseph, *The Sword and the Shield*, 90–91; Lewis, *Shadows of Youth*, 106–11.

8 Joseph, *The Sword and the Shield*, 90.

9 Clayborne Carson, *In Struggle: SNCC and the Black Awakening of the 1960s* (Cambridge, MA: Harvard University Press, 1995), 20.

10 Robin D. G. Kelley, *Hammer and Hoe: Alabama Communists during the Great Depression* (Chapel Hill: University of North Carolina Press, 1990).

11 Payne, *I've Got the Light of Freedom*, 243.

12 Payne, 246.

13 Ransby, 70.

14 Payne, *I've Got the Light of Freedom*, 88.

15 Payne, 93–94.

16 Lewis, *Shadows of Youth*, 13.

17 Joseph, *The Sword and the Shield*, 89–90.

18   Myles Horton, with Herbert and Judith Kohl, *The Long Haul: An Autobiography* (New York: Teachers College Press, 1990), 57.

19   Mie Inouye underlines that "by the end of the 1930s, Highlander staff estimated that they had served about two thousand people in twenty-one CIO, AFL, and independent unions. Six alumni had been elected presidents of their union locals, twenty-two had become full-time union organizers, and many more had assisted in or directed local union membership drives and strikes." Mie Inouye, "The Highlander Idea," *Jacobin*, April 13, 2019, https://www.jacobinmag.com/2019/04/highlander-folk-school-tennessee-organizing-movements.

20   Aldon D. Morris, *The Origins of the Civil Rights Movement: Black Communities Organizing for Change* (New York: Free Press, 1984), 70.

21   Alinsky and Myles Horton knew each other and exchanged several letters in the late 1950s, but it never led to more substantial partnerships between the two organizations. See box 5, folder 75, UIC.

22   Inouye, "The Highlander Idea."

23   Payne, *I've Got the Light of Freedom*, 68.

24   Carson, *In Struggle*, 45.

25   Carson, 71.

26   Howard Zinn, *SNCC: The New Abolitionists* (1964; repr., Chicago: Haymarket Books, 2013).

27   Payne, *I've Got the Light of Freedom*, 237.

28   McAdam, *Freedom Summer,* 125.

29   Carson, *In Struggle*, 51.

30   Jack Minnis, "The Care and Feeding of Power Structures," ca. 1963–1964, 8, box 46, folder 654, UIC.

31   Mike Miller, "What Is an Organizer?" ca. 1963–1964, Civil Rights Movement Archive, https://www.crmvet.org/docs/miller-organizing.pdf.

32   Carson, *In Struggle*, 51, 103.

33   SDS, *The Port Huron Statement* (New York: Students for a Democratic Society, 1964), 24.

34   Wini Breines, *Community and Organization in the New Left, 1962–1968: The Great Refusal* (New Brunswick: Rutgers University Press, 1989), 57.

35   Breines, 124, 80.

36   Quoted in Breines, 128; Frost, *An Interracial Movement of the Poor,* 7–25.

37   Breines, *Community and Organization*, 131.

38   Breines, 133.

39   Quoted in Frost, *An Interracial Movement of the Poor,* 149.

40   Frost, 73–79.

41   Andrew Kopkind, "Of, by and for the Poor," in *The Thirty Years' Wars: Dispatches and Diversions of a Radical Journalist 1965–1994* (London and New York: Verso, 1995), 8–14.

42   Frost, *An Interracial Movement of the Poor,* 84–85.

43   Undated pamphlet, ca. 1966, box 23, folder 1, W. Alvin Pitcher papers, University of Chicago Library, Special Collections Research Center, Chicago (hereafter Pitcher archives).

44   Breines, *Community and Organization*, 137.

45   Frost, *An Interracial Movement of the Poor,* 85, 87.

46   Quoted in Breines, *Community and Organization*, 127.

47 Kopkind, "Of, by and for the Poor," 12.

48 Jennifer Frost, "Organizing from the Bottom Up: Lillian Craig, Dovie Thurman, and the Politics of ERAP," in *The New Left Revisitied* (Philadelphia: Temple University Press, 2003), 92–109.

49 Frost, *An Interracial Movement of the Poor*, 72.

50 Frost, 77.

51 Craig Calhoun, ed., *Sociology in America: A History* (Chicago: University of Chicago Press, 2007).

52 Frost, *An Interracial Movement of the Poor*, 72; Horwitt, *Let Them Call Me Rebel*, 525–26.

53 Martin Bulmer, Kevin Bales, and Kathryn Kish Sklar, eds., *The Social Survey in Historical Perspective: 1880–1940* (Cambridge and New York: Cambridge University Press, 1991).

54 Breines, *Community and Organization*; Sara Evans, *Personal Politics: The Roots of Women's Liberation in the Civil Rights Movement and the New Left* (New York: Vintage Books, 1980); Frost, *An Interracial Movement of the Poor.*

55 Frost, *An Interracial Movement of the Poor*, 78.

56 Breines, *Community and Organization*, 143.

57 Frost, *An Interracial Movement of the Poor*, 40, 41.

58 Michael S. Kimmel, *Manhood in America: A Cultural History* (New York: Oxford University Press, 2018).

59 Frost, *An Interracial Movement of the Poor*, 173, 176.

60 See, for instance, Rennie Davis's later engagement in the antiwar movement in David Farber, *Chicago '68* (Chicago: University of Chicago Press, 1994), 71–74.

61 John D. McCarthy and Mayer N. Zald, "The Trend of Social Movements in America: Professionalization and Resource Mobilization," in *Social Movements in an Organizational Society: Collected Essays*, ed. John D. McCarthy and Mayer N. Zald (1973; repr., New Brunswick: Transaction Publishers, 1994), 364.

62 Joyce M. Bell, *The Black Power Movement and American Social Work* (New York: Columbia University Press, 2014), 67.

63 Orleck and Hazirjian, *The War on Poverty*, 11.

64 Thomas J. Sugrue, *Sweet Land of Liberty: The Forgotten Struggle for Civil Rights in the North* (New York: Random House, 2009), 367–74.

65 Alan Altshuler, *Community Control: The Black Demand for Participation in Large American Cities* (New York: Pegasus, 1970).

66 Sugrue, 398.

67 Noel A. Cazenave, *Impossible Democracy: The Unlikely Success of the War on Poverty Community Action Programs* (Albany: SUNY Press, 2007).

68 Joshua Bloom and Waldo E. Martin, *Black against Empire: The History and Politics of the Black Panther Party* (Berkeley: University of California Press, 2014), 36.

69 Orleck and Hazirjian, *The War on Poverty*, 20.

70 "Non-professionals and Community Action," ca. January 1965, box 693, folder 2, WC archives.

71 This paragraph borrows from the core argument made in Bloom and Martin, *Black against Empire.*

72 Joseph, *The Sword and the Shield*, 257.

73 Helgeson, *Crucibles of Black Empowerment*, 22.

74 Peniel E. Joseph, ed., *Neighborhood Rebels: Black Power at the Local Level* (New York: Palgrave Macmillan, 2010), 8.

75 Robert O. Self, *American Babylon: Race and the Struggle for Postwar Oakland* (Princeton: Princeton University Press, 2005), 218. See also Timothy B. Tyson, *Radio Free Dixie: Robert F. Williams and the Roots of Black Power* (Chapel Hill: University of North Carolina Press, 2001); Jeffrey O. G. Ogbar, *Black Power: Radical Politics and African American Identity* (Baltimore: Johns Hopkins University Press, 2005); Peniel E. Joseph, ed., *The Black Power Movement: Rethinking the Civil Rights–Black Power Era* (New York: Routledge, 2006); and Tom Adam Davies, *Mainstreaming Black Power* (Oakland: University of California Press, 2017).

76 Joseph, *Neighborhood Rebels*, 15, 8.

77 The decision to expel white staff and volunteers grew out of a previous decision, taken in May, to prohibit white volunteers from organizing in southern Black communities because many Black organizers "believed that it retarded the advancement of black consciousness, solidarity, and self-reliance" and because working there was often too dangerous for whites. Hasan Kwame Jeffries, "SNCC, Black Power, and Independent Political Party Organizing in Alabama, 1964–1966," *Journal of African American History* 91, no. 2 (2006): 183.

78 Lewis, *Shadows of Youth*, 202–16.

79 Quoted in Jakobi Williams, *From the Bullet to the Ballot: The Illinois Chapter of the Black Panther Party and Racial Coalition Politics in Chicago* (Chapel Hill: University of North Carolina Press, 2003), 153.

80 Mike Davis and Jon Wiener, *Set the Night on Fire: L.A. in the Sixties* (London: Verso, 2020), 257.

81 IFCO brochure, undated, box 4Zd529, folder "IFCO, 1968–1969," Briscoe.

82 Ed Chambers to Saul Alinsky, June 25, 1968, 1, box 4Zd529, folder "Interfaith Foundation for Community Organization, 1967–1968," Briscoe; "Saul Alinsky Project Runs into Trouble," *National Register*, June 23, 1968, box 4Zd529, folder "IFCO, 1968–1969," Briscoe.

83 Quoted in Horwitt, *Let Them Call Me Rebel*, 508.

84 Saul Alinsky to Lucius Walker, July 2, 1968, box 4Zd529, folder "IFCO, 1968–1969," Briscoe.

85 Joseph, *Neighborhood Rebels*, 11.

86 Bloom and Martin, *Black against Empire*, 181, 182, 196; Paul Alkebulan, *Survival Pending Revolution: The History of the Black Panther Party* (Tuscaloosa: University Alabama Press, 2007); Donna Murch, *Living for the City: Migration, Education, and the Rise of the Black Panther Party in Oakland, California* (Chapel Hill: University of North Carolina Press, 2010).

87 Williams, *From the Bullet to the Ballot*, 128, 126.

88 Williams, 127–29; Jakobi Williams, "Bob Lee (1942–2017)," *Jacobin*, March 31, 2017, https://www.jacobinmag.com/2017/03/bob-lee-black-panthers-fred-hampton-chicago.

89 Williams, *From the Bullet to the Ballot*, 146.

90 Helgeson, *Crucibles of Black Empowerment*, 16, 17.

91 "Portfolio," September 1966, 1, box 23, folder 8, Pitcher archives.

92 L. Witmer, "Kenwood Oakland Community Organization," November 1967, box 23, folder 8, Pitcher archives.

93 "KOCO progress report," October 13, 1966, 1, 4, box 23, folder 8, Pitcher archives.

94   James Alan McPherson, "Chicago's Blackstone Rangers," *Atlantic*, May 1969, https://www.theatlantic.com/magazine/archive/1969/05/chicagos-blackstone-rangers-i/305741.

95   Curtis Burrell, "A Statement to the Black Community," June 17, 1970, box 755, folder 19, WC archives.

96   Murch, *Living for the City*.

97   US Census, "CPS Historical Time Series Tables," table A-1, https://www.census.gov/data/tables/time-series/demo/educational-attainment/cps-historical-time-series.html.

98   Joseph, *Neighborhood Rebels*; Max Elbaum, *Revolution in the Air: Sixties Radicals Turn to Lenin, Mao and Che* (London and New York: Verso, 2006); Matthew J. Countryman, "'From Protest to Politics': Community Control and Black Independent Politics in Philadelphia, 1965–1984," *Journal of Urban History* 32, no. 6 (2006): 813–61; Cedric Johnson, *Revolutionaries to Race Leaders: Black Power and the Making of African American Politics* (Minneapolis: University of Minnesota Press, 2007); Dan Berger, *Outlaws of America: The Weather Underground and the Politics of Solidarity* (Oakland: AK Press, 2005).

Chapter 6

1   Austin is now a majority Black neighborhood.

2   Joseph Heathcott, "Urban Activism in a Downsizing World: Neighborhood Organizing in Postindustrial Chicago," *City & Community* 4, no. 3 (2005): 277–94.

3   Rebecca K. Marchiel, *After Redlining: The Urban Reinvestment Movement in the Era of Financial Deregulation* (Chicago: University of Chicago Press, 2020).

4   Studs Terkel, "Interview with Gale Cincotta," July 7, 1977, Studs Terkel Radio Archive, https://studsterkel.wfmt.com/programs/gale-cincotta-discusses-community-organizing-fair-housing-and-loan-practices.

5   Joan Ecklein, *Community Organizers*, 2nd ed. (New York: Wiley, 1984), 1, vii.

6   Harry C. Boyte, *The Backyard Revolution: Understanding the New Citizen Movement* (Philadelphia: Temple University Press, 1980), xiii.

7   Gary Delgado, *Organizing the Movement: The Roots and Growth of ACORN* (Philadelphia: Temple University Press, 1986).

8   Peg Knoepfle, ed., *After Alinsky: Community Organizing in Illinois* (Springfield, IL: Sangamon State University Press, 1990).

9   Garrow, *Rising Star*, 1–41.

10   Satter, *Family Properties*.

11   Miller is probably the best-known advocate for claiming Alinsky as an important figure for the left, a position he has consistently defended over the years. See, for instance, Mike Miller, "Alinsky for the Left: The Politics of Community Organizing," *Dissent* 57, no. 1 (2010): 43–49.

12   Knoepfle, *After Alinsky*; John Kretzmann and John McKnight, *Building Community from the Inside Out* (Evanston, IL: Center for Urban Affairs and Policy Research, 1993). See also Sen, *Stir It Up*, for more historical context.

13   Garrow, *Rising Star*, 241–42, 281–83.

14   Barbara Ferman, *Challenging the Growth Machine: Neighborhood Politics in Chicago and Pittsburgh* (Lawrence: University Press of Kansas, 1996), 13.

15   Mark R. Warren, *Dry Bones Rattling: Community Building to Revitalize American Democracy* (Princeton: Princeton University Press, 2001).

16   Delgado, *Organizing the Movement*, 64.

17   The seven stages are research and analysis; initial contact through systematic door knocking; establishing an organizing committee and a clear issue to campaign around; preparing a neighborhood meeting; holding the meeting; organizing actions to build pressure; and evaluating the actions.

18   Quoted in Atlas, *Seeds of Change*, 39.

19   Boyte, *The Backyard Revolution*; Harry C. Boyte, Heather Booth, and Steve Max, *Citizen Action and the New American Populism* (Philadelphia: Temple University Press, 1986); Harry C. Boyte and Frank Riessman, eds., *The New Populism: The Politics of Empowerment* (Philadelphia: Temple University Press, 1986); Robert Fisher, *Let the People Decide: Neighborhood Organizing in America* (New York: Twayne Publishers, 1994).

20   Michael Stewart Foley, *Front Porch Politics: The Forgotten Heyday of American Activism in the 1970s and 1980s* (New York: Hill and Wang, 2013), 5.

21   Boyte, *The Backyard Revolution*, 7.

22   In 1978, for instance, Joseph F. Timilty, chair of the federal National Commission on Neighborhoods, which was established a year earlier in the wake of the National Neighborhood Policy Act to promote neighborhood survival and revival, stated "emphatically that much more authority can be better exercised, many programs can be better administered, and a higher proportion of public funds can be better spent at the neighborhood level." Quoted in Randy Stoecker, *Defending Community: The Struggle for Alternative Redevelopment in Cedar-Riverside* (Philadelphia: Temple University Press, 1994), 252–53.

23   Josh Pacewicz, *Partisans and Partners* (Chicago: University of Chicago Press, 2016); Elisabeth Clemens and Doug Guthrie, eds., *Politics and Partnerships: The Role of Voluntary Associations in America's Political Past and Present* (Chicago: University of Chicago Press, 2010).

24   Boyte, *The Backyard Revolution*, 61, 8.

25   On how competing visions and definitions of a shared entity work as a binding force, see Pattillo, *Black on the Block*.

26   Edward T. Chambers, *Roots for Radicals: Organizing for Power, Action, and Justice* (New York: Bloomsbury Academic, 2003).

27   Heathcott, "Urban Activism in a Downsizing World." For a thorough history of block clubs and Black-led neighborhood-based civic efforts on Chicago's West Side, see Amanda I. Seligman, *Chicago's Block Clubs: How Neighbors Shape the City* (Chicago: University of Chicago Press, 2017).

28   Dana R. Fisher, *Activism, Inc.: How the Outsourcing of Grassroots Campaigns Is Strangling Progressive Politics in America* (Palo Alto: Stanford University Press, 2006), 11–15.

29   Jackie Kendall and Steve Max, interview with author, March 16, 2017.

30   Delgado, *Organizing the Movement*, 123–61; Atlas, *Seeds of Change*, 37–46.

31   Gary, Delgado, *Beyond the Politics of Place: New Directions in Community Organizing in the 1990s* (Oakland, Applied Research Center, 1993).

32   Sen, *Stir It Up*, xxvii–xxviii. Another important institution that pushed for the recognition that organizing work could not do away with ideology was the Grassroots Policy Project, which was founded in 1993 by Richard Healey. A former antiwar activist, Healey was a leader in the New American Movement, which merged with the Democratic Socialist Organizing Committee in 1982

into the newly formed Democratic Socialists of America. See Richard Healey and Sandra Hinson, "Bringing Back Ideology," *Forge*, July 22, 2020, https://forgeorganizing.org/article/bringing-back-ideology.

33 Lilian Mathieu, "The Space of Social Movements," *Social Movement Studies* 20, no. 2 (2021): 193–207; Doug McAdam, Sidney Tarrow, and Charles Tilly, *Dynamics of Contention* (Cambridge and New York: Cambridge University Press, 2001).

34 Jim Field, interview with author, March 15, 2017.

35 Field, interview with author.

36 In the case of Roman Catholicism, for instance, the number of people becoming priests, nuns, and monks steadily declined in North America and western Europe in the second half of the twentieth century.

37 Richard A. Schoenherr and Annemette Sorensen, "Social Change in Religious Organizations: Consequences of Clergy Decline in the U.S. Catholic Church," *Sociological Analysis* 43, no. 1 (1982): 23–52; Robert Bauman, "'Kind of a Secular Sacrament': Father Geno Baroni, Monsignor John J. Egan, and the Catholic War on Poverty," *Catholic Historical Review* 99, no. 2 (2013): 298–317.

38 Madeline Talbott, interview with author, February 25, 2016; Atlas, *Seeds of Change*, 48–51.

39 Talbott, interview with author.

40 Andrew Kopkind, "ACORN Calling: Door-to-Door Organizing in Arkansas," *Working Papers for a New Society*, summer 1975, 19.

41 Elbaum, *Revolution in the Air*.

42 Ben Joravsky, "Community Organizers. A Community That Needs Organizing," *Neighborhood News*, May 14, 1993, box 10, National Organizers Alliance archives, University of Maryland Libraries, Special Collections and University Archives, College Park (hereafter NOA archives).

43 Sandra M. O'Donnell, "Is Community Organizing...."

44 Bureau of Labor Statistics, US Department of Labor, *Economics Daily*, "The Last Private Industry Pension Plans," January 3, 2013, https://www.bls.gov/opub/ted/2013/ted_20130103.htm.

45 Warren, *Dry Bones Rattling*, 86.

46 William Sander and William Testa, "Educational Attainment and Household Location: The Case of Chicago's Lakefront," *Economic Perspectives* 34, no. 4 (2010): 116–29.

47 Delgado, *Organizing the Movement*; Sen, *Stir It Up*.

48 Warren, *Dry Bones Rattling*, 90.

49 Fred Brooks, "Racial Diversity on ACORN's Organizing Staff, 1970–2003," *Administration in Social Work* 31, no. 1 (2007): 27–48.

50 Mark R. Warren and Richard L. Wood, *Faith-Based Community Organizing: The State of the Field* (Jericho: Interfaith Funders, 2001), https://comm-org.wisc.edu/papers2001/faith/faith.htm.

51 Bell, *The Black Power Movement*.

52 Talbott, interview with author.

53 Frank Dobbin and Erin Kelly, "How Affirmative Action Became Diversity Management: Employer Response to Antidiscrimination Law, 1961 to 1996," *American Behavioral Scientist* 41, no. 7 (1998): 960–84; Frank Dobbin, *Inventing Equal Opportunity* (Princeton: Princeton University Press, 2009).

54 Brooks, "Racial Diversity on ACORN's Organizing Staff."

55 Garrow, *Rising Star*, chaps. 39–40.
56 Boyte, *The Backyard Revolution*, 46.
57 Abbott, *System of Professions*, 293.
58 Ecklein, *Community Organizers*, 3.
59 See, for instance, Mark G. Hanna and Buddy Robinson, *Strategies for Community Empowerment: Direct-Action and Transformative Approaches to Social Change Practice* (Lewiston, NY: Edwin Mellen Press, 1994); George Brager, Harry Specht, and James L. Torczyner, *Community Organizing* (1973; repr., New York: Columbia University Press, 1987); Rachelle B. Warren and Donald I. Warren, *The Neighborhood Organizer's Handbook* (Notre Dame, IN: University of Notre Dame Press, 1977).
60 Alinsky, *Rules*, 7.
61 In 1967, for instance, several former ERAPers (Jill Hamberg, Paul Booth, Mimi Feingold, and Carl Wittman) published a ninety-five-page pamphlet called *Where It's At: A Research Guide for Community Organizing*, distributed by a number of radical presses and organizations, which an investigator from the US Senate called "a complete guide to the would-be community organizer for finding out any and all facts relating to any specific community so that radical groups can compile information that could enable them to organize and control any number of aspects of community life." United States Senate Committee on Government Operations Permanent Subcommittee on Investigations, *Riots, Civil and Criminal Disorders: Hearings before the Permanent Subcommittee on Investigations of the Committee on Government Operations, United States Senate, Ninety-First Congress, First Session, Pursuant to Senate Resolution 26, 91st Congress, June 18, 24, and 25, 1969*, vol. 19 (Washington, DC: US Government Printing Office, 1969), 4049.
62 Abbott, *System of Professions*, 54; Andrew Abbott, "Linked Ecologies."
63 Ecklein, *Community Organizers*, viii.
64 Michael Reisch and Stanley Wenocur, "The Future of Community Organization in Social Work: Social Activism and the Politics of Profession Building," *Social Service Review* 60, no. 1 (1986): 70–93.
65 Schutz and Miller, *People Power*, 43, 48.
66 Schutz and Miller, *People Power*, 44.
67 Frost, *An Interracial Movement of the Poor*, 92.
68 Jo Freeman, "The Tyranny of Structurelessness," *Berkeley Journal of Sociology* 17 (1970): 151–65.
69 Delgado, *Organizing the Movement*, 181.
70 Gregory D. Squires et al., *Chicago: Race, Class and the Response to Urban Decline* (Philadelphia: Temple University Press, 1989).
71 Boyte, *The Backyard Revolution*, 46.
72 Abbott, *System of Professions*, 79–85.
73 Warren and Wood, *Faith-Based Community Organizing*.
74 Kendall and Max, interview with author.
75 Quoted in Frost, *An Interracial Movement of the Poor*, 170.
76 McAdam, *Freedom Summer*, 204.
77 Elizabeth Clemens, *The People's Lobby: Organizational Innovation and the Rise of Interest Group Politics in the United States, 1890–1925* (Chicago: University of Chicago Press, 1997).
78 Heather Booth, interview with author, May 25, 2018.
79 Kendall and Max, interview with author.

80   Kendall and Max, interview with author.

81   Mike Miller, *A Community Organizer's Tale: People and Power in San Francisco* (Berkeley: Heyday, 2009).

82   "What Is the Chicago Community Organizing Cooperative?" ca. 1992, box 10, folder "Newsletter," NOA archives.

83   Invitation letter, 1994, box 9, folder "Gathering—1994," NOA archives.

84   "It's a Big World—Somebody Has to Change It!" *Ark*, fall 1993, 2, box 2, folder "Chicago Arts," NOA archives.

85   *Practicing What We Preach: The National Organizers Alliance Guide to the Policies and Practices of Justice Organizations*, first draft, ca. 2000–2001, box 4, NOA archives.

86   Kim Fellner to Gary Delgado, May 26, 1992, 1, box 9, untitled folder, NOA archives.

87   "It's Time. The National Organizers Alliance," letter sent to unknown recipients, ca. January 1993, box 9, folder "Originals," NOA archives.

88   Kim Fellner, "Reintegrating the Movement: What's Our Vision," *Social Policy*, winter 1993, 56, box 9, folder "Originals," NOA archives.

89   "2005 Summary Description. National Organizers Alliance Pension Plan," undated, i, addendum, box 1, folder 3, NOA archives.

90   Letter to members, March 19, 1996, box 10, NOA archives; "NOA Justice Pension Plan Coordinator/Organizer," ca. 1999, box 1, folder "Women's Group, IV," NOA archives.

91   "National Organizers Alliance Forges New Connections for a New Era," press release, May 1, 1993, box 10, NOA archives.

92   Wade Rathke to Kim Fellner, August 20, 1992, box 9, folder "Untitled— November Group, 1993," NOA archives.

93   The only example I found in the archives is the attempt that Terry Mizrahi, from the Education Center for Community Organizing at the Hunter College School of Social Work, in New York, made to host NOA in the early 1990s. How the partnership proposal was turned down is unclear.

94   Kim Fellner to Lance Lindblom, October 30, 1991, box 9, folder "Untitled—SC Nominations," NOA archives.

95   "Minutes of the Meeting of South Side Organizers," June 7, 1994, 4, box 1, folder "NOA Initiatives: Fundraising & Organizing Planning Group—1997, Meeting Notes and Agendas," NOA archives.

96   Daniel M. Russell, *Political Organizing in Grassroots Politics* (Lanham, MD: University Press of America, 1990), 123.

97   David Menefee-Libey, *The State of Community Organizing in Chicago* (Chicago: Center for Community Research and Assistance, 1985), 1.

98   *Midwest Academy Organizing Manual* (Chicago, 1984).

Chapter 7

1   Barack Obama, *Dreams from My Father: A Story of Race and Inheritance* (1995; repr., New York: Broadway Books, 2004), 133.

2   Sheingate, *Building a Business of Politics*; Bruce A. Desmarais, Ray La Raja, and Michael S. Kowal, "The Fates of Challengers in U.S. House Elections: The Role of Extended Party Networks in Supporting Candidates and Shaping Electoral

Outcomes," *American Journal of Political Science* 59, no. 1 (2014): 194–211; Kim Moody, *On New Terrain: How Capital Is Reshaping the Battleground of Class War* (Chicago: Haymarket Books, 2017); Skocpol, *Diminished Democracy.*

3   Edward T. Walker, *Grassroots for Hire: Public Affairs Consultants in American Democracy* (Cambridge, UK: Cambridge University Press, 2014), 192.

4   Adolph Reed, *Class Notes: Posing as Politics and Other Thoughts on the American Scene* (New York: New Press, 2000).

5   Frances Fox Piven and Richard Cloward, *Poor People's Movements: Why They Succeed, How They Fail* (New York: Vintage, 1977); Edward T. Walker and John D. McCarthy, "Legitimacy, Strategy, and Resources in the Survival of Community-Based Organizations," *Social Problems* 57, no. 3 (2010): 315–40.

6   Giving USA Foundation, "Giving USA 2018: The Annual Report on Philanthropy for the Year 2017" (Chicago, 2018).

7   Megan E. Tompkins-Stange, *Policy Patrons: Philanthropy, Education Reform, and the Politics of Influence* (Cambridge, MA: Harvard Education Press, 2016); Karen Ferguson, *Top Down: The Ford Foundation, Black Power, and the Reinvention of Racial Liberalism* (Philadelphia: University of Pennsylvania Press, 2013); Joel L. Fleishman, *The Foundation: A Great American Secret; How Private Wealth Is Changing the World* (New York: PublicAffairs, 2009).

8   Charles T. Clotfelter and Thomas Ehrlich, eds., *Philanthropy and the Nonprofit Sector in a Changing America* (Bloomington: Indiana University Press, 2001).

9   Joan Roelofs, "How Foundations Exercise Power," *American Journal of Economics and Sociology* 74, no. 4 (2015): 655.

10   Robert Reich, *Just Giving: Why Philanthropy Is Failing Democracy and How It Can Do Better* (Princeton: Princeton University Press, 2018), 143.

11   Ellen Condliffe Lagemann, *Philanthropic Foundations: New Scholarship, New Possibilities* (Bloomington: Indiana University Press, 1999).

12   Alan Rabinowitz, *Social Change Philanthropy in America* (New York: Quorum Books, 1990); J. Craig Jenkins and Abigail Halcli, "Grassrooting the System? The Development and Impact of Social Movement Philanthropy, 1953–1990," in *Philanthropic Foundations: New Scholarship, New Possibilities*, ed. Ellen Condliffe Lagemann (Bloomington: Indiana University Press, 1999), 229–56; J. Craig Jenkins and Craig M. Eckert, "Channeling Black Insurgency: Elite Patronage and Professional Social Movement Organizations in the Development of the Black Movement," *American Sociological Review* 51, no. 6 (1986): 812–29.

13   Rabinowitz, *Social Change Philanthropy in America*, 51.

14   "Strengthening the Community Organizing Field," July 11, 1995, box 1, folder "National Network of Grantmakers," NOA archives; Larry Parachini, *The Partnership to Fund Organizing: An Evaluation of the Project Prepared for the National Network of Grantmakers, the National Organizers Alliance, the Southern Empowerment Project*, January 1998, 1, box 1, folder "Untitled," NOA archives.

15   Jerome L. Himmelstein, *Looking Good and Doing Good: Corporate Philanthropy and Corporate Power* (Bloomington: Indiana University Press, 1997).

16   "NOA Pension Program: Summary," ca. 1996, 3, box 10, NOA archives.

17   Ferguson, *Top Down*; Susana A. Ostrander, "Moderating Contradictions of Feminist Philanthropy: Women's Community Organizations and the Boston Women's Fund, 1995 to 2000," *Gender and Society* 18, no. 1 (2004): 29–46; Joan Marie Johnson, *Funding Feminism: Monied Women, Philanthropy, and the Women's*

Movement, 1870–1967 (Chapel Hill: University of North Carolina Press, 2017); Susan Watkins, "Which Feminisms?" *New Left Review* 109 (2018): 5–76; Jenkins and Eckert, "Channeling Black Insurgency."

18 Joan Roelofs, *Foundations and Public Policy: The Mask of Pluralism* (Albany: SUNY Press, 2003).

19 Tim Bartley, "How Foundations Shape Social Movements: The Construction of an Organizational Field and the Rise of Forest Certification," *Social Problems* 54, no. 3 (2007): 229–55.

20 Warren and Wood, *Faith-Based Community Organizing*; Robert O. Bothwell, "Foundation Funding of Grassroots Organizations" (Washington, DC: National Committee for Responsive Philanthropy, 2000), https://comm-org.wisc.edu/papers2001/bothwell.htm.

21 Gary Delgado, *Beyond the Politics of Place: New Directions in Community Organizing in the 1990s* (Oakland: Applied Research Center, 1994). For a lengthy critical review of Delgado's book defending the legacy of Alinskyism, see Mike Miller, "'Beyond the Politics of Place': A Critical Review," *Comm-Org* (blog), October 9, 1996, http://comm-org.wisc.edu/papers96/miller.html.

22 David Garrow, *Rising Star: The Making of Barack Obama* (New York: William Morrow, 2017), 219.

23 Lawrence J. Engel, "The Influence of Saul Alinsky on the Campaign for Human Development," *Theological Studies* 59, no. 4 (1998): 636–61; Robert Bauman, "'Kind of a Secular Sacrament': Father Geno Baroni, Monsignor John J. Egan, and the Catholic War on Poverty," *Catholic Historical Review* 99, no. 2 (2013): 298–317.

24 Woods Charitable Fund, *A Report for the Year 1985*, 4. In author's possession.

25 William S. McKersie, "Local Philanthropy Matters: Pressing Issues for Research and Practice," in *Philanthropic Foundations: New Scholarship, New Possibilities*, ed. Ellen Condliffe Lagemann (Bloomington: Indiana University Press, 1999), 329–58.

26 University of Chicago, Special Collections Research Center, Irving A. Spergel papers, box 5, folder 5, *Woods Fund of Chicago: Evaluation of the Fund's Community Organizing Grant Program*, report written by Sandra O'Donnell, Yvonne Jeffries, Frank Sanchez, Pat Selmi, April 1995, 7.

27 Woods Fund of Chicago, "Increasing Organizing Capacity on the South Side: The First Two Years of the Woods Fund of Chicago's South Side Initiative" (Chicago: Woods Fund, 2007).

28 Center for Impact Research, "Community Organizing in Three South Side Chicago Communities: Leadership, Activities, and Prospects" (Chicago: Woods Fund, 2004), 7.

29 Woods Fund of Chicago, "Increasing Organizing Capacity on the South Side," 2.

30 Woods Fund of Chicago, 3.

31 Woods Fund of Chicago, 24.

32 Center for Impact Research, "Community Organizing in Three South Side Chicago Communities: Leadership, Activities, and Prospects," 6.

33 Travis, interview with author, February 7, 2017.

34 James C. Scott, *Weapons of the Weak: Everyday Forms of Peasant Resistance* (New Haven: Yale University Press, 1985).

35 Warren and Wood, *Faith-Based Community Organizing*.

36 "Report Card on Progressive Funders," undated, box 1, folder "NOA Initiatives: Think Tank Committee," NOA archives.

37 Woods Fund of Chicago, "Increasing Organizing Capacity on the South Side."

38 See, for instance, Kim Fellner, Ellen Furnari, and Terry Odendahl, "Money Talks," *Ark*, no. 6, January 1996, 32, box 2, folder "Chicago Arts," NOA archives. Fellner was NOA's coordinator, and Furnari and Odendahl worked with the National Network of Grantmakers. All three announced the joint effort by both organizations to "work together to leverage more money into progressive organizing."

39 "Looking for the Right Answers from the Left Foundations," *Ark*, no. 11, June 1998, 30–38, box 2, folder "Chicago Arts," NOA archives.

40 Doug Henwood, "Take Me to Your Leader: The Rot of the American Ruling Class," *Jacobin* 41 (spring 2021): 49–72.

41 "Looking for the Right Answers," 37.

42 Jane McAlevey and Bob Ostertag, *Raising Expectations (and Raising Hell): My Decade Fighting for the Labor Movement* (London and New York: Verso, 2014), 19–26.

43 Kendall and Max, interview with author.

44 McAlevey and Ostertag, *Raising Expectations*, 25.

45 "Looking for the Right Answers," 36–37.

46 Author's field notes, Chicago, April 2, 2016.

47 L. A. Kauffman, *Direct Action: Protest and the Reinvention of American Radicalism* (London and New York: Verso, 2017), ix.

48 Deborah Gould, *Moving Politics: Emotion and ACT Up's Fight against AIDS* (Chicago: University of Chicago Press, 2009); Paul Lichterman, *The Search for Political Community: American Activists Reinventing Commitment* (Cambridge and New York: Cambridge University Press, 1996).

49 Kim Feller, "Organizers Shut Down WTO: Crowd Gasps," *Ark*, no. 15, spring 2000.

50 Jacquelien van Stekelenburg, Conny Roggeband, and Bert Klandermans, eds., *The Future of Social Movement Research: Dynamics, Mechanisms, and Processes* (Minneapolis: University of Minnesota Press, 2013).

51 Zeynep Tufekci, *Twitter and Tear Gas: The Power and Fragility of Networked Protest* (New Haven and London: Yale University Press, 2017), x.

52 Political scientist and democratic socialist Alyssa Battistoni writes that when she learned how to organize she practiced "exercises like 'stake, take, do,' which lays out a sequence of questions for you: What is at stake for you? What will it take to win? What will you do about it?" And she points out that certain prescriptions and rules govern such seemingly mundane action: "You have to start with what matters to you and the person you're organizing before jumping into how hard it's going to be and why they should do it anyway." Alyssa Battistoni, "Spadework: On Political Organizing," *n+1*, spring 2019, https://www.nplusonemag.com/issue-34/politics/spadework.

53 Debra C. Minkoff, *Organizing for Equality: The Evolution of Women's and Racial-Ethnic Organizations in America, 1955–1985* (Philadelphia: Temple University Press, 1995).

54 Kenneth T. Andrews and Bob Edwards, "Advocacy Organizations in the US Political Process," *Annual Review of Sociology* 30 (2004): 493.

55 Skocpol, *Diminished Democracy*.

56 Steve Jenkins, "Organizing, Advocacy, and Member Power: A Critical Reflection," *WorkingUSA* 6, no. 2 (2002): 56–89.

57 Lichterman, *The Search for Political Community*.

58 Delgado, *Organizing the Movement*, 219.

59 Garza, *The Purpose of Power*; Layng Szakos and Szakos, *We Make Change*.
60 Woods's annual reports indicate that overall grantmaking declined between 2004 and 2014, from $3.5 million to $2.5 million, but grants classified as "Intersection" remained above a $1 million threshold. By contrast, community organizing grants, which became the second-largest giving category in 2005, ahead of policy, peaked at just over $1 million in 2007 and then declined continuously through 2012. Changes in the share of each of the grant-making categories confirm the centrality of donations classified as "Intersection," which between 2004 and 2014 consistently account for more than 40 percent of total giving, even exceeding 50 percent in 2010 and 2012.
61 Vanessa Tait, *Poor Workers' Unions: Rebuilding Labor from Below* (Cambridge, MA: South End Press, 2005), 44. Haymarket published a new edition of Tait's book in 2016.
62 Tait, 102.
63 Tait, 106.
64 On rank-and-file labor militancy in the 1970s, see Aaron Brenner, Robert Brenner, and Cal Winslow, eds., *Rebel Rank and File: Labor Militancy and Revolt from Below during the Long 1970s* (London and New York: Verso, 2010); Staughton Lynd and Alice Lynd, eds., *Rank and File: Personal Histories by Working-Class Organizers* (Chicago: Haymarket Books, 2011); Lane Windham, *Knocking on Labor's Door: Union Organizing in the 1970s and the Roots of a New Economic Divide* (Chapel Hill: University of North Carolina Press, 2017).
65 McAlevey, *No Shortcuts*.
66 Tait, *Poor Workers' Unions*, 191.
67 Ruth Milkman and Kim Voss, eds., *Rebuilding Labor: Organizing and Organizers in the New Union Movement* (Ithaca: ILR Press, 2004).
68 Jarol B. Manheim, *The Death of a Thousand Cuts: Corporate Campaigns and the Attack on the Corporation* (New York: Routledge, 2001). The title of Manheim's book quotes labor leader Richard Trumka, who was elected secretary-treasurer of the AFL-CIO in 1995: "Corporate campaigns swarm the target employer from every angle, great and small, with an eye toward inflicting upon the employer the death of a thousand cuts rather than a single blow." See also McAlevey, *No Shortcuts*, 50–58; Tait, *Poor Workers' Unions*, 1–20.
69 The profiles of the people who led these departments are significant. In 1998, former ULU organizer Kirk Adams replaced Richard Bensinger at the helm of the Organizing Department (Bensinger had led the Organizing Institute from its creation to the mid-1990s). In 2000, Adams was replaced by Mark Splain, who had started out as a community and welfare organizer in the 1970s before working for ACORN's ULU in the early 1980s. In 2002, Splain was replaced by former ACORN organizer Stewart Acuff.
70 Bruce Nissen, "The Effectiveness and Limits of Labor-Community Coalitions: Evidence from South Florida," *Labor Studies Journal* 29, no. 1 (2004): 67–88; John Krinsky and Ellen Reese, "Forging and Sustaining Labor-Community Coalitions: The Workfare Justice Movement in Three Cities," *Sociological Forum* 21, no. 4 (2006): 623–58.
71 Quoted in Tait, *Poor Workers' Unions*, 202.
72 Steve Early and Larry Cohen, "Jobs with Justice: Mobilizing Labor-Community Coalitions," *WorkingUSA*, 1997, 49–57.

73   Tait, *Poor Workers' Unions*, 191.

74   Atlas, *Seeds of Change*, 99–117; Amanda Tattersall, *Power in Coalition: Strategies for Strong Unions and Social Change* (Ithaca: ILR Press, 2010), 63–103.

75   Marc Doussard and Jacob Lesniewski, "Crossing Boundaries, Building Power: Chicago Organizers Embrace Race, Ideology, and Coalition," *Social Service Review* 91, no. 4 (2017): 585–620.

76   William Sites, "Beyond Trenches and Grassroots? Reflections on Urban Mobilization, Fragmentation, and the Anti-Wal-Mart Campaign in Chicago," *Environment and Planning A: Economy and Space* 39, no. 11 (2007): 2632–51.

77   Robin D. G. Kelley, *Race Rebels: Culture, Politics, and the Black Working Class* (New York: Free Press, 1996), 232–33.

78   Dan Clawson, *The Next Upsurge: Labor and the New Social Movements* (Ithaca: ILR Press, 2003).

79   *Politics & Society* published McAlevey's piece alongside three critical responses. Jane McAlevey, "The Crisis of New Labor and Alinsky's Legacy Revisiting the Role of the Organic Grassroots Leaders in Building Powerful Organizations and Movements," *Politics & Society* 43, no. 3 (2015): 1–41; Stuart Eimer, "The Crisis of New Labor and Alinsky's Legacy: Some Questions, Comments, and Problems," *Politics & Society* 43, no. 3 (2015): 443–46; Paul Osterman, "Building Progressive Organizations: An Alternative View," *Politics & Society* 43, no. 3 (2015): 447–52; Kim Voss, "Same as It Ever Was? New Labor, the CIO Organizing Model, and the Future of American Unions," *Politics & Society* 43, no. 3 (2015): 453–57. McAlevey later published her own response to the commentary on her personal website: https://janemcalevey.com/wp-content/uploads/2015/09/responding-to-the-commentaries-081315.pdf.

80   Stephanie L. Mudge, *Leftism Reinvented: Western Parties from Socialism to Neoliberalism* (Cambridge, MA: Harvard University Press, 2018).

81   Sheingate, *Building a Business of Politics*, 3.

82   Caroline W. Lee, Edward T. Walker, and Michael McQuarrie, *Democratizing Inequalities. Dilemmas of the New Public Participation* (New York: New York University Press, 2015); Michael McQuarrie, "No Contest: Participatory Technologies and the Transformation of Urban Authority," *Public Culture* 25, no. 1 (69) (2013): 143–75; Caroline W. Lee, *Do-It-Yourself Democracy: The Rise of the Public Engagement Industry* (Oxford and New York: Oxford University Press, 2015).

83   This was the argument made at the time by Harry Boyte and people from the Midwest Academy / Citizen Action milieu. See Boyte, Booth, and Max, *Citizen Action*.

84   Moody, *On New Terrain*, 130.

85   Kendall and Max, interview with author.

86   Bernard Ohanian, "Troublemakers in Training," *Mother Jones*, January 1988, 43.

87   Barbara Ferman, *Challenging the Growth Machine: Neighborhood Politics in Chicago and Pittsburgh* (Lawrence: University Press of Kansas, 1996), 112.

88   Ben Joravsky, "Gardner's Run: Harold Washington's Former Political Aide Is in a Four-Way Race for City Clerk," *Chicago Reader*, February 14, 1991, https://www.chicagoreader.com/chicago/gardners-run-harold-washingtons-former-political-aide-is-in-a-four-way-race-for-city-clerk/Content?oid=877108.

89   Gary Rivlin, *Fire on the Prairie: Chicago's Harold Washington and the Politics of Race* (New York: Henry Holt, 1992).

90 Ferman, *Challenging the Growth Machine*, 107–9; Rivlin, *Fire on the Prairie*.

91 Ferman, *Challenging the Growth Machine*, 13.

92 Nicole P. Marwell, "Privatizing the Welfare State: Nonprofit Community-Based Organizations as Political Actors," *American Sociological Review* 69, no. 2 (2004): 265–91; see also Nicole P. Marwell, Erez Aharon Marantz, and Delia Baldassarri, "The Microrelations of Urban Governance: Dynamics of Patronage and Partnership," *American Journal of Sociology* 125, no. 6 (2020): 1559–1601; Michael McQuarrie and Nicole P. Marwell, "The Missing Organizational Dimension in Urban Sociology," *City & Community* 8, no. 3 (2009): 247–68.

93 Nicole P. Marwell, *Bargaining for Brooklyn: Community Organizations in the Entrepreneurial City* (Chicago: University of Chicago Press, 2007), 11.

94 Jeremy Levine, "The Privatization of Political Representation: Community-Based Organizations as Nonelected Neighborhood Representatives," *American Sociological Review* 81, no. 6 (2016): 1252.

95 Levine, 1254.

96 Clarence N. Stone, Robert P. Stoker, and John Betancur, eds., *Urban Neighborhoods in a New Era: Revitalization Politics in the Postindustrial City* (Chicago: University of Chicago Press, 2015); Lee, Walker, and McQuarrie, *Democratizing Inequalities*.

97 Rosanne, interview with author, February 15, 2016.

98 In France, a wealth of studies have been conducted since Mattei Dogan's groundbreaking work on recruitment paths to French political careers in the 1960s. In the UK, various works published in the 1980s and 1990s addressed the issue, such as Pippa Norris and Joni Lovenduski's *Political Recruitment: Gender, Race, and Class in the British Parliament* (Cambridge, UK: Cambridge University Press, 1995). In the US, however, the topic has been framed in a different fashion, with the hegemonic rational-actor model precluding engagement with sociological analyses that look at social constraints and determinants. Instead, in the wake of Joseph Schlesinger's seminal *Ambition and Politics*, published in 1966, the question has been primarily defined in terms of political ambition.

99 Ta-Nehisi Coates, *We Were Eight Years in Power: An American Tragedy* (New York: Penguin, 2018).

100 Mark Wild, *Renewal: Liberal Protestants and the American City after World War II* (Chicago and London: University of Chicago Press, 2019).

101 Helen Shiller, *Daring to Struggle, Daring to Win* (Chicago: Haymarket Books, 2022).

102 Peter Dreier, "From Organizer to Elected Official," *Huffington Post*, October 9, 2008, http://www.huffingtonpost.com/peter-dreier/from-organizer-to-elected_b_124971.html.

103 David K. Fremon, *Chicago Politics Ward by Ward* (Bloomington and Indianapolis: Indiana University Press, 1988).

104 McAdam, Tarrow, and Tilly, *Dynamics of Contention*.

105 Ruth Milkman, "A New Political Generation: Millennials and the Post-2008 Wave of Protest," *American Sociological Review* 82, no. 1 (2017): 2.

106 Pierre Bourdieu, *Distinction: A Social Critique of the Judgment of Taste*, trans. Richard Nice (Cambridge, MA: Harvard University Press, 1984), 316.

Conclusion

1   "Author Dave Eggers in conversation with President Barack Obama," November 20, 2018, https://www.youtube.com/watch?v=N7ZHDoNhScY.

2   Edward McClelland, "Challenges to the Obama Center Might Work This Time," *Chicago Magazine*, August 14, 2019, https://www.chicagomag.com/news/august-2019/why-challenges-to-the-obama-center-might-work-this-time.

3   Heather Cherone, "Want to Serve on Chicago's New Police Oversight Board? Deadline to Apply Is Friday," WTTW, January 31, 2022, https://news.wttw.com/2022/01/31/want-serve-chicago-s-new-police-oversight-board-deadline-apply-friday.

4   Black feminist groups that have claimed Baker's legacy include Ella Baker's Women Center, Ella's Daughters (now defunct), and more recent organizations associated with the Movement for Black Lives. On a democratic socialist take on spadework, see Battistoni, "Spadework." Spadework was also the name of a short-lived consulting firm founded in 2019 that "[recruits] talented, diverse, and motivated organizers for campaigns across the country" and connects the labor force with potential hirers (https://dothespadework.com/about-us).

5   And because of the credentializing mechanisms at play in social work from the 1910s on, it is most likely that the "community organizers" who worked in war camps during World War I and in community-organization-oriented social-work institutions during the 1920s were also college graduates, even though I did not find hard data to substantiate this insight.

6   Alan Abramowitz and Ruy Teixeira, "The Decline of the White Working Class and the Rise of a Mass Upper-Middle Class," *Political Science Quarterly* 124, no. 3 (2009): 391–422.

7   US Census Bureau, "CPS Historical Time Series Tables," table A-1, Years of School Completed by People 25 Years and Over, by Age and Sex: Selected Years 1940 to 2021, 2022, https://www.census.gov/data/tables/time-series/demo/educational-attainment/cps-historical-time-series.html.

8   "This CEO Wants to Reduce Emissions by Turning Buildings 'into Teslas,'" CBC News, February 24, 2022, https://www.cbc.ca/news/science/what-on-earth-blocpower-electrifying-buildings-1.6363098; David Freedlander, "On Behalf of the Plutocrats," *Curbed*, November 25, 2020, https://www.curbed.com/2020/11/kathy-wylde-partnership-for-new-york-city.html.

9   McAlevey, *No Shortcuts*, 19, 38.

10   See, for instance, Charles Korr, *The End of Baseball as We Knew It; The Players Union, 1960–81* (Chicago: University of Illinois Press, 2002); Joseph M. Turrini, *The End of Amateurism in American Track and Field* (Urbana: University of Illinois Press, 2010); Graham Curry and Eric Dunning, *Association Football: A Study in Figurational Sociology* (New York: Routledge, 2015).

11   Nina, interview with author, April 13, 2016.

12   Sheingate, *Building a Business of Politics*; Dennis W. Johnson, *Democracy for Hire: A History of American Political Consulting* (Oxford, UK: Oxford University Press, 2017).

13   A useful resource in that regard is Dean Spade's *Mutual Aid: Building Solidarity during This Crisis (And the Next)* (London and New York: Verso Books, 2020), particularly chap. 5, "No Masters, No Flakes."

14   Mike Davis, "Trench Warfare," *New Left Review* 126, November–December 2020, 30.

15   Clément Petitjean and Julien Talpin, "Tweet and Doorknocks: Differentiation and Cooperation between Black Lives Matter and Community Organizing," *Perspectives on Politics* 20, no. 4 (2022): 1275–89.

16   Sean Campbell, "Black Lives Matter Secretly Bought a $6 Million House," New York Magazine, April 4, 2022, https://nymag.com/intelligencer/2022/04/black-lives-matter-6-million-dollar-house.html.

17   See, for instance, Hahrie Han, *How Organizations Develop Activists: Civic Associations & Leadership in the 21st Century* (Oxford, UK: Oxford University Press, 2014); Hahrie Han, Elizabeth McKenna, and Michelle Oyakawa, *Prisms of the People: Power & Organizing in Twenty-First-Century America* (Chicago: University of Chicago Press, 2021).

18   Spade, *Mutual Aid*, 111–12.

19   Ransby, *Ella Baker*; Inouye, "Starting with People Where They Are."

20   Kay Lehman Schlozman, Sidney Verba, and Henry E. Brady, *The Unheavenly Chorus: Unequal Political Voice and the Broken Promise of American Democracy* (Princeton: Princeton University Press, 2012); Andrew Perrin and Alanna Gillis, "How College Makes Citizens: Higher Education Experiences and Political Engagement," *Socius* 5 (2019): 1–16.

INDEX

ABOUT HAYMARKET BOOKS

Haymarket Books is a radical, independent, nonprofit book publisher based in Chicago. Our mission is to publish books that contribute to struggles for social and economic justice. We strive to make our books a vibrant and organic part of social movements and the education and development of a critical, engaged, and internationalist Left.

We take inspiration and courage from our namesakes, the Haymarket Martyrs, who gave their lives fighting for a better world. Their 1886 struggle for the eight-hour day—which gave us May Day, the international workers' holiday—reminds workers around the world that ordinary people can organize and struggle for their own liberation. These struggles—against oppression, exploitation, environmental devastation, and war—continue today across the globe.

Since our founding in 2001, Haymarket has published more than nine hundred titles. Radically independent, we seek to drive a wedge into the risk-averse world of corporate book publishing. Our authors include Angela Y. Davis, Arundhati Roy, Keeanga-Yamahtta Taylor, Eve L. Ewing, Aja Monet, Mariame Kaba, Naomi Klein, Rebecca Solnit, Olúfẹ́mi O. Táíwò, Mohammed El-Kurd, José Olivarez, Noam Chomsky, Winona LaDuke, Robyn Maynard, Leanne Betasamosake Simpson, Howard Zinn, Mike Davis, Marc Lamont Hill, Dave Zirin, Astra Taylor, and Amy Goodman, among many other leading writers of our time. We are also the trade publishers of the acclaimed Historical Materialism Book Series.

Haymarket also manages a vibrant community organizing and event space in Chicago, Haymarket House, the popular Haymarket Books Live event series and podcast, and the annual Socialism Conference.

ALSO AVAILABLE FROM HAYMARKET BOOKS

Class Struggle Unionism
Joe Burns

Elite Capture
How the Powerful Took Over Identity Politics (and Everything Else)
by Olúfẹ́mi O. Táíwò

Let This Radicalize You
Organizing and the Revolution of Reciprocal Care
by Kelly Hayes and Mariame Kaba

Rehearsals for Living
Robyn Maynard and Leanne Betasamosake Simpson
Foreword by Ruth Wilson Gilmore, afterword by Robin D. G. Kelley

Saving Our Own Lives: A Liberatory Practice of Harm Reduction
Shira Hassan, foreword by adrienne maree brown
Introduction by Tourmaline

SNCC: The New Abolitionists
by Howard Zinn

Speaking Out of Place: Getting Our Political Voices Back
David Palumbo-Liu

ABOUT THE AUTHOR

Clément Petitjean is an associate professor of American studies at the Université Panthéon Sorbonne, in Paris. He holds a PhD in sociology. He's published his work in academic journals such as *Perspectives on Politics* and the *European Journal of Cultural and Political Sociology* and popular outlets such as *Jacobin*, *Contretemps*, and *Le Monde diplomatique*.